Wakefield Press

Turning Points

Robert Foster and Paul Sendziuk are both Associate Professors in the School of History and Politics at the University of Adelaide. Robert Foster works especially in the area of Australian and comparative Indigenous History and his most recent book, co-authored with Amanda Nettelbeck, was *Out of the Silence: The History and Memory of South Australia's Frontier Wars*. Paul Sendziuk has particular expertise in the history of Australian immigration, public health and disease. He is the author of *Learning to Trust: Australian Responses to AIDS*. They are currently writing a history of South Australia.

Turning Points

Chapters in South Australian History

Edited by

Robert Foster and Paul Sendziuk

Wakefield Press

Wakefield Press
16 Rose Street
Mile End
South Australia 5031
wakefieldpress.com.au

First published 2012
Reprinted 2017

Cover design by Liz Nicholson, designBITE
Typeset by Wakefield Press

National Library of Australia Cataloguing-in-Publication entry

Title:	Turning points: chapters in South Australian history / Robert Foster and Paul Sendziuk (eds).
ISBN:	978 1 74305 119 1 (paperback).
Notes:	Includes index.
Subjects:	South Australia – History.
Other Authors/ Contributors:	Foster, Robert. Sendziuk, Paul, 1974– .
Dewey Number:	994.23

Contents

List of Illustrations

Acknowledgements

The authors would like to thank the Vice-Chancellor of the University of Adelaide, Professor James McWha, the Executive Dean of the Faculty of the Humanities and Social Sciences, Professor Nick Harvey, and the Head of the School of History and Politics, Professor Clem Macintyre, for providing the financial and logistical support that allowed us to stage the 'Turning Points' public lecture series in July and August 2011. Thanks to Mirna Heruc and Elizabeth Pascale of Art and Heritage Collections at the University of Adelaide for committing their time and resources to assist in the promotion and staging of the series. Particular thanks to Clare Parker of the History Discipline, who not only helped in the organisation of the event, but also provided valuable assistance in proofreading and indexing the manuscript. Thanks to the Art Gallery of South Australia for providing us with the images used in the lectures and the book. Our deep gratitude goes to the speakers themselves for generously offering their time. We would also like to acknowledge the members of the public who came to the lectures on a series of cold winter nights and demonstrated the depth of community interest in South Australian History. Finally, we would like to express our continuing appreciation of Wakefield Press for supporting the lecture series and for undertaking to publish this volume.

I

Turning Points in South Australian History

ROBERT FOSTER & PAUL SENDZIUK

The year 2011 was the 175th anniversary of European settlement in South Australia; not one of the marquee commemorations in the grander scheme of things, but more than sufficient to encourage a reflection on that history. To this end a group of eminent Australian historians, either South Australians or scholars whose work engages South Australian history, were invited to take part in a series of public lectures in which they were asked to address the theme 'Turning Points in South Australian History'. This book is the outcome of that lecture series, reproducing all of the lectures as scholarly chapters, along with some others specially written for this collection. Each of the contributors were invited to approach the task as they saw fit, and the chapters vary in style from standard scholarly histories, to more free-form reflections on the topics they chose.

What are 'Turning Points'? Martin Crotty and David Roberts recently addressed this question in their book *Turning Points in Australian History* and conceded that they used the concept somewhat loosely to encompass not just points in time that might have produced 'a marked divergence from previous ideas, developments and practices', but also 'crucial moments', 'milestones' or 'watersheds' in the unfolding of history.[1] We adopt a similar approach here. It is not possible in a volume such as this to comprehensively survey the history of the state, but by engaging it from the perspective of 'Turning Points', we can at least sample some of that history's key features and developments.

Perhaps our first turning point is the very establishment of South Australia itself, in the sense that its origins differ markedly from those of the earlier Australian colonies. Indeed, this idea of a 'sense of difference' is often seen as emblematic of the state's history. Derek Whitelock's book *Adelaide 1836–1976: A History of Difference* is overtly guided by the theme: Adelaide's 'distinctiveness', he writes, lies 'entwined in the city's historical origins'.[2] While Whitelock addressed the theme with direct reference to Adelaide, it is nonetheless evident in histories of the state itself, such as Douglas Pike's classic account of South Australia's foundation, *Paradise of Dissent*.[3] What was that difference? In a nutshell, the narrative is that South Australia was established independently of the earlier Australian colonies, outlawed the importation of convicts, was based on rational economic principles, and was a pioneer of social and political reform. There is a measure of truth in these claims, and South Australians, especially in the 19th century, took great pride in their story, as Foster and Nettelbeck's chapter demonstrates. However, history conceived as a triumphant parade of progress is inevitably shallow, and obscures a more complex, often fraught, but ultimately much more interesting truth. The diverse contributions in this volume tease out some of those complexities.

The second chapter in this book, written by Bill Gammage, goes to one of the most fundamental turning points of all, the way the nature of the land itself was changed by European colonisation. Born in Narrandera and resident of Canberra, Bill Gammage nonetheless spent most of his academic career at the University of Adelaide, where he nurtured and encouraged a generation of Australian and, particularly, South Australian historians. His first book, *The Broken Years* (1974), is a study of the experiences of Australian soldiers in the First World War, and has become a classic of Australian war literature. Throughout his career Gammage has continued to explore Australia's experience of war, but he has also maintained a long-time interest in Australian Indigenous history, and that is the theme he explores here. In his chapter, 'The Adelaide District in 1836', Gammage makes the claim that what the settlers saw when they first arrived on the Adelaide Plains was an environment carefully crafted by its Aboriginal owners through the use of fire. While the idea that Aboriginal people used fire to facilitate hunting and gathering is now an orthodoxy,[4] Gammage takes the argument much further and suggests that fire was used as a tool of quite sophisticated land management.

Born in Tasmania, where he first studied convicts, Henry Reynolds soon travelled north to James Cook University in Queensland, and turned to the study of Australia's Indigenous history. His first book, *The Other Side of the Frontier* (1981), was a ground-breaking study of frontier violence between Aboriginal people and Europeans in Australia. In the years that followed, Reynolds' work has surveyed the many dimensions of race relations in colonial Australia. Perhaps the most influential of his books is *The Law of the Land* (1987), which re-assessed the history of Aboriginal rights to land in Australia. In his chapter 'South Australia: Between Van Diemen's Land and New Zealand', Reynolds re-visits this story and reminds us of what a pivotal role the settlement of South Australia played in that history. As the colony of South Australia was being planned, reformers in the British government, who had successfully turned against slavery, now turned their attention to the rights and welfare of Aboriginal people across the Empire. The prospective colony of South Australia was put under the microscope, and the planners were asked, among other things, to make provision for Aboriginal rights to land. This was, Reynolds argues, Australia's 'first land rights movement'. The argument Reynolds first made in *The Law of the Land*, and which he re-tells here, would eventually become significant in the Mabo decision of the High Court (1992), which led to the recognition of Native Title in Australia.[5]

Paul Sendziuk grew up on the Western Australian goldfields and developed a keen awareness of how the 'little states', such as WA and South Australia, are generally neglected by authors of national histories. In co-convening the 'Turning Points' lecture series, and co-editing this book, he is pleased to reveal what is often left out. As a relatively recent emigrant to Adelaide, and bringing the scepticism of an outsider, Sendziuk is well placed to observe the way in which South Australians construct their identities and take particular pride in the 'free' origins of their state. This became the starting point for his chapter, 'No Convicts Here', which unravels the myth of South Australia's convict-free foundation. His findings are quite remarkable: not only did convicts find their way to South Australia, but the fledging colony transported the worst of its own criminals to New South Wales and Van Diemen's Land. South Australian authorities devised various means of deterring the emigration of escaped and emancipated convicts and expirees, and sought to punish those who came, seemingly with little success.

Robert Foster teaches in the School of History and Politics, and Amanda Nettelbeck in the School of Humanities, both at the University of Adelaide. Since the 1980s, Robert Foster, a student of Bill Gammage, has written extensively on Australian, and especially South Australian, Indigenous history. Amanda Nettelbeck, whose first book was *Reading David Malouf* (1994), shifted her attention to Australian colonial literature, and then Australian Indigenous History in the 1990s. Individually and collaboratively, Foster and Nettelbeck have written numerous books and articles on the history of relations between Aboriginal people and settlers in colonial South Australia. Their most recent book, *Out of the Silence: The History and Memory of South Australia's Frontier Wars* (2012), explores not only the nature and extent of frontier violence in South Australia, but also how that story has been remembered. Their chapter in this volume, 'Proclamation Day and the Rise and Fall of South Australian Nationalism', explores South Australia's sense of 'difference' in the nineteenth century through the lens of Proclamation Day ceremonies. While it might sound strange today to speak of South Australian 'nationalism', we should remember that until Federation all the Australian colonies were independent and self-governing parts of the British Empire. As Anthony Trollope observed of the Australian colonies in the 1870s, they are 'determined to be separate ... They are Victorians, or Queenslanders, or men of New South Wales'.[6]

In her chapter titled 'Sex and Citizenship: From Ballot Box to Bedrooms', Susan Magarey takes as her subject two key turning points in the advancement of women in South Australia: the move towards the admission of women to political citizenship (via the right to vote) and to economic citizenship (via access to paid work). While the campaigns that secured the right to vote for women in the 1890s and the passing of legislation against discriminatory employment practices in the 1970s came some eighty years apart, Magarey discerns that they were linked by a common concern about sex and were both underpinned by the need to reconceptualise female sexuality. In order to understand how the two legislative reforms came about, the author asks us to consider a range of explanations that are political, structural and cultural in nature. Magarey grew up and worked in South Australia, being one of the founders of the Research Centre for Women's Studies at The University of Adelaide, and has a personal connection to the stories that she relates; she was involved in the Women's Liberation Movement that helped secure the anti-discrimination legislation in the 1970s and one of her forebears, Dr Sylvanus Magarey, supported the women's suffrage legislation in South Australian parliament. Magarey's work here is an extension of a distinguished career in which the publication of books about women features prominently. She is the prize-winning author of a biography of Catherine Helen Spence, *Unbridling the Tongues of Women* (new edition 2010), as well as *Passions of the First-Wave Feminists* (2001), and, with co-author Kerrie Round, *Roma the First: A Biography of Dame Roma Mitchell* (2007; revised edition 2009).

Jill Roe also grew up in South Australia, on a farm near Koppio on the state's west coast. Like a lot of country kids, she came to the city where she graduated from the University of Adelaide before moving to Sydney. For most of her career she taught History at Macquarie University. These experiences perhaps gave her a more than usual sympathy for her principal subject, the novelist Miles Franklin, who also left the country behind for a career in the 'big smoke'. Her biography *Stella Miles Franklin* (2008) is an epic account of Franklin's life and a prize-winning work. Roe has also had a long association with the *Australian Dictionary of Biography* and was a long-time President of the Australian Historical Association. In this chapter she takes a more personal – 'back to Koppio' – approach to her task of examining life in rural South Australia. Rather than examining a single turn, she highlights multiple turning points; the ebbs and flows, the ups and downs, the good and the variable rhythms of country life.

From the country we move to the city, or at least to a suburb of one. The building of Elizabeth in the 1950s and 1960s was the cornerstone of Premier Thomas Playford's grand plan for the industrial and demographic development of the state. It was achieved by the importation of working-class migrants from Europe, especially the United Kingdom, and the vision of an exceptional cohort of civil servant planners who knew that South Australians needed to think differently if the state was to match the prosperity of its larger and mineral-rich neighbours. Mark Peel, the son of British migrants, brings this captivating story to life, integrating memories of his own childhood in Elizabeth. As the best historians often manage to do, Peel encourages us to look beyond the period and place in question to consider what ambitious migrants and bold urban planners might offer Australia today if only they were trusted by government to do so. Like so many of its brightest students, Mark Peel left Elizabeth and completed degrees at Flinders University, Johns Hopkins University and the University of Melbourne. He then taught History at Monash University for many years before taking up his present position as Professor of Modern Cultural and Social History at the University of Liverpool. He is the author of numerous books including *Good Times, Hard Times: The Past and the Future in Elizabeth* (1995), *The Lowest Rung: Voices of Australian Poverty* (2003), *A History of Australia* (2011), and most recently *Miss Cutler and the Case of the Resurrected Horse: Social Work and the Story of Poverty in America, Australia and Britain* (2011).

Both the author and the subject of the penultimate chapter of this volume need little introduction. The author is Neal Blewett, a long-serving member of Federal Parliament (1977–94) and a former minister in the Hawke and Keating Labor Governments. Prior to entering parliament, Blewett had a distinguished career as a political scientist and taught this subject at Flinders University. He was born in Tasmania and educated at Oxford University as a Rhodes Scholar, but raised his children and spent much of his adult life in South Australia. Blewett's subject, former premier Don Dunstan, is both a political contemporary and forebear, having entered state parliament two decades before Blewett went to Canberra; both were committed social democrats and sometimes at odds with stalwarts of the Australian Labor Party. Dunstan's support for the arts and social policy innovations, as well as his culinary and sartorial experiments, should be familiar to South Australian audiences. Less well known is the story of how Dunstan's particular brand of social democracy, and the tactics he employed, revolutionised politics in the 1960s and 1970s and were crucial in Labor gaining power at a Federal level in 1972. Neal Blewett offers a fascinating insight into this momentous period in the state's – and nation's – history, composed from an extensive array of sources and anecdotes.

John Hirst has been labelled a 'conservative' by historians who favour what might be termed the 'radical nationalist' version of Australian history. This is because he has been interested in the lives of colonial elites, as much as workers, and contradicted long-held views about the brutality of the convict system and the centrality of class and sectarian conflict in shaping Australian history.[7] But there is nothing conservative about the way in which Hirst goes about challenging established orthodoxies, nor the manner in which he presents his arguments. In many ways, the question that Hirst set himself in his chapter is the most difficult of all those chosen by the book's contributors. Rather than examining any one turning point, his aim was to illuminate what makes South Australia different.

What he discovered, however, are the ways in which the histories of the other states resemble events in South Australia much more closely than most historians have been prepared to accept. In characteristic iconoclastic fashion, he uses the occasion of the celebration of South Australia's 175th anniversary to show people in other states what they have to learn about their own origins.

2

The Adelaide District in 1836

BILL GAMMAGE

Australia's founding migrants had two primary requirements: fresh water to start a new life, and a port to stay tied to the old life – a contradiction at the heart of every settler experience. Adelaide was the last state capital site chosen, and all its predecessors had trouble with water, or a port, or both. South Australia duplicated these troubles, first on Kangaroo Island (not enough water), then at Glenelg (not a port). Finally William Light put a port on the coast and a capital on the water, as Brisbane, Perth and Melbourne had done, and as in those places thus sparked squabbles lasting years on which mattered most.

Settlers next wanted grass, and Adelaide rewarded them more richly than any other capital. There was so much grass, judiciously studded with trees, that newcomers often called the district a 'park'. Today, 'park' is never used to describe our bush, unless in the sense of National Park, which states its uses rather than its scenery. We did not have a scenery word equivalent to 'park' in 1836. On the ground and in our minds, those parks have been destroyed.

What were they like? To see how plants were distributed in 1836, we follow the first settlers from Kangaroo Island to Adelaide, then down the coastal plain and fringing hills to Encounter Bay. The plant distribution in this district, indeed in all Australia, was not natural, but made.[1] To make it, Aborigines worked with the country where it suited, but where it didn't suit they changed the country, most obviously by replacing trees with grass. They managed every inch of ground, not with equal frequency, but with equal thought, for every inch was made by a Dreaming ancestor and had to be kept as it was. Not for these careful managers was any notion of wilderness or its equivalent, *terra nullius*: that was made by Europeans after 1836. That wilderness exists now but not then conveys how momentous a turning point the British coming was.

We now know things about Australia's plants that newcomers in 1836 did not. We know how densely eucalypts and scrub grow without fire. We know too that most native plants tolerate fire, and that many encourage it. Thus in colonial paintings and words we can see the effects of fire that newcomers could not. What they thought natural we can see was made, by fire or no fire.

Let us examine some of those paintings. Today is the 175th anniversary of the landing of the first official settlers on Kangaroo Island, so like most of them I begin briefly there. In William Westall's *View on the north side of Kanguroo Island* (Figure 1), we see animals untroubled by humans and dense forest running to the shore. Westall's views on the south coast of Australia show similar dense bush around the island, because no one lived there: it was the isle of the dead. Its only decent clearing in 1836 was not there in 1802; it was made on Cygnet River later, by a runaway sailor, and was so valuable that the new arrivals stole it.[2] This dense forest shows how southern eucalypts grow without regular fire.

On the mainland, settlers first tried Glenelg, which we see in J.A. Thomas' *View from the surveyors flagstaff on the beach, Holdfast Bay* (Figure 2). At left is Black Forest, but at right the trees are curiously distributed: they box an open plain. Why? The rest is mostly grass, yet around Adelaide almost every soil grows one tree species or another, and this land grows trees now. Why so few then? The difference between then and now, and between here and Kangaroo Island, is fire. Not bushfire – most Australian plants survive that – but deliberate, repeated fire, clearing off seedlings while carefully shielding isolated belts and clumps. We are looking at Aboriginal land management.

On 16 November 1836 Mary Thomas wrote here, '[t]he country, as far as we could see, was certainly beautiful, and resembled an English park, with long grass in abundance and fine trees scattered about, but not so many as to make it unpleasant, and no brushwood'.[3] Being summer the grass was green, and wattle and banksia stood with 'tall and stately gum-trees on all sides'.[4] Inland were lagoons and the Sturt River, thick with tall reeds. The Adelaide track crossed 'level land studded with trees, and every here and there a stretch of rich meadow-land … the grass in many places three or four feet high, and the whole tract evidently of the most luxurious description'.[5] This is nothing like Kangaroo Island.

Even more striking, while some trees have been deliberately cleared, others have been deliberately left, and left in patterns: note that trees box in Thomas' painting, and foothills have tree lines along the crests, yet all but one face is grass, while all bases are forest.

In Thomas' *View of the Glenelg plains, near the hills*, we see the same plains and hills nearer Mt Lofty (Figure 3). Plain and hill grass suddenly gives way to forest, breaking the land into sharp-edged belts and clearings, with denser tree lines along the crests. This pattern demands skilful fire over a long time, yet it was common in 1836.

I call the pattern a template, a deliberate and long-term distribution of plants to locate an animal species, making it predictable for day-to-day harvest. The most obvious templates joined the grass feed to the forest shelter that kangaroos prefer. We now accept that Aborigines burnt grass to bring on green pick for grazers, but they did more. They made forest or scrub shelter not too thin or too thick, and more open near its edge than within. Beside it they put good grass, split by trees

Figure 1. William Westall, *View on the north side of Kanguroo Island*, 1802 (an7746463, National Library of Australia)

Figure 2. J.A. Thomas, *View from the surveyors flagstaff on the beach, Holdfast Bay*, 1837? (vn5924559, National Library of Australia)

so hunters could ambush prey. They left a template alone until game was quiet and abundant, then to activate it burnt a grass patch or two, knowing that when it re-shot green kangaroos would seek it out. Over centuries at least two fire regimes opened this forest, another managed the grass, and from time to time another activated the template.

A template spent much time out of commission. Hunted kangaroos become

Figure 3. J.A. Thomas, *View of the Glenelg plains, near the hills*, 1837? (an5924556, National Library of Australia)

spear-shy and move, so people lit suitably spaced templates in rotation around a circuit, luring prey from one green patch to the next. As shown in Thomas' painting (Figure 3), templates could be close, as long as those actually lit were far enough apart not to compete with each other. This system let a few animals be speared easily and selectively, as was done by families or small groups. Large gatherings needed well-timed fires and local bans years ahead to let kangaroo numbers build up, then big fires and many people to ring the country, and nets and organised drives to harvest prey.

Indigenous people were thus far from the aimless and chance-dependent hunter-gatherers most Europeans thought them in 1836, and some still think them. To burn patterns so complex in terrain so varied demands intricate knowledge of plants and fire, visionary planning, and persistence greater than anything modern Australia has imagined, or achieved.

Of course not all country was laid out for grass. Some land did not allow it, and many plants and animals prefer other habitats. Swamps and reeds probably held Aboriginal Australia's richest resources. They were common, notably behind the coastal dunes from Glenelg north to Port Adelaide.[6] Settlers thought the port, prized by the Kaurna, to be a 'gloomy swamp' with little fresh water, nothing but their lifeline to Europe. Inland, some saw a plain, 'flat, swampy, and not very picturesque', but Light saw a 'fine rich-looking country with an abundance of fresh-water lagoons'. 'Belts' of wattle, mallee, sheoak and pine split the plain, and herbs and flowers sprinkled grass 'eaten with avidity by cattle' and so by kangaroos, although probably this plain was more for plains turkey, grass birds, reptiles, and yams and other tubers.[7]

Eleven kilometres southeast of the port, the Torrens curved between 'two gentle slopes … [and] Beautiful grassy plains … with a sufficiency of timber to … look well'.[8] North of the river, open forest dominated flats and hills, pines upstream, giant gums in the city and below.[9] South was a low plateau. George Kingston, Light's deputy, put his tent there,[10] then Light chose it for his city. It had more trees than the land around, but still 'very few and mostly damaged by fire'.[11] Light explained:

> The obstructions … were greater on this particular spot than any other part of the plain. It may be asked then, 'Why choose it?' I answer, 'Because it was on a beautiful and gently rising ground, and formed altogether a better connection with the river than any other place'.[12]

From this spot, grass and scrub patches led north to the river, east was grass, west mallee, centre and south grass with scrub clumps under tall eucalypts. It was *tarndanya*, a summer rest place for red kangaroos, with somewhere on it the rock of the Red Kangaroo ancestor.[13] Light designated parkland around it, but several newcomers thought parks were already there. They referred to 'park-like scenery',[14] and in the 1840s one wrote:

> This park land is a pleasant scene, and has much the appearance of English parks, being adorned in many places by large native trees growing in clumps, and having the river passing through the grounds for some distance, with handsome trees lining its banks.[15]

No bushfire could do that, and no casual burning.[16]

From the city, plains rose gently east, grassland 'scattered about with noble park-like' eucalypts.[17] Edward Stephens recalled 'a magnificent gum forest with an undergrowth of Kangaroo Grass, too high in places for a man to see over. In fact people had lost their way in going from Adelaide to Kensington',[18] and Theodore Scott declared:

> The rich green plains, not covered by dense forest, but by stately trees, rising here and there from their green foundations in the same way as they do in the noble parks of England, the pretty streams, the broad lakes, margined with beautiful shrubs and flowers … form altogether frequent scenes of interest and beauty.[19]

Figure 4. Martha Berkeley, *Mount Lofty from The Terrace, Adelaide*, c. 1840. (Watercolour on paper. South Australian Government Grant 1935, Art Gallery of South Australia; 0.851)

When the newcomers stopped fire, trees and undergrowth returned, as we see in Martha Berkeley's *Mount Lofty from The Terrace, Adelaide* (Figure 4). Although naturally forest country, the foreground has few trees, no stumps, and no undergrowth. Saplings are colonising the middle ground; here in January 1838 Alexander Imlay commented on a 'belt of small trees belonging to the Mimosa tribe, about half a mile wide'.[20] Beyond, forest sits on the plain and lower slopes – a few magnificent gums still survive there. As Thomas showed, most hill faces are grassy until their crests parade lines of trees unlike anything seen today. In 1839 Scott noted these 'gently undulating hills crowned with trees'.[21] At right, tree lines run down grass hills and zigzag across the plain.

Lest you think Berkeley invented patterns so varied, Stanley Leighton presents a similar view in *Adelaide from the north, March 1868* (Figure 5). There was yet more variety; the forest had clearings and the grass had tree clumps and belts. '[W]here Norwood and Kensington now stand', George Hamilton wrote, 'wooded glades of great beauty opened out in all directions, extending to the foot of the Mount Lofty Range'.[22] Stephens mentioned 'a nice piece of cleared land' south of Kensington, and 'a clear space of a few acres backed by noble gum trees' at about Shipster's Road.[23] Joseph Hawdon thought the scenery

Figure 5. Stanley Leighton, *Adelaide from the north, March 1868*, 1868 (an4603125, National Library of Australia)

Figure 6. John Michael Skipper, *Adelaide from the Hills*, 1838 (Watercolour on paper. Morgan Thomas Bequest Fund 1942, Art Gallery of South Australia; 0.1227)

very pleasing. Towards the sea it consists of plains studded and intersected with belts of trees. The Mount Lofty Range distant about two miles to the eastward, presents a beautiful picturesque appearance, with its various and sloping sides variegating by its shadow the luxuriant grass to every shade of green.[24]

Figure 7. Edward Charles Frome, *Adelaide and St Vincent's Gulf from Glen Osmond Road*, 1845 (Pen and ink and watercolour on paper. South Australian Government Grant Adelaide City Council & Public Donations Fund 1970, Art Gallery of South Australia; 709HP68)

Artists, like John Michael Skipper in *Adelaide from the Hills* (Figure 6), depicted these features. On the plain is a fire, sharp grass-forest edges and necks, clearings, dense tree belts perhaps following water, and open forest. The grass squares suggest the east and south parklands: you'd expect a Red Kangaroo resting place to have good grass handy. Another painting, Edward Frome's *Adelaide and St Vincent's Gulf from Glen Osmond Road* (Figure 7), confirms grassy hills and grass-forest belts on the plain.

We see this again if we turn to the hills, as is evident in John Michael Skipper's *Mount Lofty, Adelaide* (Figure 8). Without timely fire the foreground hills would be scrub or forest. As in Thomas and Berkeley, the crest at left has more trees – crests make good cover for grazers and for hunters coming up the blind side. The next hills have many more trees. James Backhouse confirmed this steady increase in tree cover:

> After crossing the grassy plains of Adelaide, the first hills ... are grassy, with a few trees, and a variety of plants. The next hills ... have trees scattered upon them ... The next hills are ... abounding in gay vegetable productions, in forest ... Some of the hills, like the plains below, are covered with ... fine Kangaroo-grass, that is green, notwithstanding the temperature has, several times lately, risen to 107 in the shade.[25]

Figure 8. John Michael Skipper, *Mount Lofty, Adelaide*, February 1838 (Watercolour on paper. Morgan Thomas Bequest Fund 1942, Art Gallery of South Australia; 0.1226)

Further, Hamilton described hills rising 'in graceful gently swelling acclivities, picturesquely sprinkled with a variety of trees until they joined the forest which crowned the lovely mountain range'.[26] But all the hills were more open than today, unless of course they are being grazed now. As George Stevenson noted, Mt Lofty Range was 'covered with fine wood and grass to the very summits. There is little or no brushwood, and the country seems in many places as if it was laid out in the first style of Capability Brown'.[27] (Brown popularised natural seeming park-like landscapes on English estates.)

Into the range, Charles Sturt found the Onkaparinga hills 'grassy, and clear of trees'.[28] Further east lay 'a beautiful, open, undulating country, with grass up to the horses manes; the trees … of large size',[29] and northeast

> a most beautiful and rich Country. The Ranges … broken into smooth grassy vallies [sic] and the more level country resembled more an English Park than any thing else … dense brushes … separate the [grassy] limestone downs of the Murray from the richer country.[30]

Grass alternating with scrub or forest, mostly unnaturally open, ran to the Murray, whereas on many Australian rivers and coasts a grass highway followed it along.

Figure 9. John Michael Skipper, *Onkaparinga, South Australia*, 1838 (Watercolour on paper. Morgan Thomas Bequest Fund 1942, Art Gallery of South Australia; 0.1208)

Figure 10. J.W. Giles, after George French Angas, *Currakalinga, looking towards St Vincent's Gulf*, 1845? (Lithograph, hand-coloured with watercolour, on paper. South Australian Government Grant, 1953 Art Gallery of South Australia; 533G28)

Figure 11. William Light, *View at Yankalillah*, 1837? (an7830519, National Library of Australia)

Turning south, in Skipper's *Onkaparinga, South Australia* (Figure 9) we see burnt foreground hills looking west across the Onkaparinga to the coast south of Port Noarlunga. There is no scrub and trees only in clumps, implying careful fire about every three years. Similarly, land near Aldinga was 'sloping grassland in front, without a single tree for 3 or 4 miles square, of a beautiful bright green in winter and spring, and a golden colour during the hotter months ... surrounded by finely wooded eminences'.[31] You see that summer gold in this painting.

Like the distant dunes, other coast country had more trees. 'The scenery about Willunga is the prettiest I have seen in Australia', Edward Snell wrote, '[t]here is a fine background of hills which at the base slope gently off to the sea, the whole covered with trees through which the roads wind and looking very much like a gentleman's park in England on a very large scale'.[32] George French Angas also depicts this area in *Currakalinga, looking towards St Vincent's Gulf* (Figure 10). Angas wrote of this view, 'the singular manner in which the trees are dotted about in all directions over the landscape, will convey a tolerable idea of much of the country of this portion of Australia'.[33] Most land was burnt in this way, for woodland or grass, 'so long and thick an herbage that it is quite laborious to walk through it ... the scenery resembles an English gentleman's park'.[34] This could not be haphazard.

We see this again in William Light's *View at Yankalillah* (Figure 11): trees or bushes are densest on crests, so were burnt variably. To flourish in this way, the hills need fire every three to four years to thin wattle and eucalypt saplings, kangaroo and similar grasses prefer fire about every three, and Drooping Sheoak, the

Figure 12. George French Angas, *Entrance to the gorge of Yankalilla, Oct 1, 1850* (an2904224, National Library of Australia)

Figure 13. J.W. Giles, after George French Angas, *Yattolinga, Oct 5, 1850* (Lithograph, hand-coloured with watercolour, on paper. South Australian Government Grant, 1953 Art Gallery of South Australia; 533G45)

foreground tree, seven to ten fire-free years to seed. So at least three fire regimes, plus others for the coastal scrub, made this land. Fire regimes were distinct, repeated, and integrated with neighbours to maintain particular plant and animal habitats.

Note the bare hills in Angas's painting *Entrance to the gorge of Yankalilla* (Figure 12). John Lort Stokes noted them as well: 'instead of a succession of forested hills and dales' further south, he 'passed over extensive treeless downs, contrasting strikingly in appearance from the woody country around'.[35] Many are still bare today, possibly because of shallow soil. On the plain, healthy grass-trees show that settlers brought to an end Indigenous fire practices quite recently, but already trees are regenerating on the hills runoff.

We see indicators of this also in Angas's painting *Yattogolinga* (Figure 13). Angas noted, '[t]his scene represents the high and bold hill between Rapid Bay and Cape Jervis ... on the right are two species of the grass tree ... on the left are young silver wattles'.[36] Wattles are rapid regenerators after fire, and here they are taking hold.

There was some scrub and undergrowth in 1836, for some plants and animals prefer it. Sturt wrote, '[o]n the other side of Mount Terrible the country is very scrubby for some miles, until, all at once, you burst upon the narrow, but beautiful valley of Mypunga [*sic*] ... covered with Orchideous plants of every colour, amidst a profusion of the richest vegetation.'[37] (Many orchids in flower signify recent fire.) But if newcomers do mention scrub it is usually to exclude it. Jane Franklin thought the land between Mt Lofty and Encounter Bay 'exceedingly pretty; in some parts not unlike an English park, grassy and lightly timbered, and quite free from scrub and underwood'.[38] Sturt found the same country 'so open that the labour of felling and clearing is wholly unnecessary'.[39] Backhouse reported it 'covered with grass, and intersected with belts of Gum-trees, and a sickle-leaved Acacia. Some of the Kangaroo-grass was up to our elbows, and resembled two years' seed meadows, in England, in thickness; in many places, three tons of hay per acre, might be mown off it'.[40] It sounds like a crop because it was, while deliberate and repeated fire made grassy woodland look natural.

Few newcomers imagined such discipline. Light thought the country 'looked more like land in the possession of persons of property rather than that left to the course of nature alone',[41] and John Morphett considered it 'very picturesque and generally well timbered, but in the disposition of the trees more like an English park than we would have imagined to be the character of untrodden wilds'.[42] Adelaide's newcomers learnt more about local people than at any other capital, yet could still think the careful construction around them 'untrodden wilds'. For manager and spoiler alike, the loss was irrecoverable.

The spoilers came not to make country, but to loot it. They fractured its uses into city, port, farm and pasture, and they transformed earth, water, plants and animals. I will cite three examples.

The Torrens

In 1836 the Torrens was a typical Australian river, shallow, spreading, often dry. A 'miserable dribbling current with an occasional waterhole', one settler called it in 1838.[43] More charitably, another wrote that in summer 'the water ceases to flow, but collects in large natural tanks or holes, some of them of great extent, and supplied by underground springs',[44] and in 1876 a third recalled, 'it may appear strange to those who have only seen the Torrens as it is now; but ... the river, like many Australian streams, became a series of lakes in dry weather'.[45] Hawdon thought the Torrens 'a very small stream of excellent water ... In the summer season this stream is found running only for a short distance below the Town, where it disappears beneath its gravelly bed'.[46] The bed spread so wide that some newcomers crossed it without seeing it, and Thomas painted where it lay without depicting it. Franklin 'saw no river whatever that was anything better than a string of water holes, the intervals between the pools being dry ground. In winter there is sometimes a continual stream. The Torrens at Adelaide is a river (so called) of this description'.[47]

These features were because the Torrens ran slow and shallow. James Hawker explained, '[a]ny number of fallen trees blocked the bed ... and here and there were patches of ti-tree'[48] which slowed the water. Clearing the bed had an immediate effect. It let the heavy 1851 rains reach Adelaide 15 minutes faster than any earlier flood, with a force that cut deep, necessitating bridges where once people stepped across.[49] In 1862 an old colonist regretted that the river had 'worn a deeper channel in the soft soil of the plains – that its yielding earthy banks are far more precipitous than they were – [and] that in summer the wide chasm of river bed is more out of proportion than it used to be, with the slender rivulet that trickles along its centre'.[50] The beds of most Australian rivers are not shallower as is commonly assumed, but deeper.

Deep rivers dried neighbouring land. Those many lagoons and lakes newcomers praised were replenished less often; plains were longer exposed to drought; and the Torrens hit the coastal swamps and reed beds with greater force. In time, the deep channels it cut might alone have drained the swamps, but settlers thought it beneficial to drain, just as with the fens in England, with great damage here and there.

Fire

Another pivotal change was to landscape fire. Until 1836 it was a friend; now it became an enemy. A few newcomers did see that fire could help. Johannes Menge saw plains 'exactly like the Parks I saw in London ... the old grass having been burnt by the natives and the new grass having grown a foot high an emerald colour out of the black gave the eyes a delightful impression ... The grass is everywhere five foot when not burned [and] bears a corn like barley'.[51] But no settler saw how close an ally fire had been, so well controlled that until 1836 people lit most fires in summer, when now it is dangerous and illegal. Newcomers considered fires terrifying that we think mild; fires which by their own accounts barely scorched canopies, and were mostly out next day.[52] Angas described hills eucalypts with their

> massive trunks blackened, in many places as high as fifteen or twenty feet from the ground, by the tremendous fires that sweep through these forests, and continue to blaze and roll along, day and night for many miles, in one continuous chain of fire. These conflagrations usually take place during the dry heats of summer, and frequently at night; the hills, when viewed from Adelaide, present a singular and almost terrific appearance; being covered with long streaks of flame, so that one might fancy them a range of volcanoes.[53]

At any time, let alone in 'the dry heats of summer', fires rising a mere 15–20 feet to blacken trunks but not canopies are not big. In 1841 the *South Australian Register* thought hills fires less fierce than those on the plains: 'the fire has evidently raged fiercely in many places, yet it never seems to attack anything but the grass and the leaves of the lower bushes, leaving the trees unscathed, the larger ones being seldom found hollow and blackened as are those on the plains below'.[54] Not even new chums thought plains fires fierce. If only fires today were so gentle.

No settler could burn with such skill, and once they built fences or stacked hay they could not burn at all. Instead for well over a century a rigid regime persisted under the slogan 'Prevent Bush Fires'. Only since the 1980s, as one capital city after another has been immolated, have we begun to see that the best fire control is to reduce fuel, and even now not everyone accepts the implications of this, and no one can do it with the skill of the Kaurna and their neighbours. What knowledge we have lost.[55]

Plants and animals

Stopping fire let trees grow. We saw this in the paintings of Berkeley and Angas. At Kensington by 1848, '[y]oung gums and wattles, not as high as the fence, began to spread',[56] and hills were being covered 'with young gum trees'.[57] In March 1839 Nathaniel Hailes found it 'easy to lose oneself in the heavily wooded city even in the daytime, and at night it was scarcely possible to avoid doing so. The maze-like character of the spot was greatly enhanced by a multitude of wattles, which occupied spaces between gum or she-oak trees'.[58] This is rapid regrowth; perhaps Hailes was in the city's west, which people were not burning in 1836 because it was *wirranendi*, 'being transformed into a forest'.[59]

In the Onkaparinga valley near Hahndorf in January 1839, Dirk Hahn saw

> beautifully-formed trees, which nature had planted there as if with the hands of a gardener. Every tree stood about 40 feet apart from the others. Some were perhaps an acre apart, so that the land could be cultivated without uprooting a single tree … I found grass three feet four inches high: they looked like our European cornfields.[60]

Figure 14. William Rodolph Thomas, *Aboriginal family group on the Onkaparinga River near Hahndorf... 1870* (vn4935828, National Library of Australia)

William Thomas depicted the valley 30 years later in his painting *Aboriginal family group on the Onkaparinga River near Hahndorf* (Figure 14). You see the scattered big trees Hahn admired, their spreading branches confirming that they grew in the open, but scrub now fills the ground. Hahn saw people burning here in mid summer 1839:

> They form a circle about twenty English miles in diameter, light fires around this area, and then direct the fire closer and closer in toward the centre of this circle. The long dry grass, bushes and young trees burn fiercely; all the animals living in this area flee toward the centre, where the savages then capture them ... the fire burned for some days; I had never before seen such a fire.[61]

Can anyone now get a fire circle to burn in on itself, let alone one 20 miles wide? Again, imagine this Aboriginal family's despair: a remnant of that 20 mile circle, templates destroyed, totems denied, land made wilderness, carers made guilty.

This ruin is what many think South Australia was like when Europeans arrived. South Australia passed its key closer settlement act, the *Waste Lands Amendment Act*, in 1869, so this 1870 scene conveys what selectors faced: no parks, but decades of back-breaking axe work. Frederick McCubbin's famous painting *Down on his Luck* (1889) shows a despondent pioneer amid dense wattle and sheoak regeneration, just as you would expect of southeast land released from fire.

But only one tree is older than 1836, a big gum, its trunk black from ancient fires. The pioneer legend rightly honours the hardy men and women who carved homes from the dense bush, but it does not follow that this is how the land was in 1836.

Stopping fire also transformed animal distribution, threatening some species while freeing others from ancient constraints. Think of Adelaide's vanished marsupials, of the birds which have gone and come, of the insects. 'The annual burnings by the natives for their hunting purposes', Menge observed, 'have destroyed not merely the impeding brushwood, but also every kind of annoying insects and injurious reptiles'.[62] Near Adelaide locusts advanced as fire retreated. According to Wilkinson, they

> were first observed close to the town, and for two years were confined to some two or three miles around Adelaide; but now they have extended their march, and bid fair to ravage the whole country ... annual burnings ... had the effect of destroying countless multitudes of insects that now are allowed to live and increase. The grass is eaten at present as soon as it appears, and during the hot weather is much too scarce to enable the fire to make a continuous line, without which very many insects must escape the flame.[63]

A final change. Burn Australia's perennial grasses and they come back green, especially in summer. Burn Europe's annuals and they die; don't burn them and they die. Their summer colours are white or cream, the colours of their dying. Settlers replaced native perennials with exotic annuals, notably grain crops, changing forever the summer colour of Australia. Impressionist painters like McCubbin, Tom Roberts and Arthur Streeton captured that colour, and that dead cream-white now frames our consciousness of our country. Let this change, visible but unseen, epitomise South Australia's first turning point.

3
South Australia: Between Van Diemen's Land and New Zealand

HENRY REYNOLDS

The year 1836 has been of particular interest to me recently. I have been writing a history of Tasmania and to deal with the colonial period I decided to concentrate on one year, and chose 1836, initially because at the very beginning of the year the young Charles Darwin visited Hobart (in fact he had his 27th birthday there). But Charles Darwin became less and less important as I read everything I could about the year. One of the many small details that I came across was that three of the ships that had arrived at Kangaroo Island sailed to Hobart while they were waiting for the arrival of the official party. Then, very early in January 1837, there were ships in Hobart ready to sail to the new colony of South Australia. This clearly indicates that South Australia must be seen in the context of the whole of Australia, and by 1836 Hobart and Sydney were already quite substantial settlements even by the standards of towns in Europe. We also need to look at the situation in England itself, because so many of the things that were decided about South Australia were being discussed in London in the mid-1830s.

Among the issues that were very important in the 1830s in both Australia and Britain was the question of policy towards the Indigenous people including the Aboriginal peoples of Canada and Australia, and the Maoris of New Zealand. This question was the subject of intense interest, debate, dispute, and anguish, in New South Wales, Van Diemen's Land and Western Australia. The South Australians, or rather the prospective South Australians, who visited Hobart in late 1836 were undoubtedly informed about the 'Black War' that had only just finished and which had seen about 200 settlers and many more Aborigines killed.[1] It had been a very intense time of conflict. In Western Australia the so-called battle of Pinjarra had just taken place.[2] In New South Wales there was the beginning of the squatting rush, and the resulting conflict with Aborigines out on the Western Plains, the most important event of which we know as the Myall Creek Massacre.[3] In light of these events it was very difficult to avoid the question of Aboriginal rights in the mid-1830s either in Australia, or in Britain. In London the question of Indigenous rights had become a major issue for both the Colonial

Office and for the government. The founding of South Australia coincided with the meetings of the House of Commons Select Committee on Aborigines (British Settlements), which issued two significant and widely read reports.[4] At the same time the Aboriginal Protection Society was founded.[5] All of this activity indicated that there was deep concern about the relations between settlers and Indigenous people and particularly about conflict over the ownership and use of land. There were the inescapable questions of why had so much conflict accompanied settlement in Western Australia, Van Diemen's Land and New South Wales, who was responsible, and what the bloodshed indicated about the very nature of Australian settlement. And there remained the abiding question of the relationship between land tenure and this deeply troubling bloodshed.

In this context, the first 50 years of Australian settlement was being judged at the very time when the final arrangements were being made for the settlement of South Australia. Much of this concern was pragmatic: if the settlement of a small place like Tasmania had cost so many lives, and the mobilisation of 2000 men for six weeks in a sweep across the island, what might be expected during the settlement of the whole continent? There was also what we would now call 'the issue of human rights' – what rights, if any, did the Indigenous people of Australia have?

It is important to remember that in this first half century the view was that the Aborigines did not have specific rights: they neither had sovereignty, nor did they have ownership over the land. When the British settled New South Wales in 1788, Tasmania in 1804, and Western Australia in 1829, the assumption was that the Crown not only became the first sovereign, because there was no other, but also the beneficial owner of all the property. That is, Australia was a *Terra Nullius.*[6]

This was an anomalous situation in the broad perspective of British colonial policy, because in North America before the settlement of Australia and during the early years of Australian settlement, there was a clear recognition of the property rights of Indians – of Indian or Native Title – and even recognition that they had a form of sovereignty: that they were domestic, dependent nations. These ideas had been recognised by the British Crown in the middle of the eighteenth century, and that recognition was passed on to the new republic in the 1790s and eventually formulated by the Supreme Court of the United States in the 1820s.[7]

So there was a change of policy that took place with the settlement of Australia in its first 50 years. Interestingly, by the 1830s, mainly as a result of what had happened in Australia, there was a turning back to that earlier policy of recognition of Indigenous rights, and this culminated most obviously in 1840 with the Treaty of Waitangi in New Zealand, under which the Maoris ceded their sovereignty, which it was accepted they had to cede, and which also recognised their property rights. This reaffirmation of traditional policy was to continue in the settlement of both Fiji, and Papua, where there was a complete recognition of Indigenous property rights. It is worth noting that had the Queensland border in the Torres Strait been drawn a little farther to the south, and the Murray Islands been included in Papua, then Eddie Mabo's ancestors would have had their property rights recognised from the very beginning of European annexation, obviating the need for the retrospective fight for them in the Australian courts during the 1980s.

My suggestion is that South Australia lay, in a figurative sense, between Van Diemen's Land and New Zealand in the way it would deal with these questions of policy towards property rights and whether the Indigenous people had human rights in a modern sense. That is, the South Australian colonists had to look at two different ways of seeing the situation. There was the old Australian way of *Terra Nullius*, or there was the new way that was already forming in policy circles in Britain. Land was clearly central to the question because the sale of land was absolutely central to the South Australian venture. There had to be land that could be sold in order for the principles of systematic colonisation to start working: in particular, money from land sales being used to bring out immigrants. But the question that arose in the 1830s was 'whose land was it after all'? Now the South Australian Colonisation Commission had no doubt that they were the beneficiaries, they were the people who were following on from what had happened elsewhere in Australia. When challenged they were able to say: look, everywhere else in Australia, even in Western Australia in the last few years there has been no recognition of Aboriginal property rights. Those great agricultural companies, the Australian Agricultural Company and the Van Diemen's Land Company, were given grants of land in the 1820s with no concern about whether there were Indigenous property rights underlying the new title.[8] This is why when the company itself and its supporters passed legislation through the House of Commons it referred to the lands they proposed colonising as 'waste and unoccupied', and 'fit for the purpose of colonisation'.[9] The prospective colonists looked back at what had gone on before, and not unreasonably so. Torrens argued that: 'hitherto in the colonisation of Australia, it had invariably been assumed that the unlocated tribes had not arrived at that stage of social improvement at which a proprietary right to the soil exists'.[10] So rather than looking for a new start, the South Australian Colonisation Commission wanted to maintain the status quo, in fact the status quo was probably essential to the whole venture. But there had been dramatic changes in the 1830s. Things had progressed, even from the time when Western Australia had been settled a few years before.

So much was new in the 1830s. Britain had not had a revolution but the so-called Great Reform Act of 1832 had enfranchised many more people and particularly the thriving middle classes of great new industrial cities. But perhaps the most significant indication of change was the abolition of slavery in 1833. Some 800,000 slaves in the British colonies were emancipated at the cost of the English taxpayer at the modern equivalent of about two billion dollars. This was an extraordinary, globally-important event. The humanitarians had taken on one of the greatest economic forces in Britain and overthrown slavery. They had shown just how powerful their campaigning could be. This was the first modern political campaign driven by a mass movement with meetings, petitions and boycotts. In 1833 alone, 5000 petitions were presented to the House of Commons, with 1.3 million signatures.[11] The humanitarians who had fought against slavery became very influential in the new House of Commons, at the very time discussions about the founding of South Australia were taking place. The new reforming Whig administration came to power in April 1835. The Colonial Office was deeply influenced by the new currents of opinion and came under the influence of two men – Lord Glenelg and James Stephen – whose families had been intimately involved in the Anti-Slavery crusade. As Stephen said, anti-slavery was a crusade which devolved on him by inheritance. It was, he said, 'of extreme importance to the happiness of mankind for which my father and my connections and friends have been living almost exclusively'.[12] But having succeeded, almost surprisingly, to bring slavery to an end in 1833 they were not intending to stop. One of the many things they did was to turn their attention from slaves to Indigenous people in the Empire, and we can trace this movement very clearly, particularly if we look briefly at the career of the man who was regarded as the liberator, Thomas Fowell Buxton, who took over from his mentor William Wilberforce and was the leader in the House of Commons in the anti-slavery crusade. He turned his attention in the 1830s, even before slavery was overthrown, to the position of Indigenous peoples within the British Empire. 'I protest', he said, 'I hate shooting innocent savages worse than slavery itself',[13] and along with others he set up the Aborigines Protection Society, the first manifesto of which said 'the abhorred and nefarious slave traffic, which has engaged for so long a period the indefatigable labours of a noble band of British philanthropists for its suppression and annihilation, can scarcely be regarded as less atrocious in its character, or destructive in its consequences than the system of modern colonisation as hitherto pursued'.[14] The most important manifestation of this movement at the very time that the settlement of South Australia was being discussed was the House of Commons Select Committee into Aborigines.

Much of the interest was in Australia, because Australia was seen as where everything had gone wrong. The humanitarians knew a lot about Australia. There had been several large collections of papers written about Van Diemen's Land, and particularly about the 'Black War', published in the House of Commons. There had also been a lot of correspondence, public and private, to the Colonial Office and to people like Buxton. Land was important as the Select Committee reported with the ringing declaration:

> it might be presumed that the native inhabitants of any land have an incontrovertible right to their own soil; a plain and sacred right, however which seems not to have been understood. Europeans have entered their borders, uninvited, and when there, have not only acted as if they are not only undoubted lords of the soil, but have punished the natives as aggressors if they have evinced a disposition to live in their own country.[15]

And these rights did not depend on how the land was used, this was simply a birthright of the people who were born in the country. But as the Committee observed, these rights were not understood in Australia and particularly in Tasmania, where the Black War had resulted. This was the burden of correspondence between Thomas Buxton, the Quaker missionary James Backhouse and the Governor George Arthur who had, after all, seen it all: the conflict on the island was concentrated in a small area in a short space of time. It had all the elements of great tragedy. At the beginning of Arthur's 12 years in Tasmania, relations between the tribes and the settlers had been largely peaceful, but between 1826 and 1831 conflict spiralled upwards. By the time he left the Colony in 1836, the Aborigines had been removed from mainland Tasmania to the islands in the Bass Strait. At the end of this period, and maybe with an eye on the new power of the humanitarians (he was a very successful bureaucrat), Arthur was very remorseful. Above all he said the policy had been bad, because there had been no recognition of the land rights of the Tasmanians, and that above all it was important to begin with a treaty, and to arrange for the purchase of land and for the compensation of the Indigenous people.

Of particular interest is a letter that was written by Arthur to Buxton in January 1835, talking about the forthcoming settlement of South Australia. Arthur had written similar things to the Colonial Office, but this was a private letter so it was much more frank. 'The importance of at once conciliating the natives, is a consideration which well deserves the attention of those gentlemen', that is, the South Australia Colonisation Commissioners. 'It is not yet too late', he declared:

> their hands are still unspotted with blood, and it is their bounden duty to take every effort under the divine blessing to preserve them from so dire an alternative, for disguise as we may, we are intruders. Under such circumstances, the sacrifices of human life, even in self defence, is peculiarly distressing. They are the native burghers of this wilderness and every contest with them must be fought within those confines, which they have inherited from their ancestors. The strangers must in every case, unless proper and equitable measures are adopted in the commencement of the settlement, be at least indirectly the aggressors.[16]

Arthur then explained a lot more about what the cost would be economically, and went on to say that

> the natives of South Australia, who are said to be numerous, cannot be expected to give up, or retire from their native hunting grounds, unless these be purchased from them, without struggle, and if blood is once spilled, I fear the worst consequences. The work of extermination may go on for many years in detail – a war of this kind is always one of extermination. Great misery will be suffered by both parties.[17]

In conclusion he declared, 'if blood be once drawn, conciliation, as I have always said, will be almost hopeless'.[18] Arthur also wrote similar, if somewhat toned-down letters, to his masters in the Colonial Office insisting on the importance of recognising the property rights of the Aborigines in the new South Australian settlement.[19]

These letters were particularly important, greatly impressing the new man at the Colonial Office, Lord Glenelg, who sent copies to the South Australian Commissioners with a warning that the content could not 'but be regarded as of the first importance in the formation of the new settlement'.[20] The Commissioners were confronted with radical and unexpected changes in policy, which overturned over 40 years of practice in New South Wales, Van Diemen's Land and, more recently, in Western Australia. Australia was no longer to be regarded as a *Terra Nullius*. Torrens was told this personally in face-to-face interviews in the Colonial Office. He was instructed that he had to arrange for an officer to be called Protector of Aborigines, who was to arrange for the sale of Aboriginal land.[21]

Far more portentous were the Letters Patent, which were issued by the King on 19 February 1836. It was the foundation document of South Australia because this was the instrument that defined the boundaries. There is no doubt about their importance. Without them there could not have been the colony of South Australia. The Letters Patent concerned many things but at the end there was a sting in the tail, as far as the Colonisation Commission was concerned. The passage read:

> provided always that nothing in these our Letters Patent contained can affect or be construed to affect the rights of any Aboriginal natives of the said province to the actual occupation or the enjoyment in their own Persons or in the Persons of their descendants of any Lands therein now actually occupied or enjoyed by those Natives.[22]

There was to be full recognition of the pre-existing property rights of the Indigenous people. If the Letters Patent were not actually drafted by James Stephen, he certainly oversaw their drafting. In a private memo written on 10 December 1835 to his Minister, Lord Glenelg, when the Letters Patent were being drafted, he wondered how the Colonial Office was expected 'to fix the boundaries of the province'. 'How this is to be done in a Terra Incognito?' he declared, 'I cannot imagine, nor how it can be done at all for any due regard to the rights of the present proprietors of the soil, or rulers of the country'.[23] It was a particularly revealing comment: there was this fundamental assumption at the very heart of the British Government that they were dealing with people who still were both the rulers of the country and the present proprietors of the soil.

For the Colonisation Commission, these attitudes were like a bombshell. They were totally unexpected. Suddenly they were told that the Indigenous people had rights and they had to be respected, their land had to be purchased not just taken.

One of the key figures, the Immigration Agent, John Brown, wrote in his diary in January 1836:

> [T]here is talk that the reason for the delay at the colonial office is the wish to bend us to some plan for the protection of the natives in order to satisfy the saints in the House of Commons. That measures should be devised and enforced for their protection and civilisation as far as possible is not only just, but politic, but that a legislature should authorise the sale of land and the formation of a colony in a part expressly declared by them for the purpose, and then as soon as people have embarked their money and spent time on such an insurance suddenly finds out that there are natives and native rights, which they … had first enquired about … is beginning at the wrong end and as just to the aborigines is unjust to the colonists.[24]

There is no doubt that the people who were planning the colony of South Australia knew that the Colonial Office was serious, knew that the world had changed completely, and they had to at least pay lip service to the property rights of the Aborigines. But there is also no doubt that they intended to deceive the Colonial Office completely. As Brown noted in his diary, 'what is to be the interpretation of the word "occupy" is the question'. And that is why in much of their literature, they phrased their statements so carefully. They talked about property rights and then said 'should such a right be anywhere found to exist' or 'were any such rights be found to exist'.[25] And that is indeed what happened. Torrens, even before the settlers had arrived in South Australia, in the middle of 1836, felt confident enough to tell another parliamentary enquiry that he did not think any property rights existed. In other words, they were looking back to the way that things had been done in Australia up to that time. They were not willing to accept that a new situation had developed. South Australia was very pleased to see itself as a new start, with land sales, immigration of respectable people, education, religion, no convicts, indeed a paradise of dissent. It may just as appropriately be called a paradise of deception.

I began with some consideration of what had happened in Tasmania in the decade before the settlement of South Australia. Experience there showed the British the consequences of settlement without a recognition of Indigenous property rights and without a treaty. Island experience suggested that the level of conflict experienced there would be infinitely greater on the whole continent of Australia. It was also argued that New Zealand was important, because by the time the settlers had arrived in South Australia the Colonial Office was already discussing the question of the establishment of the British colony there. George Arthur, the expert on these matters after twelve years in the antipodes, was in Britain when this discussion was taking place. There is no doubt that his warnings about what would happen in New Zealand if there wasn't a treaty were taken very seriously, and the South Australian experience had shown that there had to be a document far more powerful, far more robust than the Letters Patent, and hence settlement started with the Treaty of Waitangi.[26]

Many of these questions were considered in my book *The Law of the Land*, first published in 1987. At the time I was struck by the way in which the importance of what I called 'the first land rights movement' had been forgotten. This was particularly relevant to the history of South Australia. But this history was also disregarded in the law courts. One of the only places where the issue was taken up was in the so-called Gove Land Rights Case of 1971 in the Supreme Court of the Northern Territory. In his judgement, Mr Justice Blackburn simply dismissed in an extraordinary passage the significance of the Letters Patent. He asserted the clause in particular about property rights 'was not intended to be more than an affirmation of the principle of benevolence inserted in the document and ordered to bestow upon a suitably dignified status'.[27] Now that was a truly extraordinary interpretation, given what could have been found out quite easily – although if Blackburn had turned to the ordinary histories of South Australia, he would not have found much useful information. Douglas Pike, in his classic history of South Australia's establishment, *Paradise of Dissent*, simply disregarded these issues.[28]

So, what do we make of this? Is it just that the Letters Patent and their significance was forgotten? Was it deliberately hidden? Or was it just that, given the general attitude of Australia towards Indigenous people they were simply not taken seriously? And in some ways this is what happened, although less dramatically, to the Treaty of Waitangi. From the late 19th century through to well into the 20th, it was not taken particularly seriously, but came back in the modern era to be seen as the foundation constitutional document of New Zealand. And it was not really until the Mabo judgement in 1992 that people began to take the question of Aboriginal property rights in Australia seriously.[29] You will all remember how many people, including many lawyers, were taken aback by the Mabo judgement, and who strongly believed there could be no native title in Australia. First Mabo, and then the Wik judgement in 1996, changed the way we perceived the past as well as the way we consider the present and imagined the future. Because there was a misunderstanding, or even ignorance, about the Letters Patent and where they had come from, there was also a misunderstanding of the importance of the Aboriginal reserves, set up in many parts of South Australia in the middle of the 19th century. Their establishment was typically seen as an act of benevolence, rather than a result of holding back land that had belonged to the Aborigines in the first place. Nor was there an understanding of the reservations in the pastoral leases in South Australia, the Northern Territory and Western Australia which were almost totally disregarded for 150 years.[30]

The fact that the Letters Patent were overlooked is not completely surprising. In the recent book *Coming to Terms: Aboriginal Title in South Australia*, edited by Shaun Berg, there is a preface by three leading Aboriginal men who declare:

> for all of us we need to understand why the laws have failed to protect our rights to land. It makes no sense to ask why our native rights to our land were protected in Letters Patent but not in reality. The legal implications of the Letters Patent and other founding documents of the state have been a burning issue with us. To us it is unfinished business. It is something that the government of South Australia has to come to terms with.[31]

We need to remember that the Letters Patent referred to lands in actual occupation or enjoyment, and although it may have been possible before Mabo to say that such phrases simply did not mean anything, that is no longer a viable option.

As I understand it, there are at present ongoing and frustrating negotiations with the South Australian government concerning Indigenous rights to land. It may be useful to remember that it was not the politicians who resolved the question of Aboriginal land rights. The Hawke government in the 1980s promised to introduce land rights and gave up. I do not think we would have had land rights now if it had depended on Australian parliaments. It was the High Court in 1992 and 1996 that brought about the great breakthrough. But there seems to be no doubt that the founding documents, which defined the boundaries of South Australia, also recognised the property rights of the Indigenous people, and I think they are as important in their way as the Treaty of Waitangi. It seems to me that the very honour of South Australia is at stake; I think it is unavoidable that eventually South Australia will have to come to terms with those founding documents and with the present day Indigenous people.

4

No Convicts Here: Reconsidering South Australia's Foundation Myth

PAUL SENDZIUK

On the 175th anniversary of European settlement in South Australia it is not surprising that historians should seek to understand and to celebrate the decisions and factors that set the colony on a unique trajectory. Authors in this volume have, for example, noted the effect of South Australia having no established church, relatively few Irish and Catholics, and a system of land distribution that prevented squatters from gaining a firm hold on land so that farming flourished, at least while the thin soils held out. To this list might be added the scarcity and unpredictability of rainfall, which curtailed agricultural expansion, and the failure of gold to be found in quantities sufficient to spark a rush, like those in New South Wales, Victoria and Western Australia, which denied South Australia the extraordinary demographic and economic growth experienced by those colonies. And, of course, there was the unique nature of South Australia's foundation according to the principles of 'systematic colonisation', which sought the importation of a balance of capital and labour but not, under any circumstances, convicts.

It is this final and most celebrated feature that intrigues me. To this day, South Australians proudly proclaim the 'free' origins of their state, implicitly evoking the 'convict stain' and applying it to their neighbours across the border long after most of them have stopped feeling ashamed of their penal heritage. Soon after I arrived to live in Adelaide in 2005, I attended a performance at the Festival Theatre by a Tony-award winning star of stage and screen that was interrupted by an audience member objecting to a well-worn gag about Australians being descended from criminals. 'No convicts here, mate', the man shouted, inspiring applause and cringing in equal measure. A student of mine, researching the activities of escaped and former convict workers in South Australia, was later told with no less confidence by a State Library staff member that nothing would be found because 'we didn't have convicts here'. Behind such remarks, repeated in history books, newspaper articles and on talkback radio, lies a certain pride: that South Australia's founding fathers, and its residents who fought to prevent the introduction of convicts, were more enlightened than their counterparts in neighbouring colonies who maintained the system of convict transportation for much too long. Pride, also, that since South Australia was spared the presence of convicts, its streets were safer, its children uncorrupted, and its society more genial and refined.

This sense of pride has a long lineage. It is discernible in the writing of Thomas Horton James, who reflected on his time in South Australia in 1838, just two years after the colony's foundation:

> Next to the delightful mildness of its climate and the simple state of its society, there is nothing which so strongly recommends the new Colony of South Australia, as its entire freedom from convicts and *convictism*. Perhaps it might be called the most distinguishing feature in the whole picture, and the very one which gives it so vast a superiority over the old penal Colonies of New South Wales and Van Diemen's Land … [W]hen one is away from those great lazar houses, and can contemplate, at a distance, the leper-like ghastliness and deformity of convict society in those Colonies, the friends of South Australia may congratulate themselves with the highest satisfaction, that the moral virus of contamination is for ever excluded from their shores – they may go on their way rejoicing, and call down blessings on the heads of those good men who first framed the constitution of the new Colony, and to whom they are so deeply indebted for a riddance of such a pestilence.[1]

James continued:

> There are no huge barracks in Adelaide full of wicked and condemned men – no female factories or penitentiaries – no enormous jails and permanent gibbets in the public streets – here are no poor-houses often calling for enlargement – nor lunatic asylums with their drear and solitary cells, offering their living sepulchres to the sad victims of vice and rum! Nothing of this kind; and as a gentlemen said the other day, with all its newness, and with all the unavoidable inconveniences peculiar to so recent a settlement, I would rather settle in South Australia, with £100 a year, than live amongst the contagion of convicts in New South Wales or Van Diemen's Land, on an income of £200![2]

Echoing this sentiment, in 1845 local surveyor George Warren wrote to his uncle in Scotland:

> We want labourers but will rather still want than lay the foundation of convictism. We have hitherto boasted of our society compared with Sydney and Van Diemen's Land, and not without justice. Parties coming from Sydney to say nothing of Van Diemen's Land are quite astonished how peaceable quiet and orderly streets of Adelaide are at night. Here a man may go about at any time as safe as in Scotland. The almost total absence of locks and bars in the country speaks for itself and the fact that old lags are ashamed to be thought so shows the general tone of morals here which would not long continue if one third of our inhabitants were old convicts.[3]

Over the next fifty years, the prospect of South Australia uniting with the convict-tainted colonies of the east and west to form the Commonwealth of Australia was enough for many South Australians to oppose the idea of federation.4 But what if the pride of South Australians – both those who proclaimed the superiority of South Australian society and our friend at the Festival Theatre – was misplaced? What if the motives of the colony's planners and early settlers in rejecting convicts were less than pure, and their exclusionary measures less than successful? What if convicts had found their way to South Australia after all?

It would be comforting to believe that South Australia's founders and early residents rejected penal settlement because they felt the sentence of transportation to be excessively severe, that the discipline required to maintain order and work efficiency among convicts fostered cruelty and brutality, and that the entire system, in which convict men and women were assigned to work for government and landowners in order to secure the profitability of colonialism, was akin to slavery. This is how the transportation system and penal settlement is often depicted now. But these were not, by and large, the views of colonial planners and early residents of South Australia, nor even of those who argued for the cessation of convict transportation in the eastern colonies in the 1830s, 1840s and 1850s. The convict system was not brought to an end in New South Wales and Van Diemen's Land because it was considered to be cruel and wicked, but because its economic benefit had become less evident. The perceived moral corruption of convict-based society deterred British capital investors and the emigration of free men and women. Maintenance of penal institutions and garrisons of troops drained the treasury. And assigned convicts proved to be less than ideal workers: convicts found various ways to resist the demands of their masters,[5] and some were insufficiently skilled, so that many landowners complained the cost of keeping convicts outweighed the benefit derived from their labour. Since the cost of land was cheap and small parcels of it were given away to convicts at the conclusion of their penal sentences, it was also considered too easy for emancipated convicts to become land owners, resulting in an inadequate supply of labour and the inflation of its price.[6]

Having had time to study the experience of the eastern colonies, South Australia's planners and early settlers were familiar with these facts. Edward Gibbon Wakefield and other proponents of 'systematic colonisation' knew that a plentiful supply of dependable and skilled labour would be required if land in South Australia was to be cultivated efficiently and profitably. The importation of convicts would work against this. Instead they established a system by which the purchase of land was largely restricted to capitalist investors by selling it at a high price, consequently ensuring that labourers were unable to acquire it easily. Money from the sale of the land was then invested in an emigration fund that paid for the passage of migrant workers: free men and women, who represented a steady source of dependable labour. Wakefield and his supporters had noted how 'respectable' men were unwilling to invest in, or emigrate to, New South Wales and other convict colonies while landholding ex-convicts 'were elevated to the station of gentlemen, who neither by conduct or character, were entitled to any such distinction'.[7] For wealthy emigrants, then, one of the appeals of systematic colonisation was that South Australian society would more closely resemble that of England, with each class kept distinct and separate. Its appeal for honest working men and women (as well as landholders) lay in the assurance that they and their children would not be exposed to the supposedly morally corrupting influence of convicts, nor to the likelihood of having to work among convicts or of having them serve in the home.

These attractions featured prominently in material that sought to recruit land buyers and migrant labourers to the fledging colony. A publication issued by the South Australian Company in 1838, for example, extolled the virtues of the Act of Parliament that established the province, noting '[t]he 22nd section [of the Act] is of great importance to the new colony, securing it from the great obstacle by which emigration to New South Wales and Van Diemen's Land has been seriously impeded; namely, their convict population.'[8] Furthermore, arrangements made under the Act for the sale of land and the emigration fund 'secures many very important advantages':

> First: having provided a sufficient supply of free labour, the Act of Parliament declares that no convicts shall be sent to the settlement, and thus the Colonists are protected from the enormous evils which result from the immorality and profligacy unavoidable in a penal settlement.[9]

The desire to maintain South Australia's commercial advantage by excluding convicts was also evident when colonists mobilised to oppose developments in other colonies that threatened to facilitate the admission of convicts to South Australia. In June 1845, for instance, a notice was issued in Van Diemen's Land that allowed – indeed, encouraged – conditionally pardoned convicts to emigrate from the colony. Fearing an influx of such men and women, South Australians petitioned the British Government to order the notice be rescinded. In a letter to Lord Stanley, South Australia's Governor, George Grey, wrote:

> I fear that when it is known that large numbers of persons holding conditional pardons are flocking to this settlement, many most respectable families who emigrated here in the full belief that no persons would be permitted to pass into South Australia from the neighbouring colonies who could not have gone to any other part of Her Majesty's dominions, will become seriously alarmed as to the effect that this circumstance may have upon the future prospects of their children; and they will also be apprehensive, and probably not without reason, that other respectable persons will be deterred from emigrating to a settlement in which a numerous class of individuals holding such conditional pardons is known to exist.[10]

In his submission to the British Colonial Secretary, and writing on behalf of the Committee of the South Australian Society (an association of land proprietors), J.H. Croucher added: 'the great estimation which South Australia enjoys as a field for emigration, is owing in great part, to the healthy moral tone of its population; and that to permit the introduction of persons stained with crime and familiar with vice, is to inflict on it one of the greatest evils that can possibly befall a rising settlement'.[11] In a subsequent letter, Croucher reminded Gladstone that

> the colonists of South Australia, not being indebted to the Crown for their lands, but having purchased and paid for every acre they possess, some of it at a very high rate, are entitled to have their rights and privileges preserved inviolate ... The effect of the obnoxious measure in question in depreciating the value of all kinds of property in the colony, and in interfering with the due reward of the honest labourer, is too obvious to require particular notice.[12]

Clearly it was perceived that the success of systematic colonisation and the recruitment and prosperity of landholders and labourers depended on keeping convicts out. Economic self-interest more greatly determined South Australians' stance against the introduction of convicts than did any humanitarian concerns about the ethics of transportation or the welfare of convicts. In the above case, the British Government was unimpressed with the pleas of South Australians and declined to order that the notice be rescinded. It did, however, impose one new condition: that a conditionally pardoned convict must 'not return to the country or colony from which he had been transported'.[13] In doing so it secured its own position, as the majority of convicts emanated from the UK. Britain's response served only to antagonise South Australians and led to further anxiety about the viability of the colony.

Had South Australians been concerned about the severity of transportation or the welfare of convicts – who, as we have seen, were described as loathsome and evil and likened to pestilence – they would not have been so ready to transport their own criminals elsewhere. For while South Australians fought vociferously to prevent the importation of convicts to their territory, they were happy to exile their own criminals to New South Wales and Van Diemen's Land until those colonies stopped accepting convicts. South Australia inherited British laws that allowed for the sentence of transportation to be passed on those found guilty of certain crimes. It proceeded to do so, sentencing 264 criminals to transportation (with two men suffering this fate twice).[14] The majority of these convicts were sent to Van Diemen's Land, though 60 were transported to Sydney prior to the cessation of transportation there in 1840. They were conveyed by small coastal traders that sailed between Port Adelaide, Sydney, southern NSW (now Victoria) and Van Diemen's Land, with their assigned destination largely determined by the itinerary of the next available vessel.[15] The majority of those transported, some 178 people, were convicted of theft.[16]

The first public meeting to discuss ending such arrangements did not occur until February 1851. Opinion grew and in late 1851 the government responded with the passage of the Transportation Commutation Bill, which received royal assent and was made law in January 1852, thus providing for the automatic commuting of all transportable offences to prison sentences with hard labour. This necessitated building a new gaol because Adelaide did not then have the capacity to accommodate such prisoners.[17] British enthusiasm for transportation had waned by this time, especially after the discovery of gold in NSW and Victoria in 1851 made these desirable destinations for men and women looking to improve their fortune. As British Secretary of State for the Colonies, Sir John Pakington, explained: 'It would appear a solecism to convey offenders, at the public expense, with the intention at no distant time of setting them free, to the immediate vicinity of those very gold fields which thousands of honest labourers are in vain striving to reach.'[18]

Having failed to persuade the neighbouring colonies to secure their borders, South Australia went about protecting its own through a range of legislative measures. These measures, aimed at preventing or dissuading escaped or former convicts from entering the colony, were extreme in some cases, and by 1865 they undermined South Australia's boast of being more civilised and just than its neighbours. Until 1839, there were no practical means to deal with the apprehension and return of convicts who had escaped from across the border. This was rectified with the passing of the *Act to Facilitate the Apprehension in South Australia of Convicts Escaping from the Neighbouring Penal Settlements.* It was not a benign piece of legislation. It allowed for convicts – including petty thieves who had received tickets-of-leave or conditional pardons – to be returned to their penal colony where they faced corporal punishment for absconding. In reality, South Australia had neither adequate surveillance nor manpower to enforce the law, so apprehension orders were generally reserved for the most notorious or serious offenders whose recapture carried significant rewards.

Once convict transportation to the Swan River colony began in 1850, South Australian authorities felt the need to strengthen the existing legislation. The *Act to Prevent the Introduction into the Province of South Australia of Convicted Felons and other Persons Sentenced to Transportation for Offences against the Laws* (1858) allowed for a Justice of the Peace or constable to arrest any person suspected of entering South Australia from another colony while under sentence of the Crown. This legislation was replaced with a revised Act in 1865 that went further by including in the category of 'offenders illegally at large', former convicts whose sentences had expired in the previous three years.[19] Thus, even free men and women were considered to be 'illegally at large' and prohibited entry into the province if they carried the convict taint. Under both the 1858 and 1865 Acts, persons proven before a local magistrate to be 'illegally at large' could be sentenced to additional terms of hard labour in a South Australian prison before being deported. Both Acts allowed for ships to be searched upon arrival at South Australian ports and for passengers to be detained until the status of each had been determined. The penalty for ship masters who brought with them prohibited persons was £100 in 1858 then £500 in 1865, while stewards or sailors found aiding or abetting 'offenders illegally at large' could be fined £100. South Australians found to be harbouring or concealing such offenders incurred a penalty of £100 or faced imprisonment for up to 12 months.

These were not the only deterrents for escaped or former convicts. There is evidence to suggest that on facing trial for crimes committed in South Australia, offenders with convict pasts received harsher sentences than those without. Steven Anderson and I have written elsewhere about how seven of the first eight Europeans hanged in South Australia were escaped or former convicts. For some, this punishment was disproportionate to the crime or to the strength of evidence against them.[20] Two men, Henry Curran and George Hughes, were executed for stealing £5 during a robbery in which a firearm was discharged – a crime that might have warranted a lesser sentence. The colony's newspapers rejoiced at their demise. 'However abhorrent such scenes may be to humanity', wrote the *Adelaide Chronicle* after the public hangings, 'it is absolutely necessary that the hardened villains who escape from punishment in the neighbouring colonies be taught that they have no triflers to deal with here – that there is a determination, on the part of the Government, to protect to the utmost, the lives and properties of its constituents'.[21] The *South Australian Register* proselytised further:

> We trust that this execution will bring under the notice of Government the absolute necessity that exists for preventing the wholesale importation of convicts from the neighbouring colonies, which has existed almost since the establishment of this colony.[22]

Afterwards came the execution of Thomas Donelly, who was justly convicted of killing an Aboriginal man. Donelly was condemned to die for this crime, and the case against him drew on the testimony of an Aboriginal boy. Both of these occurrences were unique at the time.[23] Whereas other Anglo-Australians who killed Aborigines evaded detection or conviction at court due to other white settlers (including police) helping to conceal their crimes,[24] Thomas Donelly, a former convict, was afforded no such protection.

Another former convict, William Wright, was found guilty of murder and then executed following a trial in which evidence strongly suggested that he was provoked before fatally stabbing a man 'long known to the police as a violent and dangerous character'.[25] In a rare instance of compassion, the *Adelaide Times* protested against the sentence: 'We solemnly believe that there could scarcely be found another English lawyer of moderate attainments in his profession, who would not have charged a jury, that a crime perpetrated in hot blood, in the presence of a considerable number of witnesses, is manslaughter, and not murder.'[26] Yet even after a petition was sent to the Governor pleading for the commutation of his sentence to imprisonment for life, leniency was not forthcoming.

Analysis of the type of European offenders whose death sentences were commuted to life imprisonment in the first 25 years of white settlement in South Australia supports the argument that ex-convicts were treated differently. Where the background of offenders can be accurately determined, it is apparent that only three of ten ex-convict offenders sentenced to death were shown mercy by the Governor.[27] Conversely, 14 of 15 Europeans without a convict background (some 93.3%) had their death sentences commuted to life imprisonment.[28] Some of these 'non-convict' offenders (like their convict counterparts) had prior convictions, which somewhat eliminates this as a mitigating factor. Moreover, several non-convict offenders had committed serious crimes for which, given the time, one might have expected them to pay the ultimate price. John Wilson, for example, was found guilty of shooting at a constable with intent to commit murder whilst trying to escape police custody, yet he evaded the hangman's noose.[29] John Jones (alias John Downs) and Francis Howard were convicted of jointly assaulting their victim and stealing £8 – more than the amount taken during the robbery for which Curran and Hughes were hanged – but their death sentences were commuted to imprisonment with hard labour.[30] In the case of another 'non-convict' offender, Joseph Hawkshaw, who burgled the home and shop of J.L. Dorion, the jury recommended mercy because Dorion's premises were not well protected and 'invited burglary'.[31] In none of the cases involving escaped or former convict offenders were the victims so blamed for the crimes perpetrated against them.

One must obviously be cautious in drawing conclusions from a relatively small number of cases, but this analysis certainly suggests a bias in sentencing, possibly reflecting an intention to deter escaped and former convicts from residing in South Australia. Coupled with the passing of legislation that sought to exclude emancipated convicts and discriminated against free men and women whose sentences had recently expired, the evidence undermines the notion that South Australia was a 'paradise' for those fleeing persecution. Derived from the time in which South Australians took pleasure in denigrating the moral corruption at the core of convict colonies, this evidence is also at odds with claims that South Australia was a superior society that, above all else, maintained fairness, equality, and personal liberty.

It should now be apparent that convicts – be they escaped, emancipated or expirees – did indeed come to South Australia. In fact, their occupation of the territory that became South Australia most likely predates the arrival of Governor John Hindmarsh and the first fleet in 1836. Whalers and sealers set up semi-permanent camps in the islands and bays at the fringe of the southern mainland as early as 1803 and these camps were known to contain or be supplied by emancipated and escaped convicts (like similar settlements in Van Diemen's Land).[32] For instance, Captain George Sutherland, who sailed the *Governor Macquarie* to Kangaroo Island in 1819, reported:

> There are no natives on the island; [but] several Europeans assemble there; some who have run from ships that traded for salt; others from Sydney and Van Diemen's Land, who were prisoners of the Crown. These gangs joined after a lapse of time, and became the terror of ships going to the Island for salt, &c., being little better than pirates. They are complete savages, living in bark huts like the natives, not

cultivating any thing, but living entirely on kangaroos, emus, and small porcupines, and getting spirits and tobacco in barter for skins which they lay up during the sealing season. They dress in kangaroo skins without linen, and wear sandals made of seal skins. They smell like foxes.[33]

Peter Cunningham, surgeon on the *Recovery* during both the 1819 and 1823 convict voyages to Australia, also remarked on the island's inhabitants:

> Here a small colony of runaway convicts some years ago took up their residence, and still obtain a precarious livelihood from the kangaroos, seals and shellfish wherewith the island abounds, deriving occasionally a few European necessities by bartering the skins they produce with the vessels that call, and by assisting to collect their cargoes.[34]

After Adelaide was established, police were sometimes sent to Kangaroo Island to apprehend escaped convicts, who were often harboured by long-time residents with shady pasts. Inspector Alexander Tolmer recounts several trips that he made to the island, meeting escaped convicts whose absconding he ignored because they serviced him with information that assisted with more important inquiries.[35]

Escaped and former convicts also set up camp in the thickly forested hills surrounding Adelaide. A miller, John Dunn, passing through this country in 1840, wrote: 'We reached Crafers where a shanty had been set up by a man from Tasmania and this place was a haunt of all the escaped convicts who had made their way to South Australia.'[36] Tom Dyster, an historian of the Adelaide Hills, asserts '[t]he tiers in the 1840s were at once a garden of Eden and a repository for rogues ... Escaped convicts from Tasmania with nothing to lose after years of bestial treatment by guards who regarded them as scum, were not likely to treat with geniality intrusions upon the haunts of their new-found freedom.'[37]A more sympathetic account is given in letters sent home to family in the early 1840s by Benjamin Boyce, a working-class lad from Lincolnshire who jumped ship at Adelaide and hid out with convicts in the hills for a short period.[38] Boyce established a fond friendship and a small business with one of the former convicts, William Holland, who had been sentenced to transportation to Van Diemen's Land for 14 years and, Boyce claims, had come to South Australia as an expiree. Boyce noted that Holland had married and become relatively prosperous, having purchased land and livestock.[39]

Then there were convicts who chose to reside in Adelaide and terrorised the dreams of town officials. Proclamations and despatches issued by governors, speeches delivered by judges, and articles published in the press all pointed to the disturbing presence of convicts from the earliest days of the settlement. In June 1837, when the colonists numbered less than 2000, Magistrate Edward Stephens expressed his concern about the convict population (it is unclear whether he was referring to emancipated or escaped convicts or expirees), claiming that 'upwards of 40 of these men' were already known in the colony and urging Governor

Hindmarsh to do something about the situation.[40] Judge Henry Jickling was similarly ill-tempered, complaining that his court was full of convicts on trial for various offences.[41] In late 1837, Hindmarsh wrote to the British Secretary of State, Lord Glenelg, seeking approval to institute a police force, for which no funds had been set aside because the colony's founders believed a convict-free settlement populated by landowners and carefully selected emigrant labourers would remain law-abiding. Hindmarsh explained: 'the number of bad characters that are daily arriving from Encounter Bay, and I suspect very much from the interior, and of course suspected to be runaway convicts, make it necessary not only that a strong police body should exist, but that we should not be altogether deprived of a military force'.[42] In a half-yearly report issued in 1840, Hindmarsh's successor, George Gawler, reiterated that '[a] military force, or a police force approaching it in organisation, is absolutely necessary in a country in which natives, bushrangers, a large body of escaped convicts and whaling sailors are to be kept under control.'[43] In Gawler's opinion, '[t]wo-thirds of the prisoners in our gaol have invariably consisted of escapees from New South Wales, whilst one half of the remaining third has usually been composed of runaway sailors from vessels in the Port.'[44] His words reached the British House of Commons where T.F. Elliot, one of the Colonisation Commissioners, said that he supposed the number of convicts that came to South Australia was 'not inconsiderable'.[45] (Elliot included 'time-expired men' within the category of 'convicts'.)

It is clear, therefore, that from overland or by ship convicts did come to South Australia. But we can be less certain about how many and to what effect. Three main obstacles impede this investigation. First, since South Australians so conscientiously maintained the myth of the colony's convict-free status and of their freedom from the convict stain, they exerted little energy in documenting the activities and achievements of the escaped and emancipated convicts and expirees who did come. The state archives and libraries of Queensland, New South Wales and Tasmania have displays and websites devoted to biographies of both their most infamous and prosperous convicts, while South Australia has no such resources.[46] What remains are police and court records that, by their nature, are skewed to only reveal the worst of convict behaviour. Add to these, official statements such as those quoted above, which were issued with a clear agenda – to secure soldiers and funding for police – and which therefore may overstate the number of convicts present and almost certainly exaggerate their depravity.[47]

The second problem for historians concerns the way in which use of the word 'convict' has changed over time. Once the terms 'convict' and 'prisoner' carried two separate and distinct meanings: 'convict' was shorthand for a criminal who had been transported to Australia from elsewhere in the British Empire, while 'prisoner' referred to someone who was not necessarily a convict but had been imprisoned for a crime. But the two words began to be used interchangeably by the 1850s. Therefore, in cases where little supplementary information survives, the use of the word 'convict' in police and court records, press reports and private correspondence offers no certainty as to the person's background.

Finally, and perhaps most significantly, we know so little about escaped or ex-convicts in South Australia because they went to great lengths to hide their former identities (with good reason, given the discrimination they faced). Were it not for the distinguishing scars of the whip's lash or convict tattoos, or their recognition by other emigrants with whom they had associated in the penal colonies, most former convicts could have successfully blended with the rest of society. This proved to be easier than one might have expected. For instance, two escaped convicts, Josiah James Rogers and Thomas Jones, were selected to form part of the colony's first paid police force in 1838. The Acting Governor expressed his 'surprise and displeasure' upon their eventual discovery but, because the work was so poorly-paid and replacements hard to find, the two men were allowed to remain in the force.[48] Another man, Frederick Waller (alias Charles Fleetwood, alias George Rees), was appointed Superintendent of Convicts (i.e. prisoners) at the Adelaide Gaol on 1 July 1853, where he was charged with overseeing the prisoners' hard labour. On 11 November he absconded with £357 of government money that he had received from the Central Road Board in payment for stone broken by the prisoners. Waller was traced to Melbourne and then to Sydney, where he was apprehended and brought back to Adelaide for trial. During this time Waller was found to have been a convict himself, having been transported from England and, on account of good behaviour, serving as a clerk in a convict stockade. Waller had simply fabricated a new identity and the credentials that secured his position in Adelaide. He admitted at the trial to absconding with the money only because there were prisoners in his charge who recognised him from Van Diemen's Land.[49]

Despite these obstacles for the historian, it is possible to get a sense of the contributions made by convicts to colonial life in South Australia by undertaking painstaking work in archives and by following references to possible convict sightings and encounters in texts published at the time. These traces certainly suggest a degree of bad behaviour by escaped and freed convicts in South Australia, but they also point to rich contributions that were vital in securing the future of the colony. For example, escaped and former convicts, keen to lay low and consequently willing to take on unpleasant work in remote and inhospitable areas, joined parties of whalers and sealers and serviced them with provisions. Whaling was the colony's first export earner, with oil and bone from a single whale fetching between £500–600 in 1838.[50] As wool and wheat production absorbed capital for several years before returning profit, it was whaling and sealing, supported by convict labour, that helped keep currency circulating in the colony when bankruptcy threatened.[51]

Escaped and former convicts also performed valuable service in the agricultural and pastoral industries. Thomas Horton James, who we heard above proclaim the superiority of the convict-free colony, did admit that some convicts had found their way overland from Port Phillip and Portland Bay. Furthermore,

> others have even arrived, a thousand miles, driving cattle from the higher branches of the Murrumbidgee. All of them are generally what are called handy fellows, and more or less bring a good deal of knowledge with them, such as how to put up fences and stock-yards, build huts, split palings, &c.; and they get a capital living by working half the week in bush carpentering, sawing, brick-making, and fishing. That tall young man yonder, with his long pit-saw across his shoulders, glittering in the sun, and his mate with him, are both from New South Wales, and were either convicts or the descendants of convicts in that colony. They now are earning good wages as sawyers in the Mount Lofty range, and the pair of them last Sunday morning received eighteen sovereigns for their previous week's work in the bush. Nine pounds a week, each, for a working man![52]

In February 1837 land agent John Morphett reported: 'We have already at least 15 men come here as labourers from the convict colonies of Sydney and Van Diemen's Land, whose knowledge and course of life will be decidedly useful; that is to say stock keepers, shepherds and paling & shingle splitters.'[53] Others such as Simpson Newland at Encounter Bay, Christina Smith at Rivoli Bay and the Reid family at Gawler, also testify to the helpfulness of ex-convict labour in splitting timber for building and fencing, constructing houses and tending livestock.[54] Eliza Mahoney, the daughter of Samuel Reid, recalled how 'with the introduction of sheep and cattle overland from New South Wales, and by sea from Tasmania (then called Van Diemen's Land) there came ticket-of-leave and time-expired men, who we employed, and who understood building huts much better than the emigrants, and we never had more honest, more industrious servants'.[55]

The skills and knowledge that convicts brought with them to the virgin farmlands, forests and seas of South Australia were important, and this, coupled with the fact that they were generally willing to do arduous, dangerous and poorly-paid jobs, were the reasons why some escaped convicts, upon detection, were not turned in by employers. Writing in the 1870s, John Wrathall Bull recalled '[t]he free settlers as well as Government officials were glad to employ banished men (not asking if they were expirees or runaways) who had been well trained to work as convicts, and were skilful splitters, sawyers, fencers, and builders of huts.'[56] As we have seen, even the Police Commissioner turned a blind eye to escaped convicts forming part of his police force.

Ex-convicts also became active in commercial and civic life in Adelaide. I am in the process of tracing the life histories of 60 such men and women, whose stories I hope to share in a subsequent publication. Here I would like to focus briefly on just three men, Joseph Broadstock, Emanuel Solomon and Jack Foley. The lives of Broadstock and Solomon are quite astonishing, and suggest what might have been achieved by other ex-convicts with a similar degree of endeavour and success in concealing their pasts. The story of Foley is more ordinary but no less illuminating.

Joseph Broadstock, from a family of nail-makers in West Bromwich, was convicted of theft and assault and sentenced to seven years' transportation when just 19 years of age.[57] Arriving in Van Diemen's Land aboard the *Isabella* in November 1833, he was assigned to work for settlers. He served his complete sentence without committing further crimes, gaining a ticket-of-leave in 1837 and his Free Certificate in 1840.[58] Almost immediately he set sail for Port Phillip, where he became a publican and lodging house keeper in Melbourne. He married Elizabeth Moss in 1843 but within four years the relationship had soured; in February 1847 Broadstock placed a 'Caution' notice in the *Argus* stating his wife had left without provocation and warning others against receiving 'property clandestinely removed by her from my premises'.[59] In 1848 the former convict arrived in Adelaide describing himself as a bachelor and cattleman. (It is unclear whether he took an overland route, possibly driving cattle, or whether the designation of cattleman, while well-suited to his surname, was an utter fiction.) Broadstock soon married Mary Ann Hamly (or Hamley) who bore him the first of six sons the following year. She died in 1867, aged 40, leaving Joseph to care for their family.[60] This was accomplished through a variety of profitable land and property transactions and by successfully running a number of hotels, mainly in Salisbury, at least one of which he built. Being declared a 'fit and proper person to fill the office of Councillor' for Yatala, Broadstock was elected unopposed to the position in December 1855.[61] He proved to be a community-minded man: serving on the building committee for the St John's Anglican Church and personally donating £10 to the cause,[62] becoming a member of the Central Roads Board, and being involved in the establishment then improvement of Salisbury's first primary school, erected in 1877. When Broadstock died aged 70 on 20 October 1883, his death certificate recorded his station in life as 'Gentleman'.

Emanuel Solomon was well known in Adelaide as a businessman and pillar of the Jewish community, but few if anyone in South Australia knew that he and his brother had been convicted of larceny in London in 1817 and transported to Van Diemen's Land. The conduct of the pair during their sentence was not exemplary; Emanuel received 50 lashes for escaping into a forest, 25 lashes for neglect of duty and 50 lashes for being found in possession of an iron pick.[63] On 3 March 1821 the brothers were caught stealing clothes and were sentenced to transportation to the dreaded Newcastle penal colony; both were subsequently required to serve their full sentences.[64]

Gaining their freedom, the two men went into business in Sydney as general merchants and auctioneers and accumulated property in New South Wales until Emanuel bought a share in a South Australian land grant and emigrated to Adelaide in 1838.[65] Emanuel traded as an auctioneer and merchant, and his import-export business thrived in the fledging colony. His trade was facilitated by links with his brother in Sydney and serviced by ships they co-owned that traded between Adelaide and the eastern colonies. (Their brig *Dorset* was even commissioned on four occasions to transport South Australian convicts to Sydney and Van Diemen's Land.[66]) Emanuel proceeded to develop property in the city and in 1840 built the Queen's Theatre, the first such establishment in Adelaide. His commercial activities also extended outside the city. With a partner, he purchased 85 acres of land that was subdivided to create the township of Port Pirie, and he endowed a portion of the land to be used for religious observance.[67] Emanuel was a founder of the Adelaide Hebrew Congregation and has been described as 'the paterfamilias of the Jewish community'.[68] One of his three successive wives was Irish Catholic, however, and he is fondly remembered today for providing Mary MacKillop's Sisters of St Joseph of the Sacred Heart with two Flinders Street properties in which to live after MacKillop had been excommunicated and the Sisters ordered to vacate their premises.[69] Emanuel's success in business and philanthropy earned the esteem of his peers, leading to his election as a Member for the House of Assembly for West Adelaide (1862–65) and then the Legislative Council (1867–71). When he died aged 73, on 3 October 1873, survived by his third wife, four daughters and three sons, his estate was probated at £4500.[70]

One can locate numerous newspaper reports referring to Emanuel Solomon but none (including his obituary) allude to his convict past. A report in 1845 entitled 'New Auctioneer' discusses Solomon's intention of 'again starting in Adelaide as an auctioneer'.[71] The article appears immediately below an item concerning the proposal to send Parkhurst Boys (convicted British juvenile offenders) to Adelaide, where it is noted 'the colonists had already protested against the infusion of this convict taint into the free blood of the colony'.[72] Solomon's own convict past goes unremarked.

Jack Foley (real name John or James Lovett) had a less distinguished career but still participated meaningfully in the establishment of the southern colony. In the 1820s he had been transported to New South Wales, from where he escaped and crossed the border via an overland route. Boyle Finniss, in his history of South Australia published in 1886, tells of Foley's arrival in South Australia:

> Among the arrivals by the Murray in one of the overland parties there came a man named Foley – Jack Foley, I believe, he was called. He rode a splendid horse, one of those high-bred upstanding animals which are bred in the pastures of New South Wales. He, and a comrade of similar stamp – they were called bushrangers in those days, and bore the not very enviable repute of being escaped convicts – took refuge in the scrubby ranges at the back of the point of land opposite Granite Island. Being well armed and provided with good dogs, they supplied the few settlers at Encounter Bay, who were chiefly connected with the whaling party, with fresh meat in the shape of kangaroo flesh.[73]

Foley was apprehended in Adelaide, where he had come to deliver a message to the manager of the Bank of South Australia. The superintendent of police, Henry

Inman, was summoned and arrested Foley, who was subsequently released by a magistrate who argued that, at the time, his court had no jurisdiction over offences committed outside the colony. As Arthur Haydon notes in his early history of trooper police in Australia,

> The prisoner was accordingly released, and Superintendent Inman found it no difficult matter to induce him to help in tracking the wanted men Stone and Stanley [Foley's former companions]. Not long afterwards Foley became an auxiliary member of the police force, in which capacity he rendered much valuable service. Eventually he returned to England, to end his days there.[74]

Let us return, then, to the statements made by contemporaries of Broadstock, Solomon and Foley that begin this chapter. Both Thomas James and George Warren boasted of South Australia's superiority over New South Wales and Van Diemen's Land because of the absence of convicts in their colony. James proudly declared: 'the friends of South Australia may congratulate themselves with the highest satisfaction, that the moral virus of contamination is for ever excluded their shores'.[75] They were mistaken. Convicts might not have been transported to South Australia, but they came anyway, and in good numbers. Due to the fragmentary and ambiguous documentary record, we cannot accurately deduce how many. Writing in the first year of the colony, Edward Stephens and John Morphett both indicate that escaped or emancipated convicts constituted about 1–2% of the population.[76] Given the numerous references to convicts that I have found, some of which have been cited here, I suggest this is most likely an underestimate. The convict presence was certainly significant enough to be an ongoing concern for those in power. Accordingly, civic leaders enacted laws and supported sentencing strategies that discriminated against those with convict backgrounds in an effort to deter the emigration of convicts from other colonies, all the while transporting the worst of South Australia's own criminals to penal settlements elsewhere. In doing so, the scales of justice were tipped, to the discredit of those involved. South Australian magistrates, law-makers and the colonial executive proved that they too were capable of transgressing moral boundaries. The desire to keep convicts out, or deny their presence, meant that the significant labour, commercial and civic contributions of escaped and former convicts went unappreciated. By re-examining this key turning point in the development of the colony – the decision to reject convicts, and the impossibility of denying them entry – these contributions capture our attention and encourage us to approach the question of South Australia's difference from the convict colonies with great humility.

Acknowledgement

I wish to thank Sandy Horne and Walter Marsh for their valuable research assistance.

5

Proclamation Day and the Rise and Fall of South Australian Nationalism

ROBERT FOSTER AND AMANDA NETTELBECK

On 28 December 1836 South Australia's first governor John Hindmarsh, together with a group of colonists, landed at Holdfast Bay. Although the first fleet of colonists had been arriving on Kangaroo Island since July, the decision to site the capital on the eastern shores of Gulf St. Vincent was not made until December, so when they finally came ashore at Holdfast Bay it was plainly thought that a show of ceremony was needed to underscore the moment.[1] In the afternoon the Governor met with the other members of Council. His Majesty's Orders in Council 'erecting the province of South Australia' were read out, and the oaths of office administered. Shortly afterwards, near an old gum tree, the Governor's Commission was read to an assembly of about 200 colonists and Robert Gouger, the Colonial Secretary, read aloud the Governor's first Proclamation 'announcing to the Colonists of His Majesty's Province of South Australia the establishment of the Government'. The Proclamation enjoined the colonists to act with 'order and quietness', 'respect the laws', be industrious, sober and moral, and to 'prove themselves worthy to be the founders of a great and free colony'. It also, and at great length, spelled out the rights and protections that were to be extended to the Aboriginal people of the colony. After the reading of the Proclamation and the raising of the British flag, the Marines fired a *feu de joie* and the *Buffalo* fired a fifteen-gun salute.[2] With these symbolic ceremonial acts, the new colony was effectively proclaimed, and it was these events that came to be celebrated as marking the foundation of the colony on Proclamation Day.[3]

South Australians know 28 December as Proclamation Day – or Commemoration Day as it was more commonly known for most of its history – as the anniversary of European settlement. It is observed with a public holiday and commemorated with a formal ceremony at the Old Gum Tree at Glenelg, which with its association with the idea of 'taking root in new soil', as Jim Davidson has put it, became secured over time as the symbolic marker of South Australia's foundation.[4] Today the ceremony is a modest affair: before an audience of mainly pioneer descendants and school children the founding proclamation is read aloud and invited dignitaries make speeches before going off to lunch. Lost amongst the Christmas-New Year holiday break, most people would pay it little heed and may only be aware of it through a short report in the evening news. Jim Davidson has suggested that waning contemporary interest has left it as little more than a residual celebration of a past imperial age.[5] In the 19th century, however, the significance of Proclamation Day, and what it represented, was very different; as the press of the time repeatedly proclaimed, it was South Australia's 'national day' and it was celebrated with remarkable enthusiasm. The use of the word 'national' was not an anachronism and nor should the sentiment be dismissed as mere parochialism. Constitutionally tied to Britain and fraternally linked to the other Australian colonies, South Australia nonetheless regarded itself as a nation in its own right and reflected on the qualities that distinguished it as a nation in much the same way that Australians do today when commemorating 26 January.

While all the Australian colonies had distinctive origins, South Australia, from the very outset, sought to foreground its difference. South Australia was unique among British colonies in being established by an Act of Parliament, a legal instrument employed in the belief that it would enshrine the planners' economic principles and further their social and political ambitions.[6] They overtly sought to distance themselves from the earlier-established Australian colonies. The Act, for instance, expressly outlawed the importation of convicts, and it also made provision for what was expected to be a rapid achievement of self-government. Indeed, early drafts of the Act – which the planners penned themselves – sought a degree of colonial autonomy that Colonial Office officials thought bordered on republicanism.[7] As a symptom of its belief in South Australia's robust capacity for government, for instance, South Australia was the only one of Australia's colonies to boast the establishment of a Supreme Court from the first year of its foundation. When South Australia was granted responsible government in the 1850s, along with most of the other Australian colonies, many would have regarded it as another step on the road to eventual political independence. Writing in the year that self-government was granted, the South Australian Commissioner of Police Peter Edgerton Warburton explained his reforms to the Mounted Police Force in terms of his anticipation that they 'might one day form the basis of a national army'. In this case the national army he was imagining was the army of the South Australian nation.[8] Nor was the eventual independence of the Australian colonies beyond the imagination of British statesmen. Writing in the same year as Warburton, Arthur Mills, a Tory politician in England claimed that the aim of Britain's colonial policy should be to 'ripen those communities to the earliest possible maturity – social, political, and commercial to qualify them, by all the appliances within the reach of the parent State, for present self-government, and eventual independence'.[9] The Colonial Office, even as it was extending responsible government to the Australasian colonies, was also encouraging the idea of federation.[10] For instance, Secretary of the State for the Colonies, Earl Grey, proposed uniform tariffs and a General Assembly of the

Colonies, although this imposed attempt at unification failed to gain momentum.[11] In the decades before Federation, Australia's colonies might have maintained an attachment to the British Empire, but this was an attachment which now swayed with new loyalties, not only to a developing sense of Australian proto-nationalism, but also to an ideal of regional political independence.

In 1895 the American writer Mark Twain visited South Australia and was an invited speaker at the Commemoration Day luncheon on 28 December. In his speech Twain graciously commented on his sense of privilege at being part of 'your great day – that which commemorates the founding of a new community'. Reporting on the celebrations a few days later, the *Advertiser* noted that this was the 'event of the year in South Australia', and 'seldom is such a crowd assembled as that which is annually to be seen ... celebrating the national birthday of the colony'.[12] The notion that this was a *national* birthday rather than the birthday of a colony was later mirrored by Twain in his book *Round the Equator*: in recalling his part in the ceremonies he wrote of Commemoration Day as 'the Province's national holiday, its Fourth of July, so to speak'.[13]

In the 19th century, South Australia was not alone in expressing these sentiments; to varying degrees all other Australian colonies expressed similar attitudes. In the early 1870s the English novelist Anthony Trollope came to Australia for a year and was struck by the depth and often the virulence of inter-colonial rivalry. Writing of British laws and their influence on inter-colonial trade, Trollope observed that the Australian colonies were 'determined to be separate. Australia is a term that finds no response in the patriotic feeling of any Australian. They are Victorians, or Queenslanders, or men of New South Wales.'[14] Trollope also had no doubt that eventually 'the name Australia will be dearer to Australian ears than the name Great Britain', but the time was not yet. By the last decades of the 19th century, as Ken Inglis has pointed out, each colony had its own flag, which was often referred to as a 'national' flag.[15] These things point to a depth of regionally-specific national sentiment in the last decades of the 19th century that Australian historiography has tended to overlook, perhaps because of an entrenched assumption, as Alan Atkinson points out, 'that the one and only Australian nation was born in 1901'.[16] Much of the existing literature on Australian colonial nationalism seems framed by the apparent inevitability of Federation, but prior to Federation, colonial nationalist sentiment was expressed differently from one colonial setting to another. As John Eddy puts it, the Australian colonies were 'primarily linked with London rather than each other', and cross-continental commonalities jostled with 'entrenched local patriotism'.[17] This sentiment was not necessarily expressed in terms of separation from the Empire, but in terms of self-government within the Empire. As Anne Coote has written in relation to colonial New South Wales, '[c]olonial nationalism distinguished colony from colony; [and] the imperial relationship – their imagined Britishness – could be just another layer of nationhood.[18]

How robustly did South Australian national sentiments express what Anne

Coote has called a separate sense of 'destiny and sovereignty' in the face of the building momentum to Federation? And how have those sentiments endured over time?[19] We will explore these questions through the convenient lens of 'commemoration days' because these events, marking the beginning of European settlement, might reasonably be expected to give rise to discussions about the character and distinctiveness of the respective colonies. We will suggest that in the decades leading to Federation, as well as after it, South Australia's pride in its sense of foundational 'difference' – be that real or imagined – proved it to be the most assertive from amongst all the Australian colonies in its expression of a specifically regional form of 'national' feeling.

Foundation Days across Australia

The strength and endurance of colonial national sentiment in South Australia can be measured by comparison with foundational commemorations elsewhere. New South Wales, of course, had the longest history of celebrating Anniversary or Foundation Day on 26 January. Captain Phillip's landing was first formally commemorated on its thirtieth anniversary in 1818, and the celebrations were extended and cemented with the introduction of Sydney's Regatta in 1837. Until the 1880s, Anniversary Day remained a New South Wales event that was primarily colonial rather than continental in scope, and the other colonies also expressed their own colonial national sentiment with different anniversaries.

On 1 December 1838 Van Diemen's Land held its inaugural Regatta Day, marking both its independence from New South Wales in 1825 and its 'discovery' by Abel Tasman in 1642. The anniversary had the virtue of locating Tasmania's origins a good century and a half before Captain Phillip's landing at Botany Bay; and from 1853 – which saw the cessation of transportation to Tasmania as well as the colony's Jubilee of British settlement – the annual regatta became an opportunity to celebrate the colony's liberation from the convict 'stain'. Yet although Regatta Day endured, and was reported upon as an 'event of some considerable importance' against which even New South Wales' annual regatta could not compete,[20] press reports on its occurrence were geared around the success of the races, and went largely unencumbered by commentary on the political progress of the colony itself.

Victoria also had its 'national' day in 'Separation Day', commemorated annually on 1 July, the date on which Victoria achieved separation from New South Wales in 1851. Reporting on separation in July 1851, the *Argus*' editor called on Victorians to set themselves to transforming the 'long oppressed, long buffeted' Port Phillip into Victoria, for 'we have the makings of a splendid nation'.[21] For some time, Victorians passionately supported this ideal. For one correspondent to the *Argus* in 1862, for instance, the commemoration of Separation Day was a chance to retain 'a just pride in our separate nationality'.[22] But with the approach of Federation, Separation Day would become more ambivalently regarded. On Separation Day 1882, the *Argus* noted that while Victoria's independence from

New South Wales had held importance in 1851, Victorians were now 'called upon to labour ... for federal unity'. This was not merely perceived in terms of political expediency, but as the next step that would enhance Victoria's place within the new nation. Although Separation Day continued to be marked, in 1885 Victoria erased Separation Day from its list of Public Holidays.[23]

Queensland also celebrated a 'national day' that marked its separation from New South Wales on 10 December 1859, but like Victoria's Separation Day, its observance had become half-hearted by the 1880s. On its commemoration in 1882, the *Queenslander* reported: 'The memory of our struggle for independence from the mother colony is passing away ... and as it does so, probably the day will be less generally observed'.[24] By the late 1870s it seems that observations of the day held a primarily social character,[25] and thereafter it was reported in the Queensland press primarily in terms of the holiday entertainments that took place.

Given that Western Australia was the only colony with South Australia to be established independently of New South Wales, one might expect its commemorations of Foundation Day on 1 June to have been as robust with a sense of separate origins and achievements as were celebrations of South Australia's Commemoration Day, but this seems not to have been the case. Formally commemorated since 1834 and marked as a public holiday, Foundation Day was reported in Western Australia's colonial press as the 'national holiday', just as other colonies' 'national' anniversaries were;[26] but like Queensland's Separation Day or Tasmania's Regatta Day, it was primarily noted for the 'amusements' it provided: year after year, it was reported upon not in terms of the colony's history of achievements, sense of political destiny or future goals, as was South Australia's Commemoration Day, but as an account of horse races, athletics events, balls and suppers. Unlike Victoria's and Queensland's Separation Days, Foundation Day continued to be commemorated in Western Australia to the present time, but in 2012 it was transformed into 'WA Day'. Geared towards contemporary relevance and community inclusion, WA Day has become a broad event commemorating regional achievements, but with a less powerful focus on the history of 'foundation'.

Commemoration Day in South Australia

As Ken Inglis has noted, of all the Australian anniversaries, with the exception of Anniversary Day in New South Wales, Commemoration Day in South Australia – or Proclamation Day as it would later become known – 'evoked the most enthusiasm', and South Australians were not slow to begin those commemorations.[27] On 28 December 1837, just a year after Hindmarsh's Proclamation had been read at Glenelg, the citizens of Adelaide hosted a dinner for the Governor to commemorate the event. The Governor, and then by turns all the leading men of the colony, made toasts to the colony's prosperity.[28] George Stevenson, editor of the colony's first newspaper, proposed a toast to William Wyatt, the Protector of Aborigines. He praised the fact that 'friendly relations prevailed with the

Aboriginal population', and that they were 'daily getting stronger'. 'We had', he went on, 'taken the green olive branch of peace from their hands and we had promised them as our pledges in return the rights of British subjects – the blessings of civilisation and Christianity'. He concluded his toast with the observation, 'may the benevolent intentions of her Majesty's Ministers towards the Natives be carried out (great applause)'. Wyatt, with no apparent sense of irony, responded that 'he hoped at the second commemoration of the constitution of the colony to have present a native who might thank the colonists for himself and his brethren (cheering)'.

As early as 1841 Governor Grey directed that 28 December, 'being the anniversary of the Foundation of the Colony', be observed as public holiday, and it has been observed as a public holiday on or about that date ever since.[29] Like the Anniversary days in the other colonies, the day was principally marked by leisure activities and sporting events: regattas, athletic competitions, carnival attractions and picnics. These events found a focus and a more definitive form by the mid-to-late 1850s. 1857 was South Australia's first year of Responsible Government, when it effectively became an independent, self-governing state within the Empire. It was also its 21st birthday – its 'majority' – and the press made much of the fact that the 'Young Australia' had 'now arrived at manhood'.[30] The focus of the festivities very quickly became the city of Glenelg, Adelaide's principal seaside resort and the location of the Old Gum Tree where the Proclamation was read. In that year an attempt at a more formal recognition of the event occurred when a plaque was attached to the tree to formally mark 'the spot' where the province was 'proclaimed and established' and to 'commemorate the event of the colony attaining its 21st year'. Although the plaque records that it was 'publicly affixed' by Governor MacDonnell, the day was marred by torrential rain that so delayed the Governor's arrival that the hardy souls present went ahead without him, raised the flag, 'broke a bottle or two' in honour of the event, and went home.[31]

Commemoration Day at Glenelg was celebrated with increasing gusto as the century wore on. In 1886, for example, it was reported that more than 80,000 people had travelled to the Bay by rail alone.[32] Once there, they found a city decked out in flags and bunting. Families would promenade and enjoy the carnival attractions, take part in the numerous sporting events on land and sea, and watch the evening fireworks display. The throngs who travelled to Holdfast Bay were 'drawn thither by a strong national sentiment and by the wish to perform a pilgrimage to the colony's birthplace'.[33] The notion that the train trip to the Bay was a 'national pilgrimage' is undoubtedly hyperbolic, but it does articulate an oft-expressed view that grander forms of commemoration should also mark the significance of the day. 'Festivities are forms, commemorations are ceremonies', observed the *Register* somewhat grandiloquently in 1857, 'and we would rather see them conducted in a manner worthy of a great people'.[34] Over time, such elements were added to the Day's events.

As early as the 1850s, it became customary to fire a 21-gun salute at midday.[35] This was usually carried out by the Colony's Volunteer Artillery Corps but, for the first time in 1885, it was performed by South Australia's new gunboat, *The Protector.* This proved to be an inauspicious start: while loading the eighth round the charge exploded prematurely, killing the gunner and badly wounding another.[36] In the 1860s the salute was followed by a military band striking up a rendition of *The Song of Australia*. When this new 'tradition' was reported in 1863, the press described it ironically as 'the grand old national anthem'.[37] Like celebrations of New South Wales' Anniversary Day from the 1880s, *The Song of Australia* is interesting as an example of colonial national sentiment in which an emergent sense of 'Australianness' was conjoined with regional distinctiveness. Coined by Caroline Carleton, it was the winning entry of an 1859 South Australian competition to create a patriotic 'national song'. To this day, *The Song of Australia* is sung in South Australian school assemblies as a regionally-known 'national song', yet is little known in the other states.

To add further to the formalities of Commemoration Day, the Governor often put in an appearance, sometimes escorted by a detachment of Mounted Police.[38] Despite the iconic significance of the Old Gum Tree itself, there are surprisingly few accounts in the 19th century of formal ceremonies at the site where Hindmarsh's Proclamation was read. Photographs taken of the tree in the late 19th century show that it was protected within a fenced enclosure, its arch, for a time, braced by metal struts, and Governor MacDonnell's commemorative plaque nailed awkwardly to its apex. Periodically, calls would be made for a more fitting memorial to be erected at the spot, and in 1884 a competition was held to find the best design for such a 'pioneer memorial', but none of the designs submitted were considered sufficiently worthy of construction.[39]

The elaborate ceremony at the site of the Old Gum Tree that we know today – marked by the presence of pioneer descendants, formalised by the reading of the Proclamation and dignified by the speeches of invited dignitaries – would not take its current shape until the 20th century, but its spiritual predecessor was the Old Colonist's Banquet at the Town Hall. At first these events were relatively informal and *ad hoc*: in 1851 an Old Colonist's dinner was held in a tent at the back of the City Bridge Hotel in Hindley Street, while in 1871 Emanuel Solomon hosted a dinner for 500 old colonists – all of whom 'could tell a tale or two of early struggles and privations' – in the Adelaide Town Hall.[40] Inevitably perhaps it was the 'pioneers', and the history they represented, that were becoming the centrepiece of the Commemoration Day formalities. An Old Colonists' Association was formed in South Australia's Jubilee year of 1886 and henceforth an annual Old Colonists' Banquet was held on Commemoration Day, usually at the Glenelg Town Hall. An elaborate series of toasts and speeches, reflecting on the colony's history and extolling the virtues of the pioneers, would accompany the dining. In 1899, for instance, as South Australian soldiers fought in South Africa, everyone toasted the Queen, the Mayor toasted the Governor, and the Governor toasted the South Australian contingent who, with 'the brave lion-heart of the pioneers', served King and country.[41] Coinciding with the Banquet, there would often be an exhibition of 'relics': paintings of colonial scenes, photographs, journals and assorted memorabilia. The colony's principal relic was, of course, Hindmarsh's Proclamation itself.

In the 1880s, in discussions about how most fittingly to mark the historical significance of the Day, parallels were often made to other commemorations and, on a number of occasions, to the republican sentiments of the United States' Fourth of July:

> On the Fourth of July the citizens of the United States rehearse with pride the Declaration of Independence drawn up by the pilgrim fathers of that great nation, with its central doctrine that all men are by nature born free and equal. We have no such concrete embodiment in documentary form to read to applauding crowds, but the bases of colonial life are equally clear and definite.[42]

The editor went on to suggest that the colony's founding Act provided comparable principles in its direction that the colony be 'self-supporting', 'anti-convict' and free of 'connection between Church and State'.[43] This attempt to elevate the Imperial Act of 1834 to a status equivalent to the Declaration of Independence was forlorn, but Hindmarsh's Proclamation carried a much more romantic charge. In its account of the 1890 Commemoration Day events, the *Advertiser* noted that the original Proclamation was hanging from the wall in the Mayor's parlour: 'The language of the proclamation is as noble as the sentiments it expresses, and as it has not been published for many years it will doubtless be read with interest by the descendants of the pioneers'.[44] The Proclamation was reproduced in its entirety. By 1892, the idea that the Proclamation was the colony's founding document had taken hold and the Minister of Education had arranged for a copy of it to be displayed in all school rooms within the colony.[45] In 1893, the *Register* again reminded its readers of that 'remarkable' document's noble sentiments which enjoined to colonists to 'prove themselves worthy founders of a great and free colony' – a challenge it had no doubt they had met.[46]

South Australia's national history

South Australia's National Day was not just a public holiday marked by festivities and formal ceremonies. It was also a cause for self-conscious reflection on the colony's history and progress. Year after year, in the Commemoration Day ceremonies, speeches and in often lengthy newspaper editorials, the colony's great men and women, its pioneering social and political reforms, and its unique origins would be remembered and praised, and a distinctive national narrative emerged. In asserting South Australia's distinctiveness from the other Australian colonies, the essence of the narrative became the ideal of South Australia's foundation as an independent, 'self-supporting' community, free of convicts, and inspired by ideals of political freedom and innovation:

> It is no slight gain to us as a community that the beginnings of our national life were entirely free from the convict taint, that we were not merely an offshoot of another colony, but that from the first South Australia has been an independent province, and that those who started it were men of honour and of sterling principles.[47]

In 1878 a Commemoration Day editorial not only praised South Australia's distinctiveness, but regarded it as an example for its sister colonies. The journalist observed that the 'principles upon which the colony was founded, has not only been a great success of itself, but undoubtedly a great blessing to the sister provinces of this continent', who were learning from the example South Australia was setting. South Australians had every reason to enjoy themselves on this day of 'national rejoicing'.[48] Such claims continued throughout the late 19th century and into the 20th. In 1909, for instance, the *Advertiser* observed that 'the colonisation of South Australia was the first true attempt at the utilisation of the empty lands of the Commonwealth'. While it was true that other colonies were earlier established, 'in every case the taint of convictism was present'.[49] In 1914, the *Advertiser*'s editor noted that in South Australia 'the foundation was laid very early of those free institutions which one after another was adopted in this progressive State. The ballot, the Real Property Act, religious freedom, and land reform are some of the contributions South Australia has made to the general cause of progress'.[50]

Histories of South Australia, told in the context of Commemoration Day, tended to have a formulaic quality and a familiar cast. This is no better exemplified than in the elaborate reception put on for the old colonists in the Adelaide Town Hall to celebrate the Jubilee of the colony in 1886. Sir Henry Ayers, President of the newly formed Old Colonists' Association, led off the speech-making by putting the 'pioneers' in the vanguard. Those present, he said, who had 'witnessed the inauguration of the colony' and 'having since battled with its difficulties and shared in its prosperity, are now permitted to rejoice over the results achieved'. Some, he noted, played a special part, and first among them was the explorer Charles Sturt. Second on his list was Colonel William Light, the surveyor, for selecting the site of the city. He then proceeded to enumerate a familiar list of founding fathers. He praised the modernity and industry of the colony and observed that 'it is a blessed consolation for us to know that in departing hence we shall leave this country in an immeasurably superior condition to that in which we found it'.[51] Well into the 20th century, Commemoration Day speeches and articles would eulogise exemplary pioneers, such as Sturt, and list landmark events, such as the discovery of copper or the building of the Overland Telegraph, as signifiers of the colony's character and development.

Not surprisingly, the omissions from the story were as familiar as the inclusions.

Although more than half of South Australia's Proclamation was devoted to the principle that Aboriginal people would share equal rights with settlers as British subjects, this principle was routinely omitted in 19th century Commemoration Day speeches, which quoted from the document. Occasionally the humanitarian sentiments enshrined in the Proclamation were remembered. For instance, at the Old Colonists' Banquet given on Commemoration Day in 1871, former Emigration Agent and early settler John Brown called attention to the 'justice and right feeling' extended by the colony's founders to Aboriginal people, this historical pride in South Australia's foundational intentions belying the fact that those intentions had not been realised in reality.[52] In a Commemoration Day editorial in 1914, again, the colony's founders are congratulated for the apparently 'bloodless' settlement of South Australia, which is attributed to the 'wisdom' of the Proclamation in maintaining Aboriginal people's goodwill.[53] For the most part however, if Aboriginal people were mentioned in Commemoration Day speeches at all, they served mainly to underscore how the 'early labours of those hard-working and hopeful' pioneers had transformed a wilderness inhabited only by 'natives' into the thriving colony that emerged.[54] Women too were slow to be included in the evolving pantheon of pioneers; an early acknowledgement of the contribution came in 1896 – two years after women's suffrage had been won in South Australia – in an article in which the author confessed that not all the pioneers were 'sons of Adam'; some, indeed, were 'pilgrim mothers'.[55]

In the mid-to-late 1880s, when Victoria and South Australia celebrated their respective Jubilees, and New South Wales its centenary, multiple loyalties were now manifesting themselves: loyalty to Britain, a patriotic attachment to one's new home, and fraternal bonds with neighbouring colonies, sharpened by the prospect of federation. These jostling loyalties were especially heightened in 1888 when an effort was made to celebrate 26 January as more than just Sydney's Anniversary Day, but as a continent-wide celebration of British settlement in Australia.[56] Sydney marked the event with a week of festivities and invited dignitaries from all the Australasian colonies to attend. Melbournians joined in and marked the day with a public holiday. On 1 February 1888, the *Sydney Morning Herald* basked in the reflected glory of its anniversary and cited kind things said about the colony in other Australian papers. It cited the Adelaide *Advertiser's* comment that South Australians gladly joined with Sydney in the 'national festival'. It mentioned how the Melbourne *Argus* expressed its pleasure in the fact that Anniversary Day had been observed as a holiday in Melbourne, and noted its suggestion that it take the place of Separation Day, 'which only reminds Victorians of local strife' and which was 'best forgotten'. Nonetheless, it also winced at a discordant note from another unnamed Melbourne paper:

> Victoria, it says, will not celebrate the centenary of New South Wales, because the colony is not one hundred years old, and because the Victorians "do not enjoy

> tracing their [ancestry] to the sturdy thieves and beggars who were landed on the shores of Sydney Cove when George III was king". The allusion is plain enough, and it is as insulting as it is plain.[57]

By and by, the author took consolation in the fact that our 'Melbourne and Adelaide contemporaries are seized with the Federal spirit in discussing the celebrations', and that the mingling of so many of them with the people of Sydney 'may tend to promote the unity of Australia'.[58]

A closer look at precisely what the *Advertiser* did say suggests a somewhat more conditional endorsement of the 'Federal spirit'. The editorial began by noting that 'today the colonies of Australia are a unit, and one common sentiment pervades the whole'. The author of the article, however, chose his words carefully: almost every clause that acknowledged continental unity was matched by another that underscored colonial distinctiveness:

> Each colony of the group has its own local memories and historic dates, but today particularly all of the colonial states of this continent unite in commemorating the first stage in Australian colonization.
>
> ...
>
> The bonds that unite us are more numerous and stronger than any that keep us apart. It cannot be said that today is in any sense the anniversary of a common birthday, because some of these colonies were established on quite independent terms. New South Wales, though the senior, is not the parent colony of all the other members of the group.[59]

What the article reveals is an undisputed growth in continental nationalism, alongside a still tenacious sense of colonial nationalism. In 1890 the *Register* reminded its readers that South Australia was inaugurated as a 'Province' and not a 'colony', proudly tied to the old country, but independent: 'disposed legislatively and socially to take its own course'. 'Progress', it added, 'is the inevitable destiny of South Australia. Just as we in our own day and generation look back upon the earlier period of our existence of the province as the day of small things, so in turn will our successors glance back to the year 1890, and marvel at the small beginnings from which a great nation was destined to spring'.[60]

One might expect that as the likelihood of federal union became more certain, this sense of colonial nationalism would become less pronounced, yet this was not the case in South Australia. Rather, as the prospect of a federated Australia loomed larger, a vocabulary of regional nationalism became increasingly firm in press reports of the foundational anniversary. It was not enough, the *Register* said, to merely enjoy 'the country's birthday' – meaning South Australia's birth – but 'intelligence and patriotism' needed to be put to the purpose of making Commemoration Day an occasion for 'quickening and assisting the growth of national aspirations'. In 1892, the *Advertiser* reflected on the sentiments that 'cluster around Commemoration Day' and reminded readers of the terms of South

Australia's Proclamation and the high ideals upon which the colony was built. In the future, this writer reflected, 'the recollection of past enterprise, struggling, toil and reward, will not be absent. It is the birthday of the colony that we keep, of our country, of our home'.[61] At the Commemoration Day banquet in 1896, the Commissioner of Public Works gave the customary toast to 'the pioneers' and pondered the meaning of Commemoration Day within a federated Australia. As the colony grew in population and importance, he stated, so too South Australia's foundational anniversary 'would grow in magnitude and interest, and even when the Federal Union of all the colonies took place, and South Australia was part of the Federal Government, the colony would not lose its identity, and the importance of December 28 would be increased rather than diminished'.[62] While in retrospect this seems a hopelessly optimistic view, at the time it was generally imagined that the states, rather than the Commonwealth, would be 'the predominant site of political and financial authority' within the new federation.[63]

Commemoration Day in the 20th Century

As the Commissioner of Public Works had predicted, these expressions of South Australians' national sentiment did endure after Federation, but only for a time. In the early years of the 20th century, South Australian press editorials on Commemoration Day continued to refer to the occasion as the state's 'national birthday'.[64] Even after Federation, 'national' sentiment co-mingled with attachment to the British Empire. As the *Advertiser*'s editorial put it on 'the National Birthday' or Commemoration Day in 1903, South Australia – now no longer a colony but a state in the newly federated nation – was still destined 'to become one of the brightest jewels in the British Crown'.[65] As the 20th century progressed, celebrations of Proclamation Day, as it was increasingly being called, continued with much the same shape and sense of occasion. Most notably, the official ceremonies celebrating the day not only praised the enterprise of the first settlers and the progress of the state, but continued to draw attention to South Australia's historical sense of 'difference'.[66] In 1920, the *Advertiser* reminded its readers that their state 'was the only one in the Commonwealth which was established independently by free men having high ideals', every detail planned by 'well educated, well-to-do, and ambitious men':

> who came to the new land with the promise of a free constitution in their possession, and who, in the fullness of time, obtained that constitution, broad based upon the people's will, and containing principles of freedom and democracy which were not attained by the other States until long afterwards ...[67]

Yet over the course of the 20th century, as the federation matured, the language of nationalism which had once attached itself to South Australia – 'patriotism', 'pilgrimage', 'love of country', 'our national day' – receded and began to disappear. By the 1920s, the press stopped referring to the South Australian 'nation' and increasingly referred to Commemoration Day as the anniversary of the 'Foundation of the State'.[68] South Australian nationalism more clearly became 'State loyalty',[69] making formerly proud claims of 'exceptionalism' look increasingly like parochialism. As the new century progressed, the sentiments of nationalism became unambiguously associated with the Australian nation, increasingly buttressed by the collective national experience of two World Wars and the inexorable shift of power from the states to the Commonwealth.[70] Interest in Commemoration Day itself gradually diminished; in 1926 the *Advertiser* noted that the throngs which once flocked to the Bay were now 'a dwindling band', drawn away by the 'numerous counter attractions' to which the 'ubiquitous motor car' now gave them easy access.[71]

The increasing strength of Australian nationalism was apparent in celebrations of the state's centenary in 1936, two years before the nation celebrated its Sesquicentenary. A marble panel carved for display at Holdfast Bay situated the history of South Australia within a story of the nation's broader progress, including the laying of the Overland Telegraph Line and the achievement of Federation.[72] Yet loyalty to the nation still did not preclude enduring pride in South Australia's origins as a 'jewel in the crown' of Britain's Empire. In the same month as the marble memorial was installed at the site of the first settlers' landing to celebrate South Australia's place within a federated Australia, an Empire Pageant was performed on the Adelaide Oval in November before thousands of spectators, featuring a series of tableaux that positioned South Australia's history less within the Australian nation than within the 'brotherhood' of British colonies.[73] South Australia's centenary, it seemed, provided the occasion both for looking back to colonial affiliations and for looking forward to national ones. Yet the centennial year also provided cause for reviving what had become flagging interest in Proclamation Day. On 28 December 1936, unprecedented crowds flocked to Hindmarsh's landing site of Glenelg. Since anticipated crowds were too large to gather around the traditional site of the Old Gum Tree, the 'cult of the Tree' was continued by installing a replica at the nearby oval.[74] An estimated 150,000 people gathered to witness a re-creation of Hindmarsh's landing, which was followed by a procession of floats depicting historic scenes. The pageant travelled to the Glenelg Oval where a re-creation of the reading of the Proclamation was acted out beneath a plaster-cast replica of the Old Gum Tree.[75] The floats in the pageant included all the likely suspects: Matthew Flinders charting the coast, Sturt exploring the Murray, Hindmarsh aboard the *Buffalo* reading the Proclamation, pioneers opening up the land and, in the lead, an Aboriginal scene depicting the moment before 'civilisation' arrived.

While the Proclamation's call for the colonists to found a 'great and free country' strikes a triumphant note, the passages calling for Aboriginal rights and justice must have been more discomforting. During the 1930s, as South Australia and Victoria celebrated their centenaries and the nation its Sesquicentenary, the building momentum of Aboriginal rights brought back into focus those sections of South Australia's Proclamation which dealt with the foundational rights owed to Aboriginal people as equal British subjects. The anthropologist J.B. Cleland, for instance, suggested that there could be no better way to mark the centenary 'than by honouring some of [our] obligations to the Aborigines'. He reminded his audience that 'the proclamation read by Governor Hindmarsh at the establishment of the Province dealt with the rights and protection of the natives, and only one-third with the affairs of the white inhabitants'.[76] For decades, Commemoration Day celebrations had served to remind the South Australian community of the political aspirations and ambitions of its founders, but now it also served to remind that same community of the state's foundational but unfulfilled obligations to Aboriginal people.

However, it was not until the 21st century that the Aboriginal rights endorsed by the Proclamation became centrally acknowledged in Proclamation Day ceremonies. On 28 December 2007, the Town Clerk of the Holdfast Bay Municipal Council read aloud the Proclamation at the Old Gum Tree where 171 years earlier the Colonial Secretary read Hindmarsh's Proclamation before an assembly of some 200 colonists. The audience on this day in 2007 comprised a similar number of people, many of them direct descendants of those original colonists. As the section of the document promising 'justice' to Aboriginal people was read, a protester shouted out 'What justice?' A small group of Aboriginal protesters gathered outside the park, kept in check by two Mounted Police. For a number of years now, they have used the event as a forum to voice their demands for rights to land and a Treaty. The following year, in the spirit of reconciliation, the Council invited Aboriginal people for the first time to be represented at the event; the formalities now included an Aboriginal smoking ceremony, an Aboriginal flag now flew alongside the State Ensign, and an Aboriginal Elder called for an honouring of the promise to recognise Aboriginal rights to land which is contained in South Australia's other foundational document, the Letters Patent.

Conclusion

Over the course of the 19th century and into the 20th, expressions of nationalism describe what Alan Atkinson has called a 'multiplicity of nations, of nationhood as a variously defined, mutually overlapping, frequently evanescent sense of community and place'. In the history of what we now call Australia, he observes, 'there have been many kinds of nations, and there has been nothing absolute or eternal about any of them'.[77] In the decades before Federation, different forms of colonial nationalism were manifest in the commemoration of each colony's 'national' day, but not all of these endured over time; and although each defined a distinctive sense of regional identity and pride, not all were celebrated with a distinctively articulated sense of origins and destiny. Until recently, South Australia's and Western Australia's commemorations of their own foundational days seemed to stand out in this regard. This is hardly surprising, given that they were the only Australian colonies to be established independently of New South Wales, and they did not share the associations of separation that made other colonies' Separation Days appear less politically relevant as Federation approached. Yet today, even Western Australia's Foundation Day has lost its force, and the commemoration of WA Day that now takes place on the foundational date of 1 June is more concerned with recognising the state's wider achievements than with commemorating the foundational history of its first settlement. A similar commemoration of state distinctiveness, which celebrates the state's history and development but is not continuously associated with the foundational sentiment of colonial nationalism, takes place annually in Queensland on 6 June as Queensland Day, a contemporary initiative that was instituted by the state government in 1981. A similar shift is even being mooted in South Australia. Very recently the Unley City Council passed a resolution calling for Proclamation Day to be re-named South Australia Day, with Councillor Sangster pointing out that the 'first formal settlement of South Australia did', after all, 'occur on Kangaroo Island in July', besides which, it would make the day more inclusive of all South Australians.[78] Such a change, were the momentum for it to gather pace, would see South Australia fall in step with the other Australian states.

6

Sex and Citizenship: From Ballot Boxes to Bedrooms

SUSAN MAGAREY

My subject is sex and citizenship. My focus is on two legislative events contributing to the citizenship of women: the achievement of votes for women, a first for Australia, here in South Australia in 1894, and the prohibition of discrimination against women, again a first for Australia, in South Australia in 1975. Both were crucial moves in the admission of women to political citizenship (via the vote) and to economic citizenship (via access to paid work). I will recount the stories of each event, and consider three explanations for them, explanations that I hope will provide warrant for the sub-title of this chapter – 'From Ballot Boxes to Bedrooms'. In conclusion I will pause for a moment on the question of the citizenship of men.

Political citizenship

Let us imagine that we are in Parliament House on North Terrace. It is 17 December 1894, a Monday, close to the date of the summer solstice in the southern hemisphere. The House of Assembly is debating the third reading of the Constitution Act Amendment Bill – legislation that could give votes to women, legislation that needs a two-thirds majority because it alters the constitution, legislation that has already passed the Legislative Council. Women have deluged Members of Parliament with telegrams. They are crowding into the Speaker's Gallery of the newly completed House of Assembly to hear the debate.[1] The 'Grand Old Woman of South Australia', sixty-nine year-old Catherine Spence, arrives. She is fresh off the ship bringing her home from a year of giving lectures across the world, armed with affirmations of solidarity from suffrage campaigners in the United States and England. She goes to the Ladies' Gallery and sits beside Rose Birks, Honorary Secretary of the Woman Suffrage League, signalling her support for the measure under debate.[2] Some twelve parliamentarians – members and ministers, including both current Premier Kingston and former premier John Downer – come and greet her.[3]

At four in the afternoon, some of the women retreat to hold a brief, tense meeting of the Woman Suffrage League before they go off to the Café de Paris in Rundle Street where they are having a party to welcome Miss Spence home.

Catherine Spence notices that fierce Irish Mary Lee, acknowledged leader of the women's suffrage campaign, is 'in a great dudgeon because my welcome has been arranged outside of her – and she was not adv[ertised] as speaker'. Catherine Spence placates Mary Lee so that she agrees to join them after all.[4] Their party demonstrates the extent and weight of their support for the Bill under debate so vociferously that they drown out conversation at the table of a parliamentarian near by.[5]

The party breaks up. Principal speech makers – Mary Lee, Rose Birks, Catherine Spence, and Elizabeth Webb Nicholls, President of the Suffrage Division of the Woman's Christian Temperance Union[6] – and their friends troop back down King William Street to the Parliament, heels ringing on the pavement. As the *South Australian Chronicle* will report, the House is packed, more than it has ever been before, so that 'there was a wall of beauty at the southern end of the building, and the standard of legislative eloquence was raised sympathetically'.[7]

But the Bill's supporters are not winning this night. Its opponents are still trying to talk it out. It is past midnight, after the trams have stopped running, before the government moves an adjournment until the next morning.[8] The suffragists make their way home to restless and anxious hours. For, as one of those supporters will write later, '[n]o-one, looking at the final figures, would have any conception of the intensity of the struggle, of the manifold difficulties overcome, nor of the fact that the issue was doubtful till within 12 hours of the final vote.'[9]

The vote is taken the next morning, 18 December. 'The Ayes were sonorous and cheery', reports the *Adelaide Observer*, 'the Noes despondent like muffled bells'. The count shows 31 in favour and only 14 against. The house resounds to cheers.[10]

On the morning of this momentous decision, the Adelaide *Advertiser* appeared on the streets and breakfast tables announcing that female suffrage was, essentially, about sex.

> We have always urged that the fundamental question is the sexual one. Regard women as a class, and there is no argument worthy of a moment's examination in favour of denying them the suffrage. Regard them as a sex, with an appropriate sphere of sexual activity into which voting and sitting in Parliament – the two things are complementary – cannot be intruded without injuriously deranging normal sexual relations, and the whole aspect of the question completely changes.[11]

But the vote taken a few hours later made it clear that for the majority of parliamentarians in the South Australian legislature, women were no longer to be regarded as merely 'a sex'. Women – all women, including Aboriginal women – would have the vote on the same terms as men; they had been made political subjects, just as all men – including Aboriginal men – in South Australia had been since 1857: they were political citizens, almost three decades before the women of the United States achieved such status, and nearly four decades before those of Great Britain.

Indeed, under this legislation, women could sit in the parliament as well. This was an extension of the campaign for the vote that women had not immediately sought. The constitution of the Woman Suffrage League explicitly stated that 'no claim is put forward for the right to sit as representatives'. This right resulted from Ebenezer Ward's attempt to wreck the Bill.

Ward was known as South Australia's 'silver tongue'.[12] He had been sued for divorce by his first wife and he was to be taken to court by his second wife for failing to support her and their nine children adequately. He would arrive in the Legislative Council to oppose the Married Women's Protection Bill in 1896 so drunk that he could not read the statement on the paper in front of him. A chivalrous man, a lover of women, Ebenezer Ward suffered no doubts about the essential nature of 'normal sexual relations'. God had placed women on a 'high pedestal'. There they must remain, enjoying men's worship, discharging their 'sacred functions' – tending their domestic circles, serving their husbands, caring for their children. So, he intoned, it had been in the beginning, when God told Adam to be fruitful and multiply, so it ever should be. Men were inferior creatures, base, closer to the animals, occupied 'down there' with the cloacal world of politics, business and sexual desire. To my pride and pleasure, I find one of my forebears, Dr Sylvanus Magarey, in the parliament making fun of such imagery: 'He placed her ... on a pedestal in the kitchen', he mocked, 'stood her upon a camp-oven, and armed her with a rolling-pin for a shield ... he would keep her in thraldom in the kitchen'.[13] In August 1894, in an attempt to make the Bill unacceptable to the lower house, Ward moved that its second clause – excluding women from sitting in parliament – be struck out. But he failed: the amendment was carried. And that set South Australia at the forefront of the world for more than a decade.

There have been several explanations advanced for this victory for the women suffragists in South Australia. Let me touch on three. They offer a glimpse of three successive emphases in Australian historiography.

Politics

One explanation, from the 1970s, focuses primarily on the politics of the suffrage era. It considers the polarisation of capital and labour amid industrial strife across the country at the beginning of the 1890s and the formation of political parties, initially the United Labor Party and later the conservative parties associated with nationalism and the interests of farmers and producers. This picture is much the same as anywhere else in Australia. But in South Australia there was a third political factor. That was the array of small, often short-lived, groups which were the source of the South Australian labour movement's utopianism, and its search for visions, programs and strategies that could counter exploitation and ideological domination.[14] The District Democratic Clubs and Associations, the Land Reform Leagues, the Single Tax League, the Society for the Study of Christian Sociology, the Working Men's Patriotic Association, the South Australian Fabian Society and the district Sociological Classes – all were called collectively 'the Forward Movement' or the 'Reform Movement'. In the early 1890s, they were all working strenuously for 'a distinct forward movement, lifting up instead of levelling down society'.[15] Their major fundamental link was their faith in the new social and moral order, which they believed particular reforms would bring. Their faith gave their demands – for the single tax, nationalisation of land, distribution of wealth, and justice to labour – the ring of a sacred creed. They were fervent; they were also extremely, and ecumenically, Christian. J. Medway Day, agitator for land reform and instigator of the Reform Convention held in September 1893, had been a minister in the Baptist Church. The Reverend Dr. Jeffries gave a series of discourses in the North Adelaide Congregational Church on 'The Socialism of Christianity'. The Wesleyan minister G.E. Wheatley addressed the Reform Convention on 'The Churches and Reform'. D.M. Charleston, speaking on 'The Ethics of Socialism' shared the platform with the Primitive Methodist minister J. Day Thompson, lecturing on 'The Simple Gospel'.

The Reform Movement did not, itself, achieve parliamentary representation. But in the early 1890s, the meetings and lectures of these groups, and their paper, *Voice*, spread a spirit of idealism, a receptivity to new ideas, and a readiness for change which brought to power the government of the wonderfully rambunctious radical liberal Queen's Counsel, Charles Cameron Kingston, with the support of the first Labor Party members to achieve election to the Parliament. Initially, such a government had no interest in supporting legislation for votes for women. After all, successive motions and bills considered since the first in 1885, moved by another of my forebears, Edward Charles Stirling, had been encumbered by an array of proposals to restrict women's access to the vote, by age, ownership of property or marital status.[16] Kingston and his supporters considered these measures likely to strengthen the forces of conservatism. But suffragist Mary Lee had, from the beginning, made strong connections between the Woman Suffrage League, the United Trades and Labor Council and the Forward Movement. The Forward Movement supported the suffragists. The Woman Suffrage League opposed measures introduced by conservative politicians seeking to provide a vote for only a restricted proportion of the female population. By 1894, they had persuaded the Kingston government to take it on, and to take it on as a government measure.[17] And that ensured its success.

Structure

A second kind of explanation, advanced in the 1980s, emphasised structural changes taking place in South Australian society becoming an impetus for women to claim greater rights than they enjoyed as merely 'a sex'. Such structural changes concerned women's work.[18] Their work as wives and mothers was diminishing: the marriage-rate might have been higher than the marriage-rate in the neighbouring colony of Victoria, but it was still lower than the marriage-rate in Britain or in New Zealand; and the crude birth-rate was falling, from 39% to 24.5%.[19] At the same time, there was considerable movement for a wider range of employments for women. Increased literacy, following government provision of education, and advanced schooling, even access to the university for some young women, opened up the possibilities of winning a livelihood as a telephonist or a typist in a telegraph office, or as a teacher in a government school, or even as one of those rare pioneering women in the law or medicine. Affecting a far larger number of women was the slowly-growing industrial labour market. Women who would earlier have earned their livings as domestic servants were, increasingly, moving into the industrial labour market – into laundries, into workshops making biscuits and confectionery, rolling and packing tobacco, binding books, and making paper bags. The Working Women's Trades Union, formed in 1889, organised women working as tailoresses, seamstresses and brushmakers. There was nothing easy about such jobs. But they allowed those workers greater self-determination and greater freedom of action than they had when employed as a domestic servant in another woman's household, and the pay was better. The number of women employed in domestic service in South Australia halved between 1881 and 1911, while the number employed in factories and workshops trebled between 1876 and 1911. Women enjoying such measures of self-determination and independence found their experience in direct contradiction to the images of life for women offered by men like Ebenezer Ward. That contradiction could constitute an imperative to demand basic political rights.

Culture

A third kind of explanation, developed in the 1990s, adds a cultural dimension by placing an emphasis on how women and men were speaking and writing about the position of women and relationships between women and men. This transforms the two earlier explanations I have offered into an account of something that, I would argue, is a deep change in culture. For running alongside these structural changes in women's work was an explicit critique of the double standard of sexual morality, of 'compulsory maternity', and even of marriage.

Writing as early as 1878, Catherine Spence commented that economic independence for women would eliminate the double standard of sexual morality because it would enable a woman to *choose* 'not between destitution and marriage but between the modest competence that she can earn and the modest competence her lover offers'.[20] The Woman Suffrage League was a direct descendant of the ladies' division of the Social Purity Society formed in 1882 to combat the double standard of sexual morality and one of its consequences: prostitution, particularly among young girls. In September 1885 the Social Purity Society organised a spectacular torch-lit procession through the streets of Adelaide and into the Town Hall to listen to speeches urging legislation to raise the age of consent to sixteen. The speeches were delivered by a wonderfully ecumenical array of speakers from Anglican, Roman Catholic, Methodist and Baptist churches and the Salvation Army.[21] Eliminating the double standard of sexual morality *within* marriage – known at the time as 'compulsory maternity' – required contraception. In a novella published in 1888, Catherine Spence depicted a utopian society in which 'the preventive population check' was the centrepiece of her vision of the future; birth control was compulsory.[22] Early in the 20th century, a young Adelaide medical graduate, Rosamund Benham, published a pamphlet titled *Sense About Sex, by a Woman Doctor.* Accompanying it in a plain brown wrapper was a second work called *Circumvention: A Plan of Procreative Control is Addressed as a Medical Work to Adults by a Woman Doctor.* Benham was also urging contraception, though by dint of self-control rather than the mechanical devices that were widely available. But since she was simultaneously arguing 'how essential passion is to human existence', it seems unlikely, as historian Alison Mackinnon observes, 'that the plan was enormously successful'.[23] From these, it is but a short step to a critique of marriage. The heroine of South Australian Catherine Martin's novel, *An Australian Girl* published in 1890, expresses great suspicion of marriage. 'Yes; ever since I have been able to think or observe I have been convinced that marriage is the most foolish, faulty old institution going', she remarks. Later she notes that marriage is a spoiler of friendship.[24] Catherine Martin, herself, as another historian, Margaret Allen, observes, did marry – but not until she was past the age of child-bearing.[25]

This third kind of explanation clearly shows that the *Advertiser*'s 'normal sexual relations' were undergoing challenge and change. In New South Wales, socialist-feminist poet Marie Pitt dubbed the falling birth-rate 'the Greatest Strike in World History'.[26] Demographers have since labelled this period 'the Australian family transition'. This was a deep change in society and culture. On average, Australian families have never again been as large as they were in the 19th century. This could quite properly be called the first sexual revolution in settler Australia. It was a crucial context for the campaigns for votes for women under way at the same time. What was going on in Australian bedrooms in this period – or perhaps what was *not* going on – was essential to understanding what was happening to access to Australia's ballot boxes.

Economic citizenship

Let us move on 81 years, to the *Sex Discrimination Act* of 1975. The story can be told quickly. On 29 August 1973, Dr David Tonkin, Member of the House of Assembly for Bragg, introduced a private member's Bill 'to prohibit discrimination against persons by reason only of their sex'.[27] Tonkin was at that time in opposition; earlier, a foundation member of the Liberal Movement, he was, journalist Rex Jory considered, a 'soft' Liberal.[28] He would become premier in 1979, his three years of government perhaps best known for legislation – originating with the previous Dunstan Government – which gave the Pitjantjatjara people authority to exercise broad powers over their traditional lands, despite the wishes of the mining companies.[29] Tonkin was to explain that his Sex Discrimination Bill was introduced in 'rather trying circumstances'. His mother 'was particularly interested in the Bill'. 'She was widowed', he went on,

> when I, as an only child, was five years of age, and we had quite a battle to make good. In the climate of that time, in the mid-1930s, her education and training for employment were quite unsuitable; further, even had she thought of obtaining employment (which she did on occasions) eyebrows would have been raised and it would have been considered not the done thing.

On the evening before he was to present the Bill to the Parliament, his mother was taken to hospital. On the way there she told him that she hoped that he would go ahead with introducing the Bill because of its importance to South Australia. She died that night.[30] The next morning he was on his feet in the Parliament.

Tonkin's Bill was to 'prohibit discrimination against any individual ... in employment, training for employment and in the provision of financial services and credit'. The Bill was referred to a Select Committee and then brought back to the Parliament together with the committee's report in October 1974. The report concluded that there *was* discrimination warranting action, but as implementation of the Bill would necessitate public funding for the establishment of a Sex Discrimination Board, it recommended that a government Bill rather than a private member's Bill was required.[31] Tonkin declared this 'balderdash and absolute tommy rot!'[32] But the Premier and Treasurer, Don Dunstan, intervened to affirm the government's accord with the Bill's principles and to promise that this, or another measure to the same effect, would go forward.[33]

It did, indeed, go forward after extensive homework in the Policy Secretariat of the Premier's Department. In June 1975 Dunstan introduced the government's Bill. It was a broader, stronger and more innovative measure. The government considered, said Dunstan, that it is 'easy enough to provide in legislation a principle that there should not be discrimination', but it 'is much more difficult to provide that the people discriminated against have remedies that are real rather than illusory'. Accordingly, the Sex Discrimination Board, with a chairman [*sic*] 'with extensive legal experience', and two other members, would 'have power to act in a judicial capacity, and to award damages'. It would not be bound by 'the normal rules of evidence'. It would have 'powers of inquisition, inquiry and conciliation'. This would mean that, he elaborated,

> instead of someone who has been discriminated against having to go through the tedious, involved, costly and often unsatisfactory process of trying to prove discrimination according to the normal rules of evidence before a court, here is a board that can come to reasonable human conclusions as a result of normal investigation and inquiry in a simple and effective way.

It would be 'a signal advance', Dunstan announced, 'in social legislation in this State'. It could not, he acknowledged, 'completely eradicate all forms of unfair discrimination based on sex or marital status'. But his government hoped that it would 'create a climate in which public opinion will be mobilised against this form of discrimination'.[34] It was a giant step towards women achieving economic citizenship, made by providing a means of combating the prejudices and prohibitions that had barred them from so many kinds of paid work, even – as with David Tonkin's mother – from paid work altogether.

So what explains this victory? Will the same three kinds of explanation work once again? Let us see.

Politics

The first kind of explanation points to the politics of the Dunstan Decade. Four Dunstan governments, from 1970 to 1979, transformed South Australia. He was 'one of the most charismatic, courageous and progressive Australian politicians of the 20th century', wrote one observer. 'The Nureyev of Australian politics', said another. 'A pocket Adonis', observed a third.[35] Political scientist Andrew Parkin has judged that for about five years, '[t]he Dunstan Government sponsored a period of policy innovation probably without emulation in this country.'[36] Dunstan's self-proclaimed commitment to full and stable employment; care for the aged, poor and sick; education; and balanced development for the nation's resources, included a vision of securing 'personal liberty and the opportunity for everyone to develop to the full his or her human potential'.[37] This last goal ensured his active and constructive support for measures at least to lessen *in*-equalities between women and men.

Dunstan had help, of course. The Select Committee appointed to consider David Tonkin's Sex Discrimination Bill included Molly Byrne, the first female Australian Labor Party Member of the South Australian Parliament. It also included Peter Duncan, a young firebrand with a background in student politics, Young Labor and opposition to the war in Vietnam while he was taking his Law degree at the University of Adelaide during the 1960s. Duncan won the seat for Elizabeth in the election of March 1973 and in 1975 he joined the Dunstan Cabinet as Attorney-General. His was the Bill to abolish capital punishment introduced in November 1976. He would be the minister responsible for the Sex Discrimination Board set up once the Dunstan *Sex Discrimination Act* had passed.[38]

And of course there was the Women's Liberation Movement. It surfaced early in Adelaide when, in March 1970, a group calling themselves Women's Liberation picketed the 'Miss Fresher' contest (part of the orientation week celebrations at the University of Adelaide) in protest against the objectification of women and what historian Marilyn Lake has called 'the imperative of femininity': the requirement that women be 'sweet, attractive, submissive, understanding, dependent and defenceless'.[39] Women's Liberation groups mushroomed all over Adelaide.

In 1972 another feminist force appeared, first in Melbourne but then throughout the country: Women's Electoral Lobby [WEL], less revolutionary than Women's Liberation but nevertheless committed to radical change to the position of women and relations between women and men, initially through the electoral process. WEL developed a questionnaire that its members took to all politicians, asking for their views on a range of issues of concern to women. Dunstan achieved the best score of all WEL's respondents.[40] Deborah McCulloch was active in Women's Electoral Lobby. She rushed around organising people to make submissions to the Select Committee on Tonkin's Bill. They included stalwarts of the women's movement from the pre-Women's Liberation decades: one from the National Council of Women, another from the League of Woman Voters, a third from the Union of Australian Women.[41] One witness, Jill Blewett, was a member of the Abortion Law Reform Association of South Australia, a body formed in 1968, before Women's Liberation, but also more active in its single cause than the traditional feminists.[42] Witnesses from newer organisations included members of WEL from Port Pirie and Port Augusta, as well as McCulloch herself. They also included Annette Willcox, director of the Naomi Shelter at Ovingham,[43] who – Deborah McCulloch tells me – funded this feminist refuge by soliciting donations from men in pubs during the notorious six o'clock swill.[44]

These women had to combat assertions that 'the failure to secure positions more often than not results from the fact that only a small proportion of females possess the necessary qualifications or experience', that 'often women do not apply for positions which they do not expect to get, so that ... they are themselves responsible for what others may consider to be discrimination', that 'examples of discrimination ... appear to be based on traditional attitudes rather than on any objective ground', that 'traditional attitudes frequently result from influences at home' (code for mothers), and that some employers and trades unions are reluctant to promote women to executive positions because 'it is claimed that the presence of women at meetings or other gatherings might inhibit discussion'.[45] As David Tonkin told the parliament, 'I think the suggestion was made quite openly that bad language might be used and that women would therefore be offended'.[46] There were as well witnesses who claimed that there was no discrimination against women in education, and that discrimination against women in finance and journalism was diminishing.

However, the stories told by the women won out. And once the government's Bill was in the parliament – it was 1975, International Women's Year – women had great fun with it, on both sides of politics. The Honourable Jessie Cooper, for instance, a Liberal, one of the first two women elected to the parliament, offered the Legislative Council her favourite example of discrimination. It came from a report to the Melbourne Anglican Synod on women in the ministry, it read:

> Although a woman's qualifications and abilities may be undoubted, because she is not a man her ministry must be less than total – more in the nature of a sheepdog rather than a shepherd.[47]

Structure

The second kind of explanation looks to the structure of the labour market. One of the witnesses to the Select Committee was listed as 'Miss J.A.W. Levy'. This was Anne Levy, who would be elected to the Legislative Council for the ALP in 1975. In debate on the Bill in October 1975, the Honourable Anne Levy cut through much of the nonsense and confusion about women and work by quoting from an excellent article by feminist political economist, Margaret Power. The article was called 'Women's Work is Never Done – By Men' and appeared in a mainstream publication, the *Journal of Industrial Relations*.[48] What Power's article demonstrated incontrovertibly was that the labour market was segmented by gender. In the 60 years from 1911 to 1971, between 82% and 84% of women in the work force were in occupations that were predominantly female, and large areas of employment were closed to them.[49] Further, as later analyses by the International Labor Organisation were to demonstrate, the gender segmentation of the workforce was simultaneously a segmentation between a primary and a secondary workforce. The primary workforce was characterised by high status, stable employment, high skill requirements, high earnings and good prospects for advancement. The secondary workforce, by contrast, displayed the opposite traits – low status, high turnover and employment instability, low skill requirements, low earnings and few advancement opportunities. The primary workforce was overwhelmingly male, the secondary workforce female. As Power noted: 'female occupations are those in which work relationships require men to be in authority over women and where the nature of the work is often derivative of housework, for instance, work associated with food, clothing and cleaning and work which involves caring for the young and the sick'.[50] Margaret Power's statistics were for the whole of Australia, but Anne Levy added examples demonstrating that South Australia was by no means quarantined from such analysis. This was an unanswerable case. (It still is.)

Culture

A third kind of explanation for the success of the Sex Discrimination legislation of the mid-1970s centres on its cultural context. This period was 'the dawning of the age of Aquarius', the cultural revolution of advanced industrial capitalism, an explosion of cultural and political protest against everything that smacked of established authority, restrictions on ideas and sexual repression. 'I got Life!' they sang. 'Let the sunshine in'. These were the titles of songs in the musical called *Hair*, which Jim Sharman brought from New York to Sydney in 1970; South Australian Justice Roma Mitchell took four Sydney friends with her to see it.[51] It broke a host of taboos, men appearing with wild long hair, men and women naked, singing about hashish, about racial politics, and about gay sex.

These followed the years when television brought into people's living-rooms images of students protesting against the stultifying conditions and nature of their education in the streets of Paris; images of Martin Luther King igniting crowds – 'I have a dream' he told them – during the struggles for racial equality in the United States; images of celebrations of the liberalising anti-Stalinist politics of Alexander Dubček's new regime in Czechoslovakia; and then, closer to home, images of the moratorium marches against the United States' war in Vietnam and Australia's participation in it. These years saw the birth of the counter-culture that would, over time, become the new social movements – activist collectives demanding rights and recognitions for particular identities: youth, women, blacks, gays and lesbians, and around particular political issues: the green and peace movements protesting the degradation of the environment, the proliferation of war, and the expansion of nuclear weaponry.[52]

They would not have it all their own way. For such liberalism, even libertarianism, could still encounter authoritarianism, even residual totalitarianism. Martin Luther King, we have to remember, was assassinated. Russian tanks rolled into Prague to crush Dubček's 'spring'. The United States bombed Cambodia.

Nevertheless, the cultural liberalisation of the 1970s was manifest in the movements for the liberation of women and for rights and freedoms for gay men and lesbians. These were serious causes, but many of their actions were a carnivalesque celebration of breaking all the rules. In December 1970 a group of Women's Liberationists attempted to liberate the front bar of a hotel, still considered a male preserve, where the beer was two cents cheaper than in the 'ladies' lounge'.[53] The Gay Activists Alliance staged a demonstration among the five o'clock commuters in the city, waving lilac-coloured placards, holding balloons, singing an old anthem with new words: 'Glory, glory Homosexual'.[54] Singer/songwriter Robyn Archer composed a song which not only mentioned the unmentionable, but sang it out loud at the Adelaide University Footlights Revue: 'Menstruation Blues' it was called.[55]

This kind of explanation brings into central focus an overwhelming preoccupation with sex. Women needed information about their own bodies: Women's Liberation groups acquired copies of the immortal work, *Our Bodies, Ourselves*, from the United States,[56] transcribed whole chapters onto stencils, and copied and distributed them.[57] Anne Summers pottered about the University of Adelaide campus pinning notices onto trees; they advertised a pamphlet that Women's Liberation had made from another American publication, Anne Koedt's article titled *The Myth of the Vaginal Orgasm*.[58] Women wanted sexual freedom of a kind that could only come with control of their reproductive capacities. South Australia had led the nation with its Abortion Law Reform Association (ALRA) and its achievement of legislation legalising abortion as early as 1969. Young members of Women's Liberation continued ALRA's work by running a referral service for women seeking abortions from Bloor Court.

And, of course, there was the Pill. It has often been claimed that the trigger for Women's Liberation was the appearance of the contraceptive Pill on the mass market in 1961. Certainly, it made a great difference to heterosexual relations. It was crucial to the free love of the Woodstock music and drugs scene. Men considered that they were participating in a sexual revolution. Women did, too – briefly – but rapidly found that the freedoms of the so-called 'sexual revolution' were freedoms predominantly, if not exclusively, for men, and certainly did not lead to more satisfying sexual experiences for women.[59] Moreover, as a doctor's prescription was necessary to obtain the Pill, its appearance reinforced the authority that doctors – still predominantly male – could exercise over what could be seen as women's sexual morality; some doctors refused to prescribe the Pill for women who were not married; some doctors refused to prescribe it for any women. Anne Levy had been a member of the Board of the Family Planning Association in Adelaide and remembered well the opposition that this group encountered from the medical profession: they didn't want the Family Planning Association giving out the Pill, only family doctors should be allowed to do that. 'We had lots of fights with the AMA [Australian Medical Association]', she noted.[60]

The AMA was not the only group to align itself with the residual authoritarianism of the 1950s. The general preoccupation with sex was fomented by the South Australian police and their aggressive opposition to gay men.[61] As early as 1967, the Police Commissioner, Brigadier John McKinna, had endeavoured to prevent John Bray's elevation to the position of Chief Justice on the grounds that he was a homosexual. In 1972, all of Adelaide was shaken by the tragic death of George Duncan, found on a well-known beat on the banks of the Torrens, bashed by off-duty police and thrown into the river where he drowned. Later, in 1977–8, another policeman, newly-appointed Police Commissioner Harold Salisbury, stood toe-to-toe with Dunstan on the question of the records of Special Branch – so many of which concerned sex – and his right to keep them secret from the Government.

But the forces of reaction were not winning, at least not during Dunstan's Decade. George Duncan's death was followed by efforts to decriminalise male homosexual acts. Murray Hill, a Liberal Country League member of the Legislative Council introduced the first Bill, a private member's Bill in July 1972. The third Bill was the work of Peter Duncan, this one successful in September 1975, making South Australia the first Australian state or territory to decriminalise male homosexual acts.[62] John Bray took his place on the South Australian Bench as Chief Justice. The Dunstan Government sacked Harold Salisbury, and Dame Roma Mitchell as the Royal Commission investigating this act resolved that the Government was right to do so.

Other campaigns developed as well, around the distribution of labour and power in families, around what came to be understood as patriarchal oppressions in marriage, and around demands for childcare and pre-schools. 'Smash the family', we chorused, walking down the streets in our flimsy Indian cotton shirts. Assisted by feminist Carol Treloar who had come to Adelaide to work as Peter Duncan's Press Secretary,[63] Duncan secured the passage of legislation that outlawed rape in marriage – another South Australian first – a law that attracted intense interest and controversy across Australia, indeed, across the Common Law world.[64] Assisted by WEL, the Whitlam Government introduced blame-free divorce in its *Family Law Act* (1975) and divorce rates soared. Demographers now estimate that one in every three marriages contracted during the 1970s ended in divorce, and note that from the 1970s and 1980s there has been a major increase in couples living together without being married. They note, too, a sharp decrease in the number of births that any woman might have, a phenomenon that has to be called a second 'strike against marriage'.[65] It is another 'family transition'. So, again, what this kind of explanation brings into the spotlight is a sexual revolution. This was not the sexual libertarianism claimed as an effect of the Pill, but rather a re-ordering of all the sexual and domestic relations between women and men and children, what anthropologist Peter Sutton calls 'a deep change in culture': the second sexual revolution of settler Australia. What was, or was not, happening in the bedrooms of this state thus constituted a crucial context for the achievement of women's economic citizenship, namely women's enhanced access to paid employment.

In conclusion: three quick observations.

First, and this is principally for historians: all three kinds of explanation are necessary to account for a seemingly straight forward event.

Second, we should consider the aftermaths of these two pieces of legislation. It is often observed that it took many decades for women to take advantage of the 1894 *Constitution Amendment Act* (known as the Women's Suffrage Act) allowing women to seek election to Parliament. The cause of this phenomenon is, I am convinced, the establishment of party politics. When both Catherine Spence and Mary Lee were invited to stand for election in the late 1890s, both refused, principally because they did not want to be bound by a party platform.[66] And 12 of the 19 women who sought election between then and 1959 – when Joyce Steele and Jessie Cooper were elected – campaigned as Independents.[67] Even in the decades since women began regularly contesting seats in both the state and federal parliaments, there has been some doubt about how well the political parties support women seeking party endorsement.

The *Sex Discrimination Act*, now titled the *Equal Opportunity Act*, continues to be revised and expanded often. One example: when Chris Sumner, Attorney-General in the ALP Government of John Bannon, introduced an Anti-Discrimination Bill in 1984, its scope ranged across not only sex and marital status but also sexuality, pregnancy, physical impairment and race. I would note, though, that despite the initial requirement that the Commissioner for what came to be called Equal Opportunity should be a person 'with extensive legal experience', the successive appointments to that post have *not* had such experience, but rather, have relied upon legal advice.

Third, the final note I promised at the beginning: the citizenship of men. Sociologist Bettina Cass, following a number of Scandinavian scholars, adds a third dimension to the political and economic citizenship that I have discussed. This is social citizenship. It is earned by unpaid labour in households, in the community, and in voluntary work in the human services sector of the economy.[68] Such work has a very serious economic value. In the 1990s, the Australian Bureau of Statistics estimated the market value of the 'vast non-market contributions to family and community welfare' as worth, in monetary terms, 'an amount equal to about 60% of GDP'.[69] This 'caring work' is carried out almost exclusively by women. It is also carried out in addition to any work that women perform to earn their economic citizenship in the labour market. This is the famous – or notorious – 'double burden' of women's work, and a major deficit in men's claim on full citizenship. When the Academy of the Social Sciences in Australia considered 'critical issues' facing Australia recently, they did not identify any changes in this situation.[70] I did wonder, as I filled in the present census a few weeks ago, if the return – from this 175th anniversary of white settlement in South Australia – would show any alteration in men's willingness to earn the third element of full citizenship by taking an equal part in housework and child-care.

Acknowledgement

For help with this paper, I would like to thank David Hilliard, George Lewkowicz, Anne Levy, Deborah McCulloch and Tim Reeves; for encouragement, I would like to thank Ian Purcell; and for quality control I must thank my partner, Sue Sheridan.

7

Making the Most of It: Life on the Rural Frontier in 20th Century South Australia

JILL ROE

For many South Australians, 'country life' has always meant 'the good life'. However, by now a far smaller proportion of the state's population actually live in the country than a century ago, and these days 'the good life' is more likely to mean life in the city. By the 1980s, according to Canberra political scientist Don Aitkin, 'countrymindedness' was no more.[1]

Be that as it may, at the close of the 20th century most farms were still family farms, and the land itself is more productive than ever; and as Aitkin has more recently pointed out, there have been many new recruits to country living, not only retirees seeking a quiet life, but also people associated with new industries, such as tourism and commercial fishing. Nor have country people been totally passive in the face of socio-economic change. In fact, as often as not, they have welcomed it, even mining; and as will be suggested later, these days they are increasingly laying claim to their own histories.[2]

There are several reasons for revisiting country life. The first is, surprisingly, that these days it is a neglected subject. Some of the classic works of South Australian history have dealt with the rural experience, but most were written before historians discovered 'the other side of the frontier' in the 1980s, and things have never been quite the same since. European settlement, pastoralism, and agriculture have all tended to fall into disrepute.[3]

A second reason for revisiting country life is only now coming into view, namely mining on prime agricultural land. This is currently a big bad story in Queensland, and a fraught one in New South Wales, where the Liverpool Plains and further out the iconic Pilliga Scrub, are under serious threat. So too apparently is much of Eastern Eyre Peninsula.[4]

The third reason is harder to pin down, but is no less important. The relationship between the cities and country is now quite disproportionate in Australia due to the economic rationalism of the 1980s, which meant the country was left to fend for itself, even though its wellbeing affects us all. As political scientist Judith Brett put it in a recent *Quarterly Essay* entitled 'Fair Share: Country and City in Australia', it is time to bring the country back in.[5]

In this book we are invited to reflect upon, and identify, 'turning points'. Presumably this refers to something more than just change, for example, something dramatic like the declaration of war. However, that sort of benchmark does not sit so easily with the rhythms of rural history, so in this chapter I will be approaching the subject gradually, focusing especially on my place of origin and current research interest, Eyre Peninsula, with reference to other regions from time to time. I will also be paying attention to social and cultural history, both of which I believe to be more important than is usually recognised, and to women in rural society. The chapter comes in three sections: first something personal, a trip to Eyre Peninsula in 2007, then a look at the popular museum movement there, and finally, the bigger picture and a quick run towards the 21st century to conclude. Due acknowledgement is made at the outset of the first peoples of Eyre Peninsula, the Nawu, Banggarla, and Wirangu, for whom the turning point came very early, in 1839, when the land takers arrived at what is now Port Lincoln. Any turning point for the colonisers would be much longer in the making.[6]

A trip to Eyre Peninsula

In January 2007, my friend Helen Bartley and I went back to Eyre Peninsula. Helen, a psychologist whose life began in country Wudinna, wanted especially to revisit that part. Her father, one of only four enlisted men in her immediate family to survive World War I, went there as a soldier settler in the 1920s. I wanted especially to see the far West Coast, much of it for the first time, in what turned out to be a somewhat premature preparation for this book.

We began our journey by taking the car ferry – still running then – across Spencer Gulf, from Wallaroo to Lucky Bay near Cowell. From Cowell, an old stone town with a comparatively long white history, we went cross-country, through Cleve to Rudall, taking care to locate the memorial to children's writer May Gibbs along the way. At Rudall we turned north, to see the memorial to explorer John Charles Darke (1806–1843), said to have been speared by Aborigines, and on to Buckleboo, well beyond Goyder's famous line, drawn by him in 1865 along approximately the ten inch rainfall isohyet (300 mm. p.a.). Nowadays Buckleboo is just a name on a map, at the end of a branch line, consisting of a dozen enormous wheat silos and an apparently deserted house, but on that day protected by ferocious dogs. Here I begin to appreciate how far north the rural frontier has moved in the 20th century, and to wonder about climate change.[7]

It was reassuring to get back to Kimba, once remote, but now flourishing as a stopover on the Eyre Highway, with a big galah symbol up front and masses of desert pea in flower outside the main service station. The next day it was north-west, to Wudinna, passing through Kyancutta and its museum, about which more will be said shortly. The Wudinna area too is flourishing despite the now limited rail service, due, like Kimba, to the east-west road traffic, and to rural consolidation. Not that it is a big place even now, with some 1500 people living around there at the 2006 Census. I begin to wonder if the pivot of Peninsula life has moved north. In retrospect, I think not so much of summer stubble, but of the proximity of the Gawler Ranges and Gondwanaland as tourist attractions. This is not quite the hard country often envisaged, though it was hot and hard enough at the time.

It gets harder – and hotter – further up the highway, which follows the rail to Ceduna; and there was both less and more to take in. The familiar 'Roads to Recovery' signs seemed increasingly inappropriate, especially on the dirt road to what little remains of Nunjikompita. As for the equally remarkably named Mudamuckla, the last location before Ceduna, there is not much left either and regrettably all memory of it has gone. Less than 100 people now live at the nearest port of Haslam, but, as detailed in an enjoyable work entitled *The Jetties of South Australia*, they have managed to save some of its 1911-built jetty. The Dutch almost reached this spot nearly four centuries ago.[8]

Inevitably the Stuart case comes to mind at Ceduna. I was a student at the University of Adelaide when Ken Inglis published his book on the subject in 1961; and we went out to Thevenard to look at the site. I also re-read the book (and saw the 2002 film *Black and White*) and tried to take in this perspective on the history of Eyre Peninsula. It is not easy; but you have to try. It is impossible to spend any time in Ceduna and beyond without noticing some aspect of race relations. Here too, in another guise, is the frontier, the racial frontier. Was this, I now wonder, the turning point I am looking for? Maybe. But it is very remote. However, the locals have been working on their history, with a substantial open-air museum on the edge of town.[9]

Turning south, for me there were two 'must sees' at Streaky Bay: St Augustine's Anglican Church, where the father of eminent Australian historian Frank Crowley was once rural dean, and the still rather grand Streaky Bay Community Hotel (previously Flinders Hotel), where Daisy Bates first stayed when she left hospital in Adelaide in 1945 'to be with my natives'. It may sound somewhat fanciful, but walking the Streaky Bay jetty it felt as if she was still there, in her starched collar and long black skirt, setting us all right. St Augustine's, unlike some other churches on the Peninsula, really is still there, a handsome brick and stone building, said to be an outstanding example of some 30-odd churches designed for the Diocese of Willochra by Port Pirie layman and banker William Kingsland Mallyon.[10]

Lest this approach seems somewhat self-indulgent, it is meant to convey something of the spirit of place, and to touch lightly upon some aspects of country life as it appears today. For more, we must move further down the old West Coast, passing all too quickly by its grand coastline and its conflicted pastoral history. I had of course been following the historical research on the Elliston massacre, if that is the right phrase, and went to see the site. When I saw the graduated cave-ridden cliffs, it seemed to me that without more evidence the issues must remain unresolved. Nearby, the main bay, Waterloo Bay, is another challenging spot, with seas often too rough for the old sailing ships to enter. I confess I was not brave enough to walk far along the narrow jetty by myself in the early morning. What did warm my heart at Elliston were the remains of the biennial cliff-top sculpture exhibition, and meeting some local sculptors. Was this really Eyre Peninsula, I asked myself? Perhaps there has always been something about Elliston, since Ellen Liston, one of South Australia's earliest writers, wrote pioneer tales here. In any event, the cultural turn it now represents is something else to be taken into account.[11]

Finally, en route to Port Lincoln we stopped at Dutton Bay, where another interesting museum in an old stone woolshed presented itself. We did not stop at Coffin Bay, possibly the best-known site of all those mentioned, as I had been there many times before when young and seen the site of the old Mortlock Station homestead, then on the outskirts of town. On the other hand, perhaps we should have made the effort: the fishing industry flourishes there, and it is a prime example of holiday-making. Country Australia becomes a tourist destination? By all means. So long as food production is sustained, surely.[12]

Speaking of tourism, travelling back up the eastern coast on the way back to Lucky Bay, we visited Tumby Bay, where I was born and where my parents first retired, before, like so many old farmers, moving to Adelaide. It too has a Mallyon-designed Anglican church, St Margaret's, built on land donated by the Mortlocks and now over 100 years old. It is still a small town; at first sight not much has changed. Imagine my astonishment when on that summer's day it dawned on me that Tumby Bay is now the Riviera of Eyre Peninsula. Writer Kate Llewellyn has recently sung its praises in her memoir *The Dressmaker's Daughter* (2008). If the hematite mining goes ahead nearby, as seems probable, it will be even more changed.[13]

Museums

The trip in 2007 was a working holiday. Even so, it was apparent that tourism is a well-established industry on Eyre Peninsula as elsewhere, and that the museums have become fixed points on the tourist trail. Evidently the locals are more history-minded than in my day, when it was largely a matter of 'back to' events and the oldies out in period costume. As professional historian Geoffrey Speirs reminds us, interest in Australian history has burgeoned since the 1960s, and these days local history museums are found in many towns and suburbs, and also an array of specialist museums established in the wake of the heritage movement, mostly maintained on a voluntary basis and established quite recently.[14]

The first and certainly the most unusual museum on Eyre Peninsula was the Kyancutta Museum. Its founder, the remarkable Robert Bedford, a scientist and local entrepreneur, emigrated from England at the onset of World War I and in 1915 took up land in this still remote place to grow wheat. A man of many talents, at Kyancutta Bedford established a cottage hospital, a radio station, an air service, and in 1924, a Museum of Evolution for the geological and anthropological specimens he collected on trips inland. The building and a post office are still there, but not his collection, which was dispersed after he died in 1951. Bedford was much admired throughout the region, though not at the museum in Adelaide, and thoroughly deserves the entry on him in the *Australian Dictionary of Biography*. Apart from anything else, like many early arrivals in rural and regional Australia, he cannot be stereotyped.[15]

The Ceduna museum is something else, a community in miniature, with numerous recreated historical buildings arranged around a large rectangle. In 2007, the project was well advanced, and for me its most compelling buildings were a tiny windowless lock-up and an old school room. There was a welcome domestic life dimension to the place too; unlike some country collections, the Ceduna museum is not dominated by farm machinery. But then farming is not such big deal there.

These days all the towns down the West Coast have local museums, though due to time and space considerations only brief mention can be made here. Thus, as its website states, the Streaky Bay museum reflects farming activities prior to the late 1940s, with early agricultural and related machinery on display; the museum at Elliston has a 2005 bushfire display, and a somewhat perfunctory acknowledgement of an Indigenous presence as part of a larger mural which makes it one of the few to attract wider attention; and further south there is the previously noticed and still functional woolshed museum at Dutton Bay.[16]

More must be said about Koppio. Situated amid farmland in the picturesque Koppio Hills some 40 kilometres north of Port Lincoln, the Koppio museum is also a miniature historical community, with numerous buildings on-site, as can be checked on its website. There one can inspect Koppio's one-teacher school, one of the longest surviving such schools in the state (it closed in 1970), the old White's Flat Post Office (said to be one of the smallest in the state), a Bank of Adelaide building, and more. As well, a number of display sheds house enough farm machinery and other equipment to satisfy busloads of school children.

There are several thought-provoking features to the Koppio museum or, more correctly, the 'Koppio Smithy Museum', as it is the site of the blacksmith's shop established by Ron Brennand in 1903. If I try really hard, I can just remember him shoeing draught horses. Not that my recall is important, or even very reliable. What is important is the continuity, the live history, a reminder that rural life was once very different. Once, and not so long ago, it relied on the horse.

The Koppio museum also houses a special collection. In one of the side buildings is housed an astonishing display of barbed wire, donated by Port Lincoln resident and collector Bob Dobbins. It is a permanent collection and, as I now know, contains more than barbed wire. A colleague at Macquarie University, geographer John Pickard, who has recently completed a PhD thesis on the history of fencing in Australia, writes of 'Bob Dobbins's superb collection of posts, droppers, wire, tools, etc'. The Dobbins collection, part of which is also on display at Tailem Bend, is surely unique, at least in South Australia, and probably Australia.[17]

In an interview, Bob has recalled how after an article on his collection appeared in the *Port Lincoln Times* in 1985, local people simply dumped piles of fencing wire outside his house, which he then straightened and cut into display size of eighteen inches (45 cm). He also mentioned the interest of telegraph employees, and what made a good strainer post. Strainer posts and fencing wire may not appeal to everyone, but it is apparently a collectible, and as he said, 'every wire has a price', especially in America. Moreover, and this is the point here, the coming of fencing wire heralded a profound change in rural life. For one thing, it meant the end of the shepherd, a vital figure in the pastoral age. Some shepherds may have been quite mad due to isolation; but it was they who watched over the flocks and herds that made distant pastoralists rich and, as in the case of one Stubbs and his employer Biddle of Port Lincoln in the 1840s, bore the brunt of racial conflict. Maybe the coming of wire fencing in the late 19th century – some readers may recall the brand name Lysaght, which dates from the 1880s – was not quite a turning point, but it was surely an augury of things to come. As with the blacksmith, the shepherd belongs to a bygone era.[18]

Not that change came quickly or evenly across the country. On the family farm in the late 1930s, shearing sheds might still have had stick fencing and thatched roofs. In many places, people and horses were still cheaper than machinery well in the 20th century. A lot of work would be needed to chart the decline of the rural workforce across the 20th century, though I have written about what happened on Brindabella station run by the Franklin family in New South Wales in the 1880s; and my farmer father used to say the biggest change in his life time – he was born in 1898 and died in 1975 – was the decline in the rural workforce. Regarding horses, the horse population of Australia peaked at 2.5 million in 1919; but it would be many years before local museums became the chief repositories of the sorts of trucks and tractors found at the Koppio museum. In South Australia the last horse team was disbanded in the mid-North as late as 1958, and there were still a few draught horses in agricultural areas in the 1960s.[19]

The bigger picture

The museum movement has been part of the enthusiasm all over the country for local and community history – I think also of the Pioneer Women's Hut at Tumbarumba in the Australian Alps – and it sometimes seems especially strong in South Australia. The previous state celebration, SA150 in 1986, produced a great crop of local histories in nicely produced books with catchy titles like *Gum Trees and Gullies* (Yallunda Flat), *Grain amid Granite* (the Wudinna area), and *Between Lakes and Limestone* (a history of Kapinnie and Brimpton Lakes). Such works are invaluable in many ways, and like the local museums, evidence of a deepening self-awareness. That is to say, there's now a bottom-up depth to a still to be charted regional history.

It is easy to forget how short that history really is. Although a region like Eyre Peninsula has a European history which goes back to the sealers in the 1800s, it was a very lightly populated and mostly semi-arid region until the early 1900s, when farming in the far north of the state failed as Goyder always said it would, and following closer settlement legislation in the 1890s, a minor folk movement south and west over Spencer Gulf occurred.[20]

It may be at this point that another historian would argue that technological change ensured the success of closer settlement in the early 20th century. Of course that was vital; so too was the prior State support in the case of 20th century Eyre Peninsula and elsewhere, and other examples include the rail built across the eastern mallee to Pinnaroo, and the success of Coonalpyn Downs in the 1950s. On Eyre Peninsula the surveyors and fettlers and dam builders made life on the land manageable for the newcomers. They laid out the hundreds wherein small farming could begin, built the narrow-gauge railway from Port Lincoln to Minnipa by 1915 and then Ceduna, and they constructed Tod River Reservoir in the Koppio Hills, from whence water was piped all the way up the Peninsula by 1928. But even all that was not enough to secure rural communities.[21]

There were hard times to come, but not immediately. I would argue, however, that in addition to the technology, what ultimately ensured the success of closer settlement in this last of the regions to be brought under the plough in the early 20th century was the skill of the people themselves. They were not novices. Their experience of the land did not extend as far back as in some other colonies, but it was profound. The big lessons came from the far north, where planning was not enough. Nor was optimism about that mistaken mantra 'rain follows the plough'. The people themselves had had to work it out. As was long ago shown by D.W. Meinig, they had learned the hard way what was needed just to survive – as Meinig's title has it – *On the Margins of the Good Earth.*

They were also accustomed to hard physical labour, women and men alike. It killed too many of them too soon, especially the men. Both my grandfathers are buried in Port Lincoln cemetery, dead and gone by 1916, not much more than a decade on from their arrival. Of them I have almost no imagining, though it has become clear from reading Grandmother Roe's early diaries that her husband Gilbert Roe was far more interested in trading stock than farming, and was lucky to have brought several competent workers from the Lower North with him in 1905 and to have obtained a good block in the more fertile south. As for grandfather Heath, who died of double pneumonia in 1916 aged 44, it seems he was not much of a farmer. Certainly he had no luck with access to good land; and there was no superphosphate in those days. Arriving with his family from the near North in 1905, he was unable to make things grow near Port Lincoln; and when a few years later the family moved to land leased from the Mortlocks near Tumby Bay, it was rain shadow country and the soil was sandy. When he was allocated a block up north near Wudinna in 1915, it should have turned out well, but he died a fortnight after his oldest son contracted meningitis on a visit. In both cases, it was up to the widows to make a go of it – which they did.

Mention of grandparents brings to mind political journalist Robert Murray's recent memoir, *Sandbelters: Memoirs of Middle Australia*. Murray's family finished up in suburban Sandringham in Melbourne, but they were up-country farmers in the Victorian mallee first. Murray has provided one of the richer and more realistic portrayals of that life to date, another being Penelope Hetherington's account of the Loveday family's attempt to establish itself on Upper Eyre Peninsula during the interwar years in *The Making of a Labor Politician* (some readers may recall Ron Loveday, the author's father who much later became Labor Minister for Education, 1965–68). In *Sandbelters*, Murray recalls the women of that first generation on the mallee lands as matriarchs: 'They often approached life as the chief executive of a large household, eyes out for problems to overcome and for efficiency.'[22]

That struck a chord. My grandmothers were old and unwell by my time – they both died in the early 1950s – but they were held in awe by their large families, especially it seemed by the men; and Grandmother Roe's diaries are an eye opener for the modern reader. They are not grand, just a brief, daily record of work and weather and incident, written up neatly with pen and ink in Woods' Daily Scribbling Diaries. It is from them that we know Gilbert Roe was usually off after the horses. One striking aspect of such records is the difference between men and women's work, and how much the latter did.

The discovery of a new source is the historian's delight. Whereas there are numerous published sources on the daily round of country men – one to be particularly recommended is Colin Thiele's *Sun on the Stubble* (1961), a portrayal of boyhood in the interwar years in the Barossa Valley – extended accounts by country women are less easy to come by. More often their working lives are briefly touched upon in contributions to collections like *Eyre Peninsula Ramblings*, another Jubilee 150 publication, or survive in family records, such as Anna Roe's diaries.[23]

Here are some main points from Anna Roe's early diaries, the years 1905–07, when she was in her late 30s with six children and just settled on lower Eyre Peninsula. Washing and ironing took up at least a whole day (though she seems to have had some kind of washing machine, a 'western washer' she called it, which she didn't think much of). Sewing and mending and darning for a large family could also fill up a whole day. Preparing for Sunday was a mammoth exercise. Here is what Anna Roe records they were all doing on Saturday 3 June 1905, some three months after arrival (and by the way the person referred to as Dan was Dan Singh an Afghan worker they took over with them): 'Great shakes today – Dan grubbing Father carting some clay Jack drilling and the cook very busy at the flour three turns [*sic*] of bread one of scones one of tarts one of pies one of biscuits and a big cake and 1 custard besides boiling meat vegetables and potatoes', with 76 lbs of beef recorded (well that's what it says!). Water remained a serious problem but somehow she quickly established a large garden with roses. It was quite normal for there to be up to 20 people for Sunday lunch, or dinner as it was called then, mainly men. As she wrote in another entry: 'Providing for a growing family and four men besides so many chance callers called for a constant watch on supplies'. Apparently pickled beef was a standby. Mail went off once a week: a horseman would take the half dozen letters or more she had found time to write to family back on the mainland to Bolah Shah's store over the hills for despatch. Letters were a lifeline. This touches on the issue of distance, a special paradox in centralising South Australia.

There's more. Briefly, regular church services were held within a couple of years, a school established, and a sports oval created in the hills. When the rail came through in 1907, the whole family went to see the engine and trucks pass along, 'a great day', wrote our diarist, as of course it was. These were people who knew what was needed to make a rural community work.

Rural society on the West Coast seemed to be shaping up well by the 1920s. In South Australia the Lower North and the Mallee communities were growing lots of improved quality wheat, and new land in the granite belt around Wudinna in the northwest attracted young farmers from the south. Some research suggests that even the returned soldiers did as well as could be expected. The land that Edward John Eyre had described as 'a perfect desert' proved productive in places. At Kyancutta, Robert Bedford set up his airline and advocated a new state, Mrs Birdseye's legendary bus service began, and the Country Women's Association got going in Kimba. Best of all, there was by then a vast water reticulation system over almost the entire region, thanks to the EWS – the State's Engineering and Water Supply Service.[24]

The Great Depression put an end to all that exuberance. Farmers everywhere suffered the catastrophic fall in world wheat prices, and many left the land. So what might have been the turning point in rural life – a new prosperity, the coming of machinery, richer social lives – was more like a false dawn. As for women on the land, their lives were improved in the sense that family size went down, but domestic work was barely affected beyond the cities, where electricity was starting to make a difference.

That may be too bleak a view for the rising generation. In 1975, a rare account of rural life between the wars appeared in *South Australiana*, recorded by Joan Airy who grew up just north of Cowell in the interwar years. It has a nice balance of self-respect and truculence – a tone I sometime think is characteristically rural – 'We are on a farm because we like it and hope that the rural recession will never bear beat us'.[25] It did not beat her parents. Her father came from Kangaroo Island in 1911 and never owned the land that was in any event quite marginal. Nor did he ever make any money. But the way he and his wife managed their mixed farm through hard times is impressive. Nothing was wasted and whatever food would grow they grew. Joan Airy's mother could make soap and vinegar as well as meals and clothing; her father cut the family's hair, mended their boots, and nursed sick animals along with his farm work. The detailed account of Joan Airy's school days at Salt Creek School is especially valuable. The Airy recollection may be taken to stand for the transitional, and now superseded, way of life in the country.

There is no need to mourn this passing. Its significance is that rural life took a battering as did the urban working class in the 1930s; but in some respects the country people were better off, could survive more easily. And the good times were coming. I seldom go along with the idea that wars are for the good, but it must be admitted that war brought work at Whyalla for those less successful on the land, and primary production got a boost too.[26]

Then came the wool boom. Suddenly wheat-wool farmers became quite rich. We had the Korean War to thank for that: wars in cold climates were good for the wool industry. As well, a second, smaller, round of soldier settlement proved much more successful than it had been after World War I. And contrary to expectations, the post war boom lasted. Historians are agreed that a 'golden age of agriculture' eventuated in the 1950s and 1960s, and for most families, country life was at last quite comfortable.

Did the 1960s constitute a real turning point in country life? Maybe. But a balance between continuity and change is never easily struck. Even before then, the traditional markets for primary products such as wool were trending downwards; some areas of production have since closed down or been greatly cut back; and by now it is clear that the time has come to count the environmental costs. As well, a rising awareness of the claims of Indigenous people and knowledge of their ways is now challenging conventional wisdom on land use.[27]

Many people are now troubled by these developments, and rightly so. However, the family farm has survived, albeit in changing guise and smaller numbers. Many farmers are cognizant of the need for change, country women are more involved in farm management, there are new contributors to country life, and awareness of the importance of the country is rising. Moreover communications between town and country are set to improve and whatever happens, country people are inclined to believe that the good times will come again.[28]

The South Australian historian Rob Linn ended his history of rural Australia over the past 200 years, *Battling the Land* (1999), on that very note, which is also a note of warning:

> Most [country] people believe that rural communities will recover from the slough of the recent past. Whichever way the winds of fortune blow for them, their history has been a prolonged battle between people and the land. A realisation of that struggle, and of the fact that environmental forces are the primary influence on life, lies at the heart of any true understanding of the story of rural Australia.[29]

From Linn, it might be inferred that, one way or another, a major turning point is pending. Others have suggested that that point has already come. Graeme Davison, in a contribution to a research project on rural sustainability conducted in 2001–2002, concluded that: 'The current crisis in rural Australia has been a long time coming, but free-market economics and environmental crisis are the hard rocks on which two centuries of rural hopes have finally foundered.'[30]

Fortunately, as an historian it is not my role to predict the future. But historical perspectives are always relevant; they are not always encouraging. To identify turning points, for country South Australia as elsewhere, all the variables I have touched upon – demography, climate, markets, mechanisation, and gender – would have to be taken into account. Take demography: rural life may be more comfortable and communities firmly established, but it is always tough at the margins, and fewer people now work the land. Furthermore, as Judith Brett has argued in the essay cited at the beginning of this chapter, by the 1980s, under market-oriented public policies, people began to think the country probably did not matter much except for holidays, and maybe some foods. There may be a new interest now in gourmet food and high quality ingredients, especially here in South Australia, and in Tasmania.[31]

Perhaps things look different in South Australia, where water is a big issue, and the idea of a 'farmers' state' lives on. But I doubt it. Environmental degradation is a real issue everywhere, and distance is no protection these days from mindless market forces, even for Eyre Peninsula. Whatever happens, the production of food will be an ongoing issue. Now is the time to be thinking about these things, and to recognise that the resilience and adaptability country people have shown in the past will be vital to any effective response to the challenges that now confront us.

8

A Place to Grow: Making a Future in Postwar South Australia

MARK PEEL

Telling South Australia's story has often begun with an assertion of its difference and distinction, from those first arguments about the absence of the convict stain through to Douglas Pike's 'paradise of dissent'. If you have written a history of Australia, you must also think about those places in the national story at which South Australia can and indeed must take the centre stage so often occupied by the earlier colonies and the larger states to the east. In one way, it is part of a wider problem of how to capture the significance and drama of the nation's story. In the introduction to a new history of Australia that I have written with my former Monash colleague Christina Twomey, I put it this way:

> Writing Australia's history means facing a series of challenges, not least an unfortunate conviction that nothing much happened ... In that light, it is important to begin with a question: what makes Australia's history fascinating? One answer is the ways in which its first people shaped and reshaped their country, and their meetings with the newcomers who would propel that country in a new direction. The encounters between eighteenth century British and Aboriginal people came at a significant moment in the longer history of Europe's expansion and are an especially good example of the momentum of misunderstanding that so often accompanied it. Another answer is that Australia's dramas were often subtle and ambivalent. This is a place marked strongly by aspirations that may not seem immediately revolutionary but are no less interesting for that. It was and is a highly mobile society, a population full of migrants and movers and sojourners who have had to work out – with more or less success – the practical tolerances that allow people to live together. Far from the centre of the world, Australia was and is an anxiously experimental society, a place of invention and innovation, emulation and nervous introspection, a place where some people could forget where they came from, while others made the best of themselves and still others longed only to return elsewhere.[1]

So where, in that, do we fit South Australia? At what points in the national story are historians compelled to turn here for their best examples and their illuminations? In the 1830s, certainly, for the difference made by systematic colonisation, including Colonel William Light's ability – relatively uncommon among the first founders of Australia's British settlements – to insist upon a site that provided reasonable drainage, fertile land and fresh water. In the colony's first decades, for the importance of faith, but also for the fact that if migrants carried the baggage of religious dispute and difference to Australia, a good deal of it was left unpacked, so that the Anglicans, Nonconformists, Catholics and Lutherans who had struggled so intently over the boundaries between faith, citizenship and entitlement in Europe reached an agreement that established no one as particularly privileged. And in those same decades, for the ways in which the complicated process of possession, dispossession and the debates about the 'protection' of the first people was shaped by the knowledge of what had already happened in New South Wales and other Australian frontiers.

In a very interesting way, of course, this lecture series is itself a way of addressing that question of South Australia's significance across the broader range of history. I think all of the contributors would agree with me that what we are seeking to achieve is not some statement of South Australia's distinction, something that sets it apart from, or makes it superior to, its eastern and western neighbours. Histories that aim for distinction too often end up simplifying everybody's histories in order to sharpen the boundaries and diminish the similarities. Instead, I think what we are aiming to do is to focus upon some themes or some moments in which what happens here is particularly illuminating and interesting, for those circumstances in which to write South Australia's history is to say something very important and significant about Australian and indeed global history more broadly.

In thinking about what to say, I take some direction from an excellent essay by Robert Dare, in the *Wakefield Companion to South Australian History*, in which he talked about the importance of placing the state's history on the larger stage and connecting it with the wider, global currents and patterns of the past.[2] As my contribution to that effort, and by bringing together history and the more personal and family stories that tie me to this place, I want to return to the book that I wrote more than 15 years ago, *Good Times, Hard Times*, not in order to repeat it but in order to say two important things.[3] The first and briefer part of my talk is to say that, in that book, I tried to say something about a truly remarkable period in South Australia's history, a period that began in the depths of the 1930s depression and saw the development of a combination of public-minded cleverness, kindness and future planning that bears thinking about in the 21st century. The second part is to better convey something I now think I underemphasised in that book, something that is, indeed, rather underplayed in a good many South Australian and Australian histories: the importance of examining the past, the present and the future through migrants' eyes. To explain and explore both of these points, I will also return to Elizabeth, the subject of that first book, because it is in Elizabeth, I think, that we can best see a remarkable coincidence of public-minded cleverness – which Hugh Stretton luminously described as a way of governing based upon having a hard head and a soft heart – and the desire of migrants to make new lives.[4] In the paths that the migrants who peopled Elizabeth took in the 1950s and 1960s, and in what happened to some of them in the 1970s, 1980s and beyond, we see the partial fulfilment – and then the wholesale dismantling – of a particular way of thinking about security, prosperity and opportunity that might yet provide some resources for thinking about South Australia's future.

That period of development, which took South Australia from the harsh decline that is always the fate of small economies in bad times through to the relative prosperity of the 1960s, has had its highly able historians, not least Hugh Stretton, but also Kyoko Sheridan, Graeme Hugo, Susan Marsden and, more recently, John Spoehr.[5] It is upon John Spoehr, among others, that I very much rely for support in making the case for the contemporary and future significance of this period, not just for South Australia, but for all relatively peripheral and vulnerable societies. The 1930s, and perhaps especially the 1940s and 1950s, witnessed a powerful and internationally significant turning point in the fortunes of a small society, a turning point that demanded not the aping of theoretical abstractions borrowed from elsewhere but the ability to understand local problems and possibilities and respond to them with imagination and a good mix of idealism and pragmatism. One of the great advantages of peripheral societies is a capacity to experiment, to bring unusual combinations of talents to bear upon the challenges of the future. One of their disadvantages is a tendency to be afraid of innovation, to look to larger and more powerful places for guidance and affirmation. One could say that they tend towards both adventurousness and anxiety. In South Australia, in the 1940s and 1950s, with the unexpected contribution of a Liberal conservative as often derided by his own side as by his opposition, the balance swung decisively towards adventurousness. For a time, and in very important ways, South Australia benefited from an alignment of political and public service that built a future that the more timid could barely have imagined.

Call it the Playford era, call it the era of South Australia's remaking, call it the mid-century economic recovery that was followed by and in many ways laid the groundwork for the cultural and social transformations that will forever be linked to Don Dunstan. It rested on the idea that the future is a public responsibility, that the future of small and vulnerable places must be imagined and tackled differently from larger ones, and that making a better future is a challenge best met by ensuring that the energies and capacities of private enterprise are governed by the longer-term perspectives and expertise of public authority. As Hugh Stretton showed, what is sometimes described as a 'Playford approach' was actually something imagined and implemented alongside public servants and industrialists. South Australia was, for a time, steered in a way that trusted and emboldened those talented and clever public servants. From this stemmed some of this era's remarkable experiments and innovations, in housing and employment, urban planning and industrial policy. Not least of these was Elizabeth itself, a British-style new town, based upon the premises of neighbourhood unit planning, which strove to provide a new kind of residential community for a mixed population, and incorporated what were then perfectly reasonable expectations about the robustness of an industrial base devoted to motor cars, electrical goods and light engineering. No other Australian state managed so great a venture in town planning, and no other Australian state housing authority endeavoured to bring affordable housing and land, work, shopping and recreation into the kind of alignment the Housing Trust managed in its new town. And while in so many ways one agent of South Australia's transformation, Thomas Playford, could not have been further apart from another, Don Dunstan, one thing I think they shared was an abiding interest in the future, an ability to see South Australia as something other than a pale imitation of other places, and a capacity to understand that this demanded cleverness and an eye for distinctive opportunities, not defensive parochialism. Both, I think, contributed to a significant outcome: for a time, especially in the 1950s, 1960s and 1970s, in large part because of a particular form of intelligent, future-directed public activism, South Australia in general and Adelaide in particular were among the most fortunate environments on the earth in which to realise ordinary aspirations. They were something of a paradise, not this time for dissent or religious toleration, but for a particular form of social mobility.

To talk of cleverness, of experiment and innovation, is to risk being seen as turning from history to hagiography. It is important not to, and none of the able historians upon whom I draw ever did. There were aspects of development for which Thomas Playford had no instinctive feel, others for which he had antipathy, and others still in which he did not follow the lead of some of his administrators when he should have. In time, some of the choices about the future of Adelaide, Elizabeth and the state's regions would seem less sensible than others. The 'Playford Plan' was blind to some issues that it should have seen, and to problems that would in time unravel some of its successes. It was not as forward-looking in health, law or education as it was in housing and industrial development, for instance, and its activism was as shaped by the sometimes limited cultural and social horizons of its designers as the Dunstan government's activism was shaped by the very different capacities of its leaders, not least Don Dunstan himself. Playford's plan also imported into South Australia thousands of new voters who were unlikely to offer him their support. Granted, what was known as the 'Playmander' (a peculiar South Australian variant of electoral malapportionment) meant that those people, like others in Adelaide, did not enjoy the same electoral power as those in rural areas, something that made many people legitimately angry in the 1950s and 1960s. But those new voters would eventually be numerous enough to help bring that voting system down. If the rise and significance of Playford's South Australia has had its chroniclers, so have its problems, its demise and its uncertain legacy. But I think it is important to remember it for what it was, and to imagine what South Australia might have been in, say, 1940 or 1950 or 1960 had it never been undertaken. History is a discipline of hindsight, and here hindsight helps us grasp the importance of what occurred.

In the debates and discussions about Playford's South Australia, less has been made, perhaps, of another factor in this transformation, and the ways in which South Australia's postwar future was shaped by an eagerness for social and generational mobility that drew tens of thousands of Europeans to Adelaide and to other cities and towns. That desire for mobility was – and remains – a profound force. Along with the struggle for tolerance, which has seen so much change in people's relationships with each other and in their ability to be themselves, and the demand for privacy, for something like a room of one's own, the last two centuries have also been transformed by a fascinating and powerful struggle to rise and by an aspiration and an expectation that class, sect, faith, gender, culture and power should be no bar to talent. Well into the second half of the 20th century, this mobility has been experienced and interpreted in generational terms and has, of course, often been tied to migration, especially in Europe's new worlds of North and South America, Australasia and southern Africa.

Australia's history has been powerfully punctuated by long- and short-term migrations. Migration is the rhythm of its story, from the first people who arrived 50 or 60 thousand years ago in what was probably the first great human movement that involved crossing water rather than land, to the convicts and free settlers of the 19th century, the British who poured in just before the First World War and then again after the Second, the displaced Poles, Ukrainians, Latvians, Lithuanians and Estonians, the Italians and Greeks and Lebanese and Turks and Syrians, the Vietnamese, to the more recent arrivals from the Middle East, South Asia, the horn of Africa and Latin America. A migrant society is a society of risers and fallers, of success and failure, of brilliant careers and new dynasties and of people who can't mend what has been torn or replace what's been lost. And it is important to remember, too, that for many of its migrants up to and including the 1960s and 1970s, Australia was a very distant place. Migration is rarely something incidental or accidental. Migration to Australia from Europe was in some senses even more determined and purposeful. In studying what drew people here, we learn much about the power of a particular set of political instruments to not only rebuild and reshape a state but also about the nature of ordinary aspirations and hopes in a century torn by war, dislocation and turmoil.

One of the reasons to study migrants, or other outsiders and marginalised groups, is because of what they can tell us, and not just about themselves, their pasts and their journeys. Sometimes the best way to understand a culture and a society is from the outside in and the bottom up. It is to ask those people what they know and what they find out, for good and for bad. It is to ask what we find out about ourselves by asking what others saw and see, what we find out, in this case, by examining South Australia through migrants' eyes. And part of what I want to achieve here – and more broadly – is to put the single largest group, the British, back into the migrant story, because of what they shared with Adelaide's Greeks and Italians and other groups, and because of what was different. The story of Australia's migrations must of course attend to little Italys and little Vietnams, and a good deal of effort and scholarship over the last several decades has ensured that the story of Australia must also recognise the fundamental importance of its ethnic and cultural diversity. This is an attempt to add to that effort, not undermine or supplant it. It is to recognise that those postwar British were also migrants and outsiders, in a very important sense, even if they were different kinds of outsiders to the groups more traditionally identified as 'migrant' in postwar Australia. To look through their eyes is to see something just as significant.

Fortunately, I can claim some authority in speaking about British migrants. I am the child of two of them, who left England separately but arrived here together on the *Orontes* in 1956. Of course, writing a book about the history and the future of Elizabeth also meant writing about British migrants, because British migrants made up such a large proportion of the town's population. And now I have reversed my parents' migration, moving with my partner, who is also the son of two British migrants from Melbourne, to a Victorian house in a grove in south Liverpool, 25 miles from where my mother spent her childhood, surrounded by people who can't understand why anyone would migrate from Australia to Britain.

This is, in part, an attempt to redress what I now see as a deficiency in the story I told in *Good Times, Hard Times*. Writing a book about Elizabeth meant describing its transition from a 1950s new town to a 1980s "problem area" and then into a 1990s "urban redevelopment zone" deemed fit for comprehensive rebuilding. This was a way of telling important stories about class, opportunity and inequality in postwar Australia. Of course, I acknowledged and made clear that Elizabeth's story was also partly mine. My parents had come to Elizabeth in the middle of 1959. I was born there in October of that year, in a new public hospital where the maternity wards never closed. At this point, my father had just secured a job at the Weapons Research Establishment, which lay along Elizabeth's western edge. After three years of casual employment on farms and workshops and months spent unemployed, he was grateful for the job and the wages, even if it meant he had to spend days and sometimes weeks at a time at the testing ranges in Woomera. Even better, a job in Elizabeth meant you qualified to rent one of the semi-detached 'double units' built by the Housing Trust. On reflection, it was small, and spartan. But to people from 1950s Britain, it was hard to imagine what else you'd want besides three bedrooms, a large kitchen, a small parlour, an indoor toilet, a laundry sink to call your own, and a back garden with a fence around it.

Mine was a book about Elizabeth, and it was a book about a fortunate working-class generation, born in the 1950s and 1960s, who benefited from all of the opportunities our parents could afford and who were able – usually for the first time in our families' histories – to attain the security our parents had always desired. We heeded their consistent warnings about the need for qualifications and skills; some took apprenticeships and training, the boys in the car factory or the metalworking trades, the girls in hairdressing, nursing and office work. Others, like me, took advantage of our parents' ability to keep us in school.

In writing about Elizabeth, I wanted to write about the kinds of policies – in housing, urban planning, income redistribution, education, employment and welfare – that had given my generation its chances. I raised, though I did not resolve, my ambivalence about the emphasis on sacrifice, struggle and self-effacement, the narrow versions of manhood and womanhood that security demanded, and the life paths that could and could not be imagined. I recognised that for many of us, mobility and success came at the cost of disconnection. In a way, we were raised to leave Elizabeth and not look back. We were raised to see our parents' lives as having a pattern we would not repeat, to see ourselves as part of a movement away from insecurity and danger that we had to continue in our own lives, lest their sacrifices be in vain.

Yet at the same time, it wasn't meant to be an introspective book. I wanted to give a clearer picture of how and why a place like Elizabeth, which outsiders so often saw as drab and plebeian, could be so valued by the people who lived there. Above all, I wanted to write about the kind of perspective on Australia's history afforded by the successes and failures of places like Elizabeth, about what created the good times for so many ordinary people and what had turned them into hard times. I wanted to write about the forces and decisions that had made parts of Elizabeth desperately poor during the 1980s and 1990s, after I had gone, and turned it into a 'disadvantaged' place that other people, for good and bad intentions, wanted to call a 'slum'.

So, for me, Elizabeth was a kind of touchstone for some of the great stories of the last two centuries, and especially of the postwar period. Stories about opportunity and its denial, about the importance of good wages and women's endless caring labour in the fulfilment of ordinary families' aspirations, about how a group of people had taken the sometimes uncertain benefits and bounties of a clever attempt to plan a successful future and made from them what I called a 'workers' city'. What I didn't do as much was to convey Elizabeth's Britishness. I didn't look enough, I think, through migrants' eyes. It was in the book, because it had to be. There was material on the recruitment caravan that used to travel to Manchester and Leeds and Sheffield, on the voyage, and on the visit to Elizabeth by Ena Sharples of *Coronation Street* in 1964. The chapters on local life and community talked about how Elizabeth's largely migrant population had given the town some decidedly British characteristics. I noted but perhaps made too little of the fact that for much of the 1960s, Elizabeth was the single largest and most concentrated migrant settlement in Australia. In 1966, 48% of the town's 43 thousand residents were born in Britain; adding in their Australian-born children, the British made up around two-thirds of the population, a figure that was even greater in the northernmost neighbourhoods such as Elizabeth Downs and Elizabeth Field.[6]

Yet while I talked about Britishness, I didn't write enough about British migrants or British migrant culture. That was in part a deliberate decision, because in shaping the story around Elizabeth's descent into post-industrial redundancy, I particularly wanted to emphasise other issues. But I think the decision also reflected my own ambivalence about Britishness in Australia and, perhaps, the Britishness in myself. Of late, there's been a welcome surge in studies of British migrants in Australia, but the reasons for an earlier disinterest are important to canvass. The sense that the British and their Australian-born children were somehow not 'real' migrants certainly played a part. It was a confusion echoed in the language of ethnicity. There is 'Anglo-Celtic', a term I've always found bizarre. My family was English or perhaps British, but Irish Catholics were different from us. Indeed, in the culture I knew as a child, 'Anglo' was partly formed in opposition to 'Celtic'. Then there was 'Anglo-Australian', where 'Anglo' meant not ethnic, which meant not migrant. It was as if people who had arrived from Glasgow or Liverpool or west London in the 1960s or 1970s were somehow linked together with people claiming five or six or ten generations of Australian residence. But my family were migrants, and their stories were migrant stories, even if that seemed invisible to others.[7]

By the 1980s, not being a real migrant and indeed being British had begun to carry its own penalties. On the Australian left, we suffered for the British nostalgia of Australian conservatism and the Irish nostalgia of Australian radicalism. To conservatives, most of us were not the British they admired. To one side, we were the wrong kind of migrants: pampered, privileged and somehow implicated in the British nation's war on Ireland. On the other, we were the wrong kind of Britons. We were strikers and shop stewards and scousers, almost transparent from our lack of contact with the sun, with thick National Health glasses, thicker accents and quite the wrong kinds of social and political attitudes.

Of course I am generalising and simplifying issues that have been discussed in more sophisticated ways by other scholars, but in talking of the language and culture of family and neighbourhood in this way, I realise that what I didn't do in my work on Elizabeth was portray some of the most significant aspects of what was, in many ways, a remarkable place. Part of that means understanding that my own experience of migrant-ness in Australia was also remarkable. I don't think it was exceptional, because most migrants' children, whether British or Italian or Greek or Vietnamese, would recognise aspects of their own stories in it. But it was unusual, in large part because we were so thoroughly separated from Australians. So I want to take this opportunity to reflect upon how remarkable it was; I want to do here, briefly and through stories, what I perhaps did less successfully before.

One way of introducing yourself to this remarkable place is to view *A Place to Grow*.[8] This film was made by the Housing Trust in 1962 to advertise its greatest single venture and most ambitious project. It was shown at some of the Cobbers Clubs in the North of England and, according to some of my interviewees in Elizabeth, on the ships coming out. This film also became the cause of some controversy later, when people who'd moved into Elizabeth suggested that its images of golden beaches, Adelaide's vibrant 'night life' and abundant work opportunities for women were more than a little misleading. The film follows a very middle-class couple, Bob and Janet (the female actor was, I believe, a newsreader for commercial television in Adelaide). They begin with a visit to the sales office. The couple are then invited into the Housing Trust official's very impressive big red car and taken for a tour. At this point, the film becomes a little confusing, as the first couple disappear, apparently left with a "migrant family" they know, while the official visits an Australian man, a Dutch migrant and then a British couple, to emphasise the abundance of opportunity for all of the kinds of migrants eligible for housing by the Trust.

A Place to Grow does provide a good introduction to the Elizabeth that the Housing Trust wanted to advertise and display to its potential migrants. It also, I think, captures the kinds of virtues that Australians thought would be attractive to British people: the new, modern homes, the parks and shopping centres, the supermarkets with the all-important tinned pineapple, and the schools. Yet the film was rather selective. The detached family homes it depicts were, of course, the houses built for sale. The houses in which two-thirds of Elizabeth's people then lived – the semi-detached public housing rental units – appear only once and from a distance. Nor, in 1962, is there more than a brief mention of what has already become clear: that this would be a largely migrant rather than Australian town. The Housing Trust always found it difficult to lure Australians, even public housing tenants, so far from Adelaide, especially when the journey involved passing through the dusty, choking miasma produced daily by the Gepps Cross Abattoir. British, German and Dutch migrants were much easier game, especially when they were offered, as my grandparents were, a week in the hostel and a new house at Elizabeth or two years in the hostel and maybe a house in Adelaide.

In other words, the film didn't show the most remarkable Elizabeth of all. This was the migrant Elizabeth that was more characteristic of the town's northern end, which took shape during Elizabeth's 'migrant ghetto' heyday of the 1960s and early 1970s. This was my Elizabeth. My grandmother's house was in Elizabeth South, one of the oldest neighbourhoods. I call it my grandmother's house because my grandfather died before I can remember. She was a strong woman, but hard as well. I think she became steely during the war, with a husband who so enjoyed the navy that after being captured and imprisoned by the Vichy French he returned to war in 1943 and stayed away until 1946, arriving back in Devon with a clock pilfered from Germany and the makings of a small armoured car collected piece by piece from the Americans in France. Truth be told, my grandmother always frightened me a little, with her resolve and her determination. She was the only person I knew well who had migrated as a mature adult; she hated England for its class prejudices and its injustices, but she loved it for its memories, its softer colours and its lost associations.

My father was her eldest son. Thrust too early into maturity and responsibility, even his migration had been turned to family ends. He wanted to go to Seattle, to work for Boeing, but his family needed his skill for their cheap passage, and so to Australia he came, only to find that the job he'd signed on for in Yeovil had disappeared by the time he got to Adelaide. My mother left home as soon as she could, mostly, I think, from disenchantment with the life that awaited a young woman in 1950s Lancashire. She went to a London training college and then worked as a teacher in Salford and Manchester before deciding to strike out for Australia. She chose Adelaide because she rather hoped that the tall, sun-tanned, blond young man handing out leaflets for South Australia in Australia House might be typical of his type. By the time the boat made it to Adelaide, she had met and become bespoken to my father, who was tall, but not sun-tanned, not blond and not Australian. He was also travelling separately, his parents and siblings having come out three months before. All of twenty years old, he arrived in Adelaide with a suitcase, a completed mechanical apprenticeship, a spiffy new haircut, and an intended bride from the wrong end of Britain. It would have been an interesting meeting, my father, my grandmother and my mother, at the bottom of that gang-plank in 1956.

This was the extended family that moved into and formed part of migrant Elizabeth. We lived in Elizabeth North and then Elizabeth Downs. In the North, our street of semi-detached contained, from memory, one Australian family, but they were too far up the street to know well. In the Downs, our street of about 40 houses contained perhaps three 'Australian' homes. We didn't really know any of them, and their kids didn't play much with the rest of us. The different people in our streets were not Australians, but Germans and Dutch, the only other migrant groups allocated to Housing Trust properties at that time.

The Australians we met in Elizabeth were in fact mostly Aboriginal. A few were children living with foster parents, but most were families of Kaurna origin renting or buying houses from the Housing Trust. Perhaps they had few options, or perhaps they didn't share some of the prejudices against Elizabeth that were already emerging among many people in Adelaide. The striking absence in Elizabeth was white Australians, apart from a few teachers and nurses and, by the early 1970s, the first few wandering social workers. My vague recollections of meeting very few Australians as a child are happily confirmed by a much more famous Elizabeth son, rock singer Jimmy Barnes, who recalled that he hadn't met one until he was ten or eleven.[9] Of course, being from Adelaide rather complicates matters, because Adelaide English, in those days, had a more home country tone than in the eastern states. We need to remember that this was also a time when radio announcers spoke in 'educated' quasi-English voices, and before television, which came much later to Adelaide than to Melbourne, began to deliver a few Australian accents into people's living rooms. There were a few footballers; they would visit school to encourage you to bank your pocket money or buy a yo-yo or drink lots of milk. The first Australian I remember having to listen to, was a teacher in about Grade Three or Four at primary school. We found her incomprehensible; in a neighbourhood where about three-quarters of us had British migrant parents and most of the rest were called Krause, Schiller, Van Dommel or Van Der Waal, her broad Melbourne accent came as something of a surprise. The most memorable Australian of my childhood was a primary school headmaster. He was a heavy drinker and an ex-serviceman, and he was sure that we migrants didn't appreciate the full splendours of the Anzac tradition. In his concern for instilling Anzac values in migrant children, he was perhaps ahead of his time, but every April we would endure marching competitions, endless recitations of Australian war stories, and frequent reminders that were it not for the Anzacs we products of the British slums – and yes, he did use that term – wouldn't have stood a chance against Hitler.

As you can see, I learned some very interesting things about Australians from within migrant Elizabeth. Without that isolation, migrant Elizabeth would perhaps have never developed in the way it did, and it probably wouldn't have lasted as long. For most of us, Adelaide was simply too far away. In any event, Elizabeth was a place to which most city people came unwillingly, if at all. They came because they were made to work there or because they felt they had work to do. A few of them brought a sense of mission. However puzzled we were by teachers who said they'd come to help us overcome our backgrounds, we tried to give them a chance before becoming the delinquents they seemed to want us to be. It was only later that I understood what was meant, or why people from Adelaide's centre always congratulated you on 'having come such a long way'.

At the time I left the town to go to university in the late 1970s, that prejudice was rather strange, because the other remarkable thing about migrant Elizabeth was its success. In the testimonies and memories of the people I spoke to in the 1990s, and in the family stories I know myself, that success was measured in very consistent terms. For men, Elizabeth – and Australia – was defined by its jobs: decent, secure jobs with good pay and overtime. With those jobs, they could be the providers their father had often not been because of the Depression and the war, and they could experience a success that made their attachment to Elizabeth and to Australia very strong indeed.[10] For women, Elizabeth provided the opportunity of full-time mothering; however tinged that might have been by the difficulties of propelling prams up and down muddy paths, this was also experienced and remembered as a precious achievement. Full male employment and relatively good wages meant that married couples could practice the separation of responsibilities and capacities that made sense in working-class life. Most women worked before there were children and once children were in school. But their ability to stay at home with young children meant they could be the full-time mothers and carers they largely wanted to be. And in the street and neighbourhood communities of care, women who weren't mothers could still be aunties and honorary grannies, and take part in the collective mothering of dozens and dozens of late-baby-boom children by offering child care or, as was the case in our street, running informal kindergartens.

Of course, the family strategies that brought people to Elizabeth and strengthened their commitment to it didn't always work out. There were people who 'went back', though in my memory and in the stories of those I interviewed later, they were generally pitied rather than envied. For those who stayed, paths weren't always smooth. Elizabeth had its problems and its pessimists and even its malcontents. But measured by its own terms, this was a very successful place. Migrant Elizabeth, its resources, time and hopes, was organised for the future and represented in children. When they saw the films or posters about Australia, potential migrants certainly liked the images of sun, of good wages, and a country only different from your own in the greater benefits it offered. But what they responded to most were the images of babies and children, phrases such as 'Give Him a Chance in Australia', or those flickering images of children spilling out of concrete block primary schools or being vaguely attentive in high school chemistry. Give him, or her, a chance: that was a powerful motivation. It drove people, and helped them make light of the hard times. As I found in talking to Elizabeth's migrant men, and to my own father, it was the future of their children that still resonated most strongly in their decisions to migrate and to stay. It was the success of their children – success they insist could never have happened in Britain – that defined their migration as a triumph over the past.

They were right, in a way, and indeed in the same way that the Italian and Greek and Yugoslav migrants of the same period were right about their children and grandchildren, who have achieved such high levels of education and professional distinction, in the same way that the Vietnamese migrants of the 1970s and 1980s are being proved right, in the sense that the migrants of the last ten and twenty years will be proved right in their turn. The generation that came to Elizabeth as children, or who were born there in its first dozen years, were a remarkable group. As was true in most 1960s suburbs, Elizabeth's children divided into two streams. Most left school at 15, but perhaps a quarter or a third of Elizabeth's children were kept in school until matriculation, a much greater proportion than would have managed this in Britain. We were often the first generation in our families to complete secondary school. We were almost without exception the first generation to attend university or teachers college, often with the benefit of the teaching cadetships or Commonwealth scholarships that were so important then and that Labor forgot to reintroduce when they brought back university fees. For a time in the 1970s and 1980s, Elizabeth High School counted more PhDs among its matriculants than every state school in South Australia bar the academically selective Adelaide High, and more than most of Adelaide's very powerful private schools. In 1961, somewhat to the chagrin of its organisers, a state-wide survey showed that the students of the newly-opened Elizabeth High School scored the highest average IQ of any school in the state, public or private.[11] Much of that, I think, was migrant drive, migrant ambition. And when the local council decided to track some of Elizabeth's 'champions' in the early 1990s, they found something more of the migrant imprint. For a start, almost all of the lawyers, doctors, academics and other professionals who told their stories lived a long way from Elizabeth (and indeed Adelaide), having been propelled out of the town by the same forces that pushed and pulled them up the ladder of opportunity. More interesting still was the career focus of these especially successful products of migrant Elizabeth: community law, remote area nursing, social medicine.

Now, the point of all this is to say that Elizabeth was, at least for a time, a remarkable migrant community. It was a place in which an attempt to build a place for the future, in terms of housing and industry, was made successful by migrants determined to fulfil in a new world the aspirations that had dislocated them from the old world. It is remarkable for what it shares with other places better known as migrant communities. It is remarkable as a place to examine particular forms of migrant culture and Britishness in Australia, the impact of the postwar migration cohorts and the kinds of Britons who formed them, and for how those Britons made themselves into Australians, at least in some ways and to some extent. It is significant both for its extraordinary qualities and for what it represents and illustrates more broadly.

Of course, places like Elizabeth aren't meant to be remarkable. Indeed, the landscapes peopled by British migrants are often regarded as forgettable or even best forgotten. Through the distinctive combination of privilege and choice that determined our paths into Australia's cities and towns, our landscapes are outer suburban and regional, and they are full of things that were confident markers of the future in the 1950s but rather forlorn relics of the past by 1980: car factories, power plants, public housing, and technical schools. British migrant Australia ended up on the wrong side of the cultural changes of the last few decades. We're fish and chips and milky tea, not focaccia and espresso. We've ended up identified with monarchism, Anglo-chauvinism and even Pauline Hanson, however tenuous the evidence is for those claims.

But what do we see through British migrants' eyes? What do we see in Elizabeth then, and perhaps in Elizabeth now? In the paths that many of the British migrants of the 1950s and 1960s took, and especially the kind of migrants who made up British Elizabeth, we see a particular form of Australia's goodness, perhaps Australia's kindness. That kindness stemmed from a particular combination of mid-twentieth-century fears and hopes, which based a version of a better future in large degree upon memories of an anxious past. It remembered the insecurity, unemployment and inequality of war and depression, and it saw a better future stemming from decent housing, full employment and robust public education for the many, not in protecting the privileges of the few and accepting wide inequalities as inevitable and untouchable or even somehow beneficial to growth. Certainly, British migrants enjoyed a privileged access to that kindness and to that future, which meant they did not endure what other groups had to endure. But it also means they have a particular experience of, and perspective upon, the dismantling of that particular version of Australia's future. In them, we see some of the achievements of social mobility and broadly-based security, which reached further down the social scale than at any other time in modern history. We see what could happen when a small, vulnerable and peripheral place reinvented itself on a platform of public activism and imaginative, pragmatic public investment and drew to itself ambitious, mobile migrants. What we see later, perhaps, once the hard heads and soft hearts gave way to soft heads and hard hearts, is much of that disappearing, as the ladders of opportunity were drawn up and a large slice, perhaps a tenth or even a fifth, of our people, including a good many migrants, increasingly seen as 'dependent' or 'redundant'. So South Australia's migrants have something significant to tell us, about a structure of opportunity for which, whatever its faults and problems, the market, private enterprise and leaner, meaner governments have yet to provide a viable alternative.

That, I suppose, is where I would want to urge the importance of seeing through migrants' eyes. Being British didn't protect people from the forces that changed Australia into a less kind and less protective place. British Elizabeth might seem a strange quirk, something extraordinary, something, that once studied and glimpsed, can be dismissed. Certainly, if being British was all that Elizabeth stood for, if that was all we remembered and mourned, it would have become anachronistic and nostalgic by now. I would have joined the chorus gently casting aside clumsy nostalgias about bulldogs and roses and how much we'd always loved the monarchy. But there are memories of something else in Elizabeth, something profound, something that is not nostalgia because it speaks to a still vital and unfulfilled claim upon the future. We who once were there, those who are still there and those who now stand outside, can point to another memory. A memory about a place that represented so much that was being put right, in a country in which, for a good many ordinary people, migrant or not, things might yet go very wrong.

I wonder, too, if there's another way in which this history might make a difference. There are many ordinary people now who want to bring their aspirations to Australia, to bring that same desire to rise and to invest their energies, talents and efforts in the futures of their children. They're from new places, often war-scarred and torn, though not so different from the places left by the postwar displaced persons, the Dutch, the Germans, the Vietnamese, even the blitz-scarred British. The context and the mood are rather different now, perhaps especially as political leaders seem unsure whether to respond to the best or the worst of what have always been and will always be contradictory popular views about migration and refuge. In the early 21st century, such people tend to be seen as a problem, a burden, or a threat.

I hope, though, that an argument about the role of migration in the past, especially in a place like South Australia, can contribute to the intelligent discussion about the role of migration in the future. To the transformers of an earlier generation, migrants proved important and perhaps unanticipated allies in the remaking of South Australia. If we look at the looming challenges of the future – not least how to manage the fundamental issues raised by ageing and rapidly improving geriatric health, or how to imagine new ways of generating work, or how to live together equally and well – then we see challenges in which a combination of cleverness, future-mindedness and the aspirations, passions, energies and insights of the mobile might well prove decisive. It's not easy, but once again we need cleverness, a combination of future-mindedness and knowledge of the past, hard heads and soft hearts, pragmatism and idealism, all of them combinations informed and empowered by a sense of South Australia's history. One thing we can say is that here and now, in the northern hemisphere summer of 2011, in the United Kingdom in which I now live, we are again having to learn that inequality, frustration and exclusion exact a price. But I do not expect that the most imaginative solutions will come from the centre. They will more likely come from the periphery. There are, perhaps, turning points and opportunities yet to come, in which a knowledge of what made South Australia a very special place could prove very important indeed.

9

Don Dunstan and the Social Democratic Moment in Australian History

NEAL BLEWETT

The three great figures in South Australian political history so far have been the radical liberal Charles Cameron Kingston at the turn of the 19th and 20th centuries, the conservative developer Thomas Playford in the middle years of the 20th century, and the social democrat Donald Allan Dunstan in the latter half of the century. The comparisons between, and the ranking of these figures depend upon the historian's values and methodology. For the Labor historian, Ross McMullin, '[a]part from T.J. Ryan [Queensland Labor Premier 1915–19] no other Premier [in Australian history] could match Dunstan's success in spearheading the transformation of a previously conservative state.'[1] As the last of the giants of South Australian history, Dunstan's monuments lie all around us: the Festival Theatre complex, the relaxed Mediterranean lifestyle of the city and the key structures of the constitution that had been unchanged for over a hundred years before he came to power.

Yet there remains a strange ambivalence about his legacy and legend both without and within the Labor party. Professor Dean Jaensch writes in his 1989 study of modern Labor: 'The Labor party, under Whitlam and Hawke nationally and under Bannon, Cain, Burke and Wran in the states, has been involved in a transformation of organisation, style, tactics and appeals.'[2] Here we have, of all things, a South Australian political scientist assuming that South Australia's most successful modern Labor politician has had little impact on the transformation of modern Labor. The quote cannot be explained away by chronology. Dunstan outlasted Whitlam's overthrow by three years and his term as Premier overlapped that of Neville Wran. I think Jaensch is on to something here but am not sure he knows what it is. We need to ask: is his assumption correct and if so why?

On the morrow of his unexpected resignation as Premier in February 1979 one of his most persistent critics, the journalist Stewart Cockburn, wrote, '[t]he Dunstan Decade is dead, but Dunstanism as a political force and a style of leadership is almost certainly destined to rise again from the grave.'[3] But as South Australian political scientist Andrew Parkin has observed, '"Dunstanism" ... never rose from the grave'.[4] Indeed it can be argued that its fate was foreshadowed within hours of Dunstan's resignation. At a hastily put together gathering around his hospital bed, Dunstan cobbled together an agreement as to the succession. Next day the ministers and the caucus, whom he had dominated for over a decade, rejected these plans, opting for Des Corcoran as Premier, rather than Dunstan's preferred candidate, Hugh Hudson.[5] It seems, too, that he was discouraged from returning from Italy for the early election in September 1979 called by his successor, which put a premature end to Labor rule in South Australia, apparently on the grounds that 'his presence might detract from Des Corcoran's 'personal victory''.[6]

Neither in style nor substance have any of his successors followed in his footsteps. Nor in his post-parliamentary lifetime did Labor governments make much use of his talents. Neither the Bannon government in South Australia nor the national Hawke government gave him any preferment, until a modest consultancy on Aboriginal local government was offered by Bannon in 1988, followed two years later by the chair of one of his own creations, the Craft Authority of South Australia. Two of Bannon's ministers, admittedly disgruntled ones, have written that Bannon was averse to giving Dunstan any job[7] and an unnamed Labor apparatchik claimed that 'for Bannon, [Dunstan] was political poison'.[8]

But we need to be cautious here since Dunstan undoubtedly contributed to his own marginalisation. He accepted an offer to become Director of Tourism from the Cain Labor government in Victoria before the Bannon or Hawke governments had even been elected, making him unavailable for a major offer from those governments in their early years.[9] South Australians were upset that he had deserted the state, and as Dunstan was ill-suited to the role of bureaucrat and as John Cain became disillusioned with him, the Victorian experiment ended in tears and damaged his reputation.[10] His public defence of David Combe in the Ivanov affair did not endear him to the new rulers in Canberra. And when Bannon did give him a job the bitter debate that ensued led to defamation cases. A party leader seeking a quiet life would think twice before offering any position to Don Dunstan.

In death there has been much piety but little commitment. No biography has yet appeared. No recent Labor government has reflected the radical ethos characteristic of Dunstanism. One of the ministers in his government has pondered that '[t]he strange death of the Dunstan dream among Labor party power brokers is difficult to understand.'[11]

Some have explained this 'strange death' as an aversion to his style, his 'flamboyant emotionalism and theatrical flair'.[12] Brian Chatterton, who as a minister broke early with Bannon, mentions a telling shadow cabinet incident in which Bannon explained his preference for grey suits as a reaction to Dunstan's notorious pink shorts.[13] Even more than most politicians Dunstan was very much responsible for his own image. The young man first elected to parliament in 1953 at the age of twenty-six was of middling height, pale, slight, even weedy in appearance, and with a face dominated by thick horn-rimmed spectacles. Plagued by frequent illnesses, a bout of pneumonia led him to the gym. From the late 1950s he began regular workouts, daily jogging and rigorous exercises on body-building machines installed in his home in order to achieve a healthy commanding image. He put on some thirteen kilograms in muscle weight to emerge in the 1960s as the 'suave, tanned, athletic thespian ... in safari suit and contact lenses',[14] the most charismatic of late 20th century politicians, 'the Nureyev of Australian politics'.[15]

Complementing this mix was his sexual ambiguity, highlighted by a sartorial flamboyance unusual among politicians of his time. Much of the 'personal calumny ... vicious character assassination [and] gutter-level smear campaigns'[16] circulating through Adelaide during his years in power thrived on this questioning of his sexual identity. During his political career his most sustained relations appear to have been, with one possible exception, with women, which included his two wives, while another woman has published an account of their year long affair.[17] While publicly provocative – 'he seems to have young, glamorous men in attendance wherever he goes'[18] – he was privately relatively discreet during his political career. Dunstan spent the last 15 years of his life with his partner, Stephen Cheng, whom he had met in Melbourne in the 1980s.

His very immersion in the arts, a dedication unparalleled among leading Australian politicians, saw a veritable cultural renaissance in South Australia: the revitalisation of the Adelaide Festival, the completion of the Festival Centre, the establishment of professional companies in theatre, opera and dance (in many cases building on embryonic amateur companies), the setting up of the Jam Factory for crafts, and a film corporation which became the model for other states. All this had a downside. He basked in his media image as a Medici princeling presiding over his Florence of the South. At the festivals he was a star attraction: doing a Cole Porter turn with the actor Keith Michell, reciting Ogden Nash to Saint-Saëns' *Carnival of the Animals* at the Adelaide Zoo (not on the back of an elephant as the legend has it) and partying with Rudolf Nureyev. This very glamour, with his penchant for theatricalism and his sexual adventurism, have blinded some critics to the fact that he was also the most successful radical politician in Australia in the second half of the 20th century.

For 20 years Dunstan was the most dynamic force in South Australian politics transforming the Labor party, the bureaucracy and the state. He mastered the art of media management and revolutionised the techniques of electioneering. Briefly Premier from 1967 to 1968, he returned to power in 1970, the first of four successive election victories. These victories laid the foundations for a Labor hegemony in South Australia. From 1900 to 1967 the Labor party governed South Australia for only 18 years; since 1967 it has governed South Australia for all but twelve years. Dunstan dominated his cabinet (a number of whom he had personally recruited), the caucus and the party. 'What Dunstan wanted he got', said one of his ministers.[19] Yet nearly all are agreed that his approach was consensual, his cabinet collegial, his dominance stemming from his quiet authority, his talents and his achievements. With the breakdown in the relationship between two of his most powerful ministers, Geoff Virgo and Hugh Hudson, and with party dissension over uranium policy led by a cabinet minister, Peter Duncan, there were signs towards the end that this collegiality was breaking down. He left the disciplinary tasks in caucus to his loyal deputy, Des 'the Colonel' Corcoran, and the management of the party to talented party hierarchs, to whom he was always available.

He modernised and greatly expanded an antiquated and disaggregated public service ('quite primitive' in the view of one of his public service chiefs)[20] that was ill adapted to serve his demands for change. A powerful Premier's Department was built up, with talented public service figures in charge, designed to ensure effective overall coordination of the administration. Able reformers were given charge of critical departments such as community services, health and education. As has been noted: 'The goal was to have policy formulated and implemented by sympathetic servants of the highest calibre.'[21] More generally the service was opened to lateral recruitment; increasingly, merit as well as seniority figured in promotion and there were increased opportunities for women. None of this was achieved without considerable passive resistance and much criticism of 'politicisation', while at times enthusiasm may have outpaced the capacity to manage. On these foundations Dunstan became, in the view of a frequent critic, the Adelaide *Advertiser*, 'Australia's most significant social reformer of the 20th century'.[22]

It is not the rejection of his style then but the rejection of his success that is the paradox. Why has he had no emulators? A clue lies in the parallels between the post-parliamentary trajectories of Dunstan and another ALP giant, Gough Whitlam. Unlike Dunstan's resignation, Gough's martyrdom in 1975 has guaranteed him iconic status among the Labor rank and file. Yet the Labor elite, while acknowledging his status, have kept him at arm's length. Whitlam's biographer, Graham Freudenberg, writes of 'the ritual repudiation of the Whitlam Program' by successive Labor leaders.[23] The New South Wales Labor leader, Neville Wran, began the process in 1976. Facing a difficult election, he made it brutally clear that 'the welcome mat is not out for … Mr Whitlam'.[24] Hawke also explicitly rejected the Whitlam approach to governance and implicitly many of the elements of the Whitlam program.

Dunstan and Whitlam were the two pivotal figures in the remodelling of the Labor party in the 1950s and 1960s from a labourist party into a social democratic one along the lines of the British Labour party. Electorally this involved an alliance between organised labour and progressive elements in the middle classes. In terms of governing elites, it embraced a combination of trade union leaders and figures drawn from the professions and to a lesser extent small business. In policy terms it included the following elements: an acceptance of a mixed economy while retaining a moral critique of capitalism and a continuing interventionist disposition; the pursuit of a democratic polity, based on majority rule accompanied by respect for minority rights; redistributive taxation and egalitarian welfare policies;

a cultural and social alertness; and in foreign affairs an anti-colonial attitude allied with an adherence to the American alliance, which nevertheless permitted criticism of particular American foreign policies. Dunstan and Whitlam epitomised this transformation in their persons and were its leading ideological proponents. As such they were both the beneficiaries of social democracy's brief moment in the Australian sun and the victims of its collapse.

Dunstan was one of Whitlam's chief lieutenants in the social democratic transformation of the national Labor party. He led the fight to remove the Labourist commitment to White Australia. He identified early with the anti-colonial stance of post-war European social democracy, criticising the Harding administration on a visit to Cyprus, and backing Whitlam in his call for early independence for Papua New Guinea. He supported the establishment of a US communications base in North-West Australia, but courageously identified himself early with the protest movement against the Vietnam War. Enraged by the Victorian Left's rejection of Whitlam's needs-based aid for private schools, he helped mobilise the forces that brought down the Left-dominated Victorian executive, thus paving the way for Labor's federal victory in 1972.

It should be noted that this camaraderie between Whitlam and Dunstan was subject to considerable strain when they were both in power between 1972 and 1975. Relations got off to a bad start when Whitlam's first budget appeared to renege on tax relief pledges given to the wine industry and instead imposed, in Dunstan's view, crippling burdens on the industry.[25] The core of the problem, however, was Whitlam's centralist instincts allied to what Dunstan found particularly irritating, his 'fetish [for] tidiness'[26] which encouraged the Prime Minister to seek uniform solutions across the country, irrespective of state differences. Innumerable petty conflicts occurred over obligations explicit in Commonwealth tied grants, even though South Australia as the only Labor-governed mainland state was the outstanding beneficiary of the programs. A more serious conflict occurred over the Whitlam government's efforts to offset this generosity by restrictive policies as regards the general revenue grants. Dunstan believed that Whitlam's aim was 'that the States are starved of money so that they hand over their essential functions'.[27] Dunstan led the assault on this policy and through a cabal with the state Labor leaders forced Whitlam to a financial compromise at the ALP National Conference at Terrigal in February 1975. The essence of the compromise was the purchase of the South Australian railways by the Commonwealth government on extremely generous terms – a senior official in the South Australian Treasury was simply 'dumbfounded, it was just so good'[28] – and consequent technical adjustments to the revenue grants that greatly benefited South Australia.

A further breach occurred when Dunstan's bid for re-election in July 1975 was endangered by the Cairns-Morosi and Loans scandals engulfing the Federal government. Polling the weekend before the election indicated that while voters were satisfied with Dunstan, 'they wanted to express outrage at brand Labor ...

increasingly seen through the prism of the poor perceptions of the Whitlam Labor government'.[29] Dunstan, initially reluctant to dump his federal colleagues, ultimately found it necessary to declare publicly: 'They want you to think that we are to blame for Canberra's mistakes. The vote on Saturday is not for Canberra, not for Australia, but for South Australia.'[30] Whitlam seems to have grumpily acquiesced in the tactic.

But these were differences in approaches, in management, in style, not in objectives. Dunstan and Whitlam were at one in their commitment to the social democratic enterprise. It was their approach to social democracy that distinguished Whitlam and Dunstan from both their Labor predecessors and their Labor successors. Like their predecessors, Whitlam and Dunstan used the term 'social democracy' or frequently its more robust companion, 'democratic socialism', but gave it a far more precise articulation; by contrast, their successors shied away from such terminology, finding it abhorrent in a Thatcherite age. Unlike their predecessors, who were concerned with the issue of capital ownership, the social democrats held a more sophisticated version of managerial capitalism which did not focus 'simply on the evils of ownership';[31] but unlike their successors they did not assume that private management was necessarily better than public management: 'We must show people that government enterprises can be as dynamic, innovative and efficient as private sector undertakings, and in many cases are more so.'[32] Unlike many of their predecessors they did not see nationalisation as central to the Labor project but extolled the virtues of a mixed economy: '[W]e accept ... the discipline of the market place as the only basically effective general method of indicating the needs and wants of the people'.[33] But unlike many of their successors they were not so enamoured with the market as to minimise the role of government: 'We must retain our right to intervene by state action to create undertakings, to temper the market place or to remedy its failures.'[34] Above all, like their predecessors the social democrats retained a sense of the cultural deformations of market capitalism – a system propelled by greed whose rewards bore little relationship to a person's intrinsic merits or to his or her contribution to society; whereas their successors in their enthusiasm for market solutions seem too often to overlook the systemic and arbitrary inequalities inherent in market capitalism.

Social democracy was, of course, an evolutionary creed. Too many horrors littered the 20th century as a result of vanguard anti-democratic efforts to transform society for anyone, at least in advanced capitalist societies, to morally opt for such a path. As Dunstan argued, the Marxist conception of the dictatorship of the proletariat as the path to freedom was 'a load of old cobblers'.[35] 'It would not be possible', he argued in another speech, 'for a radical restructuring of this society to take place dramatically without abandoning the democratic system which has enabled us to make the progress we have.'[36] If there were to be a conflict between socialism and democracy, the social democrat must choose democracy.

Thus the nature, quality and extent of democracy in a particular society were fundamental issues for Dunstan. His relentless and unremitting struggle over 25 years to democratise the South Australian constitution defines him as a serious politician. The obstacles he faced were formidable. Since the establishment of self-government in South Australia a two-to-one ratio of non-metropolitan to metropolitan seats in the House of Assembly had favoured the representatives of rural interests. The 1936 redistribution retained this two-to-one ratio despite the significant increase of population in the metropolis. In addition it did away with multi-member electorates (which had cushioned the effects of malapportionment by permitting minority representation) and replaced them with single-member seats. This redistribution strengthened the bias in the system in favour of the conservatives and has been nicknamed the 'Playmander' after its most prominent beneficiary. As a back up, there was an upper chamber, the Legislative Council, based on a limited property franchise, accompanied by voluntary enrolment and voting, with a grossly malapportioned electoral system and with powers of veto over all legislation and with deadlock provisions so complex that the success of any confrontation was doubtful. Between 1918, when the Council became a 20-member chamber, and 1973, the ALP had never had more than four members at a time in the upper house.

Whatever that infinitely flexible term 'democratic' may mean, it cannot mean rule by a minority. Yet during the middle years of the 20th century the South Australian electoral system virtually guaranteed that the Liberal Country League, whether in a majority or a minority of the popular vote – and it is arguable that it was often in a minority – would govern the state. One of the more amusing passages in Stewart Cockburn's biography of Playford is the author's karma sutra-like contortions to square the Playmander and democracy.[37] To the struggle to democratise this system Dunstan brought gifts of oratory, tactical adroitness, attention to detail and long-term strategic vision.

Dunstan signalled the opening of the war in 1954 (his second year in the parliament) in deliberately dramatic fashion, aimed at both highlighting the issue and jolting the Labor opposition from its understandable mood of resignation. For the only time in his career he was suspended from the House of Assembly for calling Playford's 1954 redistribution proposals 'immoral' and characterising their authors likewise.[38] From then on, year after year in parliament, on the hustings, on radio and increasingly on the new medium television, at which he proved remarkably adept, Dunstan railed against the Playmander, displaying in the words of one critic 'intelligence, passion and apparent integrity'.[39]

But Dunstan's was not merely a rhetorical attack. He identified the vulnerabilities of the Playmander and set out to exploit them. Three types of seats offered Labor opportunities: first, rural seats with significant towns; secondly, rural seats on the metropolitan fringe being swamped by urban voters; and thirdly, marginal Liberal seats within the metropolis. Dunstan argued that party resources should be focused on these few key seats, and that local candidates with personal appeal beyond Labor should be recruited – hence ex-Liberals and Test wicketkeepers became candidates in such seats. Aware that constitutional issues as such had little appeal to voters, Dunstan yoked them to bread and butter issues. In the metropolis he argued that metropolitan services were neglected because metropolitan voters scarcely counted, and in the country he argued, with considerable chutzpah, that development through decentralisation was ignored for fear that bringing workers into country towns would undermine the Playmander.

The strategy worked. From 1957 the conservative majority was slowly eroded. In 1962 Dunstan wrote: 'I personally don't anticipate we will be in government in South Australia before 1965, but as the electoral situation is developing here with a drift in population, I should not think it would be later than that.'[40] He was a key player in outwitting Playford's last desperate effort to shore up his position in 1963 with a new gerrymander. By tactical abstentions Labor denied Playford the opportunity to use the Speaker's casting vote to secure the absolute majority necessary for the legislation. Two years later with a decisive popular vote of 55.0% to 36.4% Labor came to power with a slim majority of three in the 39-member House of Assembly.

With Labor now in government, the second bastion of the conservative order – the Legislative Council – came into play. Relatively quiescent during most of the Playford years, the Council was now active in frustrating Labor legislation and above all in preserving the constitutional status quo. An ambitious effort by Dunstan as Attorney-General in 1966 to resolve all the constitutional issues in a single bill was vulnerable because of its complexity. It was killed off by the Council on second reading with little sign of public lamentation. Dunstan learnt the lesson. Henceforth, while the rhetorical attack would remain two-pronged, each issue – the Playmander and the Council – would be tackled separately.

Modification of the Playmander came first, ironically, as a result of the defeat of the Dunstan government in 1968 – despite the ALP polling 52.0% of first preference votes to the LCL's 43.8%.[41] With uncertainty hanging over the ultimate result, Dunstan persuaded the Governor to allow him to retain office until the new parliament met. For six weeks Dunstan as Premier became chief agitator against a corrupted electoral system. It was perhaps his finest hour and compelled the incoming Steele Hall government to address the electoral system. Although the redistribution that then occurred still contained a substantial rural weighting, Dunstan accepted it, recognising that it was sufficiently generous to promise Labor electoral success at the next election.

With the Legislative Council now the chief barrier to his achieving his ultimate goal – one-vote-one-value – for the Assembly he upped his rhetorical attack on the Council, at first in opposition and then after 1970 in government. Year after year he lambasted the restricted franchise of the upper house, introducing bills on the issue, which though they lapsed in the Council, split the Liberal Party and hastened its disintegration. In government his attention to detail is reflected in administrative measures amalgamating the various electoral rolls thereby minimising the provisions for voluntary enrolment and voting for the Council. In addition, the computerisation of the rolls made it easier to identify potential Labor voters for the Council. Such voters were canvassed and, as Labor had focused in the 1950s and 1960s on Liberal Assembly seats weakened by social change, pressure now mounted on the Liberals in vulnerable Council seats – Midland affected by metropolitan overspill, Northern which included the Spencer Gulf industrial towns, and Central No. 2 in the Labor-voting metropolis. In the 1973 election Labor won both seats in Midland for the first time and came within a fraction of winning two in both Northern and Central No. 2.

Faced now with a potential reformist majority in the Council as a result of the Liberal split and Labor gains, and indeed with the possibility of the abolition of the upper house, the conservatives secured with Dunstan an imaginative compromise: adult franchise for the Council on the basis of a single state-wide electorate with a list system of proportional representation. There was considerable give and take by both sides, though given the strength of the Labor position it did most of the taking, the Liberals most of the giving.

Dunstan was now in a position to realise his two-decade old dream: an electoral system for the Assembly based on constitutional provision for equal electorates, determined and monitored by an independent electoral commission, whose decisions could not be challenged by parliament. This he achieved in 1975. The leading student of the South Australian electoral system has concluded that 'Dunstan could say that, essentially through his personal commitment, South Australia had the fairest electoral systems in mainland Australia and, alone of all the levels of government in Australia, had written into the Constitution provisions that the democratic bases of the systems were guaranteed.'[42] Had he done nothing else he would still have been a significant figure in the history of South Australia.

But he did much more and this brings me to Dunstan's radicalism. He was a bold, adventurous politician, willing to take risks for causes he believed in. But the risks were usually calculated; strategy and tactics were always thought through. He was the first major politician to make use of polls and surveys, but as the pollster Rod Cameron has observed, 'he never used polling as a crutch to change unpopular decisions or to mould decisions in a populist way'; for him 'market research came *after* not before, policy development'.[43] There are three aspects of the term 'radicalism' which I will use to analyse this aspect of his politics: challenging the fundamentals, iconoclastic, innovative.

His Aboriginal policies demanded a root and branch rethinking of the philosophies that had guided Aboriginal policies in Australia during much of the 20th century. Sensitised to racial prejudice through his upbringing in Fiji, he first encountered Aboriginal conditions in a 1956 visit to the Point Pearce Aboriginal Reserve, which 'appalled' him.[44] He wanted to end the paternalistic approach towards Aboriginal matters and replace it with self-determination; he wanted to end all discriminatory practices involving Aborigines; and he wished to pursue a policy of integration rather than assimilation. In opposition he took up cudgels to prevent the execution of the Aboriginal man, Rupert Stuart, for the rape and murder of a nine-year-old white girl; and he pushed Playford, with some success, to moderate the prevailing paternalism. According to John Summers, from 1965 onward 'Dunstan and his Governments were identified with the most important innovations in Aboriginal policy in Australia'.[45] The pace eased in the 1970s, partly perhaps because he ceased to be the minister directly responsible, but mainly because with the 1967 referendum the Commonwealth became the major player in Aboriginal affairs. Nevertheless issues of racial discrimination and land rights continued to figure prominently on his agenda and one of his last initiatives as premier was to introduce legislation, which, by vesting the Pitjantjatjara peoples with all their ancestral lands and the mineral rights in those lands, went further than his earlier legislation.

Influenced by the multi-ethnic nature of his own inner Adelaide constituency, he was an early and articulate exponent of the policy which came to be called multiculturalism, to such an extent that one of his successors has characterised him as 'the architect of multiculturalism nationally'.[46] Eugenia Koussidis, appointed as an ethnic officer to the Inquiry Unit in the Premier's Department in November 1975, claims, 'I was the first person in Australia to be specifically employed as an ethnic anything by any government'.[47] His cookbook published in 1976 celebrates ethnic cuisine, while he worked all his life 'to developing in South Australia the kinds of easy-going open-air civilisation Greeks, Italians and Spaniards have enjoyed for many centuries'.[48] An example of this thinking about fundamentals is a paper prepared under his authority in January 1971 which argues for a complete reframing of South Australian tourism around the concept of cultural tourism, a decade before the concept came into common use.[49] As regards civil rights and civil liberties he displayed a very 1960s sensibility and his reforms bear many parallels with those of the outstanding social democratic reformer at the British Home Office, Roy Jenkins, active at roughly the same time.

He was radical in that he was an iconoclast challenging beliefs long cherished and institutions traditionally venerated. Antiquated licensing and gambling laws were liberalised, and the Sabbath opened to shopping, sport and entertainment. Censorship laws became the most relaxed in Australia and the age of adulthood was reduced to eighteen. Since time immemorial the office of Governor had inevitably been filled by a Briton, usually with some military, naval or air force accomplishments. Dunstan ended this venerated tradition. He appointed in turn a distinguished Australian scientist, an Aboriginal pastor, and a nonconformist cleric. There is some evidence that he was disappointed in all three appointments. A more successful iconoclastic act was the Supreme Court appointment of Roma Mitchell to what had been an all male bastion – the superior courts of Australia.

Doing things first is one mark of the radical but the innovator's task is always a

Figure 15. Neal Blewett and Don Dunstan at the opening of Blewett's electoral office, 1977. Courtesy of Neal Blewett.

challenging one. For a politician it is easier to follow in the innovator's footsteps. If I might interpolate a personal note: bringing in Medicare was a much easier task because Bill Hayden had already fought the battle over Medibank. In so many areas it was Dunstan who fought the first battle. A list of his major and minor innovations in Australia makes the point: the first racial discrimination act, the first Aboriginal lands rights act, the first sex discrimination act, the first decriminalisation of homosexual acts (a measure introduced for tactical purposes as a private member's bill, but one initiated by a Labor minister and backed by all ministers in the government), the first state to put into practice federal ALP policy on needs-based aid to private schools, the first rape-within-marriage legislation, the first container deposit legislation, the first publicly funded ethnic radio station, the first officially sanctioned nude beach.

Turning to socio-economic issues, human services are often seen as the measure of a social democratic government. Here Dunstan played essentially catch-up. South Australian per capita expenditure on health, education and welfare all lagged behind the rest of the states at the end of the Playford period. By 1979 South Australian per capita expenditure in all three areas was at or near the top of the league tables, enabling a remarkable improvement in resources; two new major metropolitan hospitals were commissioned, for example, and distinctive changes in internal school architecture. A set of mental health acts in 1975 have been described as 'models of simplicity and humanity'.[50] The most remarkable changes occurred in social welfare where the Dunstan governments 'promote[d] the recognition and acceptance of social welfare as an integral part of social organisation',[51] abolishing the rather Dickensian Welfare and Public Relief Board and replacing it with a modern Department of Social Welfare (ultimately Community Welfare). Funds for the expansion of these services came from a cautious fiscal policy – 'Dunstan ran a very tight ship with Treasury',[52] from the financially beneficial off-loading of the South Australian rail system onto the Commonwealth and, for a period, the coincidence of ambitions between the Whitlam government and Dunstan Labor, a coincidence, as we have noted, not without its frictions.

On broader economic issues Dunstan, as a social democrat, was markedly interventionist. For example, he integrated the boards of the two state-owned banks and created the State Government Insurance Office to compete with private companies, and provided funds for wineries, canneries, dairy farmers and small businesses in difficulties.[53] His Attorney-General in the early 1970s, Len King, produced the most ambitious consumer protection legislation in Australia in the fields of land and house purchase, building contracts, second-hand cars, and hire purchase agreements, to which a successor later added housing tenancies. Dunstan's preference for public sector leadership is reflected in the range of new statutory authorities he established, such as the Film Corporation, the Development Corporation, the Craft Authority, and the Adelaide Festival Centre Trust.

In urban development there were significant new initiatives in nearly every year of the Dunstan period. Not always consistent – perhaps because his varying visions of the social democratic city were incompatible – his ideas changed and matured over time and were accompanied by varying administrative changes. Given 'Dunstan's quick cooperation compared to the other conservative premiers' he did well out of the funds provided through Whitlam's urban and regional development grants.[54] His Land Commission of 1973, funded by Whitlam monies, has been described as 'perhaps the most radical intervention by the public sector in Australia into the private land and housing markets'.[55] Innovatory government-business partnerships were formed for major urban development projects. An ambitious plan to build a satellite city, Monarto, in the hills east of Adelaide to ease north-south traffic congestion in the metropolis was aborted through stalling population growth and lack of Commonwealth funds. A major critique of Dunstan's urban policies concluded that they 'represent in aggregate a program of public policy making and informed policy debate unprecedented in Australia's cities'.[56]

Like all his successors as Premier, Dunstan struggled with the artificial and narrowly based industrial structure inherited from Playford, which had become increasingly unsustainable in a rationalising and globalising world. His efforts to attract major investments to the state met with little success; the grandest – a petro-chemical complex in the Iron Triangle – eluded him completely. In this he was frustrated by the nationalist aspirations of the Federal Minister for Mines and Energy, Rex Connor, and was possibly outwitted by the multinational consortium with which he was negotiating. His pursuit of industrial democracy, into which he put great effort, appears quixotic and was ultimately fruitless, indeed counterproductive in that it scared businessmen and alarmed some union leaders who feared for their prerogatives. His focus on East Asia for economic opportunities was in advance of his times, but there was little appetite for export activity in the ranks of South Australian businessmen. As the shadows fell across his premiership and over the whole social democratic project, the prospect of a vast uranium mine in the north of the state promised a way forward. But his personal concerns about nuclear policy – particularly in relation to waste disposal and the adequacy of the international safeguards – along with party opposition stymied the possibility. Whitlam had already gone, and Dunstan's standing was undermined by the economic malaise that gripped South Australia, part of a world crisis that brought in its wake the international collapse of social democracy.

The confidence and optimism of the social democrats that the future was theirs was shattered by the end of the 1970s. Keynesian economic management, on which social democrats relied, failed to function any longer, wrecked by inflation, always the flaw in the Keynesian prospectus. Efforts to reduce inflation by reducing aggregate demand did not work, or only at levels of unemployment intolerable to social democrats, while attempts to increase employment by cutting taxes and increasing public spending only worked by injecting a bigger dose of inflation into the system. Thus economies wallowed in stagflation. The problem was compounded by globalisation, which made it difficult to practice social democracy in a single country. The globalisation of capital led to demands for more competitive economies, with challenges focused on protective tariffs, industry subsidies, welfare burdens, inefficient public enterprises, rigid labour markets and tax systems ill-suited to globalisation.

The result was the rise of the philosophy of neo-liberalism throughout the western world in the 1970s. Characterised by a commitment to the market, to individualism, to small government and financial de-regulation, the neo-liberals pursued the privatisation of state enterprises on the grounds that they were inefficient, lower taxes on the grounds that taxation stifled individual enterprise, and the dismantling of an overly bureaucratic state on the grounds it bred a culture of dependency. They took from governments the weapons that dirigiste social democratic rulers had used to manage the economy – control of exchange rates and monetary policy – and backed the international rating agencies as the guardians of the fiscal rectitude of governments. By contrast with the social democrats, who tended to place society before the economy, the neo-liberals focused on the economy, for as their heroine, Margaret Thatcher, proclaimed 'there is no such thing as society'.[57]

Faced with the new zeitgeist, social democrats could either fight or compromise. In Scandinavia, where social democracy was most entrenched and resilient, the social democrats resisted but their position was eroded over the last decades of the 20th century. In Britain and Germany social democratic governments collapsed amid a sea of troubles in 1979 and 1982 respectively and, denying neo-liberalism, remained out of power for most of the rest of the century. In France the socialists under Mitterand began by defying the new consensus, then in the late 1980s, under the same leader, did a complete volte-face and embraced it.

In Australia, given the structural flaws in the Australian economy, neo-liberalism had a particularly strong intellectual appeal. Malcolm Fraser missed his Thatcher-Reagan moment leaving the way open for Labor, under Hawke and Keating. The result was perhaps the most complete accommodation with neo-liberalism of any social democratic party in the world, apart perhaps from New Zealand.[58] Most of the ingredients were there – financial deregulation, freeing the currency, removing barriers to trade, privatisation of state-run enterprises, reduction in income taxes – but all leavened by imaginative, if tight-fisted, welfare policies and carried through, unlike in Britain, with the co-operation of the trade union movement. Naturally the Liberal-National opposition supported most of the major economic reforms, since they were part of an essentially conservative agenda, which they themselves had proved incapable of carrying out under Fraser.

Whitlam's fall was directly related to issues of economic management, issues at the heart of the crisis of social democracy. Dunstan's was not. Although his popularity and authority had been diminished by the malaise in the South Australian economy, his resignation was the result of an accumulation of quite distinct issues, some of which had been long festering. The major ones seem to have been the dismissal of the Police Commissioner Harold Salisbury, itself the final event in a chain of tensions between Dunstan and the police over 20 years; the escalation of this issue by the intervention of an ex-Governor, who had fallen out with Dunstan during his gubernatorial term; the most significant challenge yet to his authority within the party – over the question of uranium mining; the pending publication of a book alleging an inappropriate liaison with a disreputable young man around town; and the harrowing death from cancer of his second wife, Adele Koh, whom he nursed at home. This accumulation of pressures brought a breakdown in his health, a dramatic collapse within the parliament, and his resignation within hours from all his offices. His personal tragedy leaves unanswered the question as to whether he could have maintained in government, as he did in private, his commitment to social democracy in the neo-liberal 1980s.

With the hollowing out of the social democratic ethos most Labor parties at the state level became even more indistinguishable from their conservative counterparts. Party competition in the 1980s was essentially managerial not ideological: it came down to which party could best manage the state's economy. In an era of narrowing competition the new leaders, unlike Dunstan, were risk averse: the adjectives most commonly used about John Bannon were 'cautious', 'moderate', 'unadventurous';[59] similarly for Neville Wran in New South Wales, the exemplar of the new style of Labor leadership, the bywords were 'moderation', 'caution', 'stability'.[60] These are in many ways admirable characteristics and may well have been appropriate during the hard-nosed 1980s; but Dunstan's rocking of the boats was not for such leaders. Power, rather than what one did with it, became the dominant motive of state Labor leaders. Wran's unauthorised biographers write, 'Wran's starting point in politics was always winning, not changing society'.[61] And in winning Wran delivered in spades. In the wake of the Whitlam debacle he won every general election he fought, two of them in 'Wranslides', and never lost a by-election. Of course Dunstan was interested in winning elections: any man who as opposition leader facilitates one premature election and as premier calls two early elections was obviously into winning, but winning was never an end in itself. The new Labor leaders sought the accolade of economic managers rather than social reformers. As a result it has been noted that Wran seldom found himself in 'the vanguard of change',[62] while the Bannon government has been charged by one academic as being 'in full flight from a comprehensive reform agenda'.[63] There was not much place in this world for a social democrat like Dunstan, no matter what his political success.

Dunstan maintained the social democratic faith to the end. He railed against 'the blind faith' in 'oxymoronic economic rationalism'[64] (his favourite term of abuse for neo-liberalism) and regretted that 'the virus [of economic rationalism] has infected ... sadly some people in both major political parties'.[65] He recognised many of the structural reforms of the Hawke-Keating governments as necessary for Australia in a globalising world and praised the Accord with the trade unions. But he disliked the rhetorical exaltation of the market and feared that too cosy a relationship with the top end of town would alienate working-class voters. While he favoured privatisation in competitive situations – he supported for example the abandonment of the two airlines policy – a major theme of his later speeches and writing was an unyielding hostility to the privatisation of natural monopolies, continuing to believe that in such situations 'public ownership performs better than private ownership'.[66] He was equally opposed to the privatisation of government services. And he warned that if the Labor party abandoned the moral critique of capitalism at the heart of social democracy, 'we will find ourselves not competing for the centre ground in politics but for the right!'[67] Some might regard that as prescient; his critics tend to see all this as a nostalgic lament for a world that had gone.

10

South Australia and Australia: Reflections on their Histories[1]

JOHN HIRST

In 1906 Alfred Deakin came as prime minister to Adelaide. He hadn't been here since the Federal convention of 1897, which met at Parliament House. On his 1906 visit he spoke to a crowd of 3000 people in the Exhibition Building on North Terrace; that is, very close to where we are now assembled. I watched the demolition of the old Exhibition from this building somewhere above us when I was a history student here in the early 1960s.

Deakin opened his speech in this way:

> I am happy to be once more in a city whose reputation guarantees to every public man the thoughtful consideration of an intelligent people.[2]

I hope Adelaide's audiences are still distinctive in the same way. I am going to talk about the distinctiveness of Adelaide and South Australia but in ways that might not be altogether pleasing. What I say about Australia might go down better. I should reveal that despite that soft-soap opening to his speech Deakin was occasionally heckled.

There is no doubt about the distinctiveness of South Australia's origins. Unlike the colonies to the east, there were no convicts, or at least none were shipped here from Britain; there was no established church, and church and state were soon separated; there were few Irish; and the squatters were not given a firm hold on the land so that farming flourished.

Paradise of Dissent (1957), the account of the founding of South Australia by Douglas Pike, is a very good book and it has a memorable title. However, the title is somewhat misleading about South Australia after its founding years. In England and Wales, the religious dissenters – the Methodists, Baptists, Quakers and Congregationalists – built chapels because they did not want to attend the churches of the established Church of England. In South Australia they ceased to be dissenters; they worshipped in churches that were of equal standing with all others. Adelaide was not a city of church and chapel-goers; it was simply a city of churches. Religious dissent lost all meaning.

I have not mentioned the Catholics; which is a very South Australian thing to do. When I learnt history here you didn't have to bother about Catholics because their numbers were small and their influence weak. But of course the Catholics enjoyed in South Australia the equality of status that the dissenting Protestants had successfully claimed for themselves.

I am myself of pure South Australian descent; I was a Methodist and I grew up in a suburb, Westbourne Park, where there was no Catholic church. Even if you add Hawthorn to Westbourne Park you will find no Romish presence. There was an Anglican church in Hawthorn, which I rather pitied for not being as well attended and lively as my own. I had no sense that the people attending St Columba's were my social superiors.

My youthful experience prepared me well for the view that South Australia was a distinctive colony. In my book on South Australia, *Adelaide and the Country* (1973), I looked to South Australia's distinctiveness to explain why the gentry families of Adelaide played a well-accepted role in the life of the city and colony. There were no convicts and few Irish to harbour resentment against these English and Scots grandees who were after all not that grand; many of them made money from squatting but squatting did not inhibit the growth of farming.

I left Adelaide, moved east and researched the histories of New South Wales and Victoria. I had left South Australia's social peace for more turbulent societies. Here there had been bitter conflicts between Protestants and Catholics and between squatters and everyone else. But looked at properly, I wrote, these conflicts were not really that severe. If you want real sectarian conflict, I said, look to Belfast or Beirut, if you want large landholders who are a real menace to the public good, look to Argentina. So this South Australian found peace everywhere. Was he influenced too much by his Westbourne Park experience? Let's have a look.

New South Wales was pastoral country. The squatters got their name because they initially squatted on crown lands beyond the boundaries without permission. Then the government, unable to remove them and not wanting to stop the expansion of the wool trade, allowed them an annual licence. Then in 1847 the British government allowed them to have 14-year leases. This is commonly regarded as a great victory for the squatters. They had actually asked for much more: they wanted to be given the land freehold as reward for their effort in pioneering it. Had they become owners of the land, as the pastoralists on the Argentine pampas did, Australian history would have been very different. Because New South Wales was a colony and because Britain's Colonial Office regarded itself as the trustee for the migrants who would come later, the lucky first comers were not to be made owners. As it was, the future of the squatters would be determined by whoever held power when the 14 years were up. Sadly for the squatters, the gold rushes intervened which massively swelled the numbers of those who did not want the squatters to get a permanent hold on the country. Gold diggers who had not made fortunes and workers in the towns demanded that they have a chance to become settlers on the land. These demands were made not on the British government but the new colonial governments, which had been granted the powers of self-government in the mid 1850s. Squatters had agitated for self-government but when it occurred it was not they who took charge but liberals and democrats, their sworn enemies. These men composed the governments that carried measures to allow small men to select land on the squatters' domain and pay for it on time payment. In Victoria, large swathes of land were taken from the squatters, surveyed, and offered to selectors. In New South Wales the would-be selector could enter the squatters' territory and peg out his claim wherever he wanted.

The land acts at first were a spectacular failure. Some small men got onto the land but under these acts the squatters were able to buy up land and transfer at least part of their run from leasehold to freehold. Every concession given to the small man they used themselves by employing dummies, men in their pay, who selected land and then transferred it to their paymaster. They bought up land at auction where the small man could not compete. They harassed selectors who got onto their land and bought them out when they failed.

General histories of Australia tend to stop the story at this point. But the story continues and has a good ending. Governments and parliaments did not give up the battle. At the outset land reform was a crusade that rallied thousands in the towns and goldfields with the hope that the squatters would be turned off their lands and every poor man would gain a farm. The issue never reached this intensity again but those selectors who had got onto the land and farmers who were still tenants kept the issue alive. They wanted more land for themselves and their sons and on terms they could afford.

So the law was changed. Tougher rules were made against dummying. Land boards examined applicants for land to test that they were genuine and not in the squatter's pay. If a dummy slipped through the Minister of Lands could simply cancel his selection. Terms for repayment on selections were made more generous so the selector could afford to take more land and spend more of his capital on improvements and machinery. Sales at auction where the big men were the successful bidders were stopped.

After these changes were made small-scale farming spread across northern Victoria and behind the Divide in New South Wales, in territory that is still the wheat belt. This transformative event of the late 19th century gets missed in the history books which for this period take as their themes trade unions, strikes, the Labor party, nationalism and Federation.

As the land laws changed, conditions became more favourable for the small man. The railways arrived which allowed them to ship produce cheaply to the cities and from there, overseas. Would the construction of railways have promoted wheat farming even if the laws had not changed? Yes, but then it would have been the squatter leasing out land to tenants to grow wheat as occurred on the Argentine pampas. In Australia most of the wheat farmers owned their land.

As we have seen, in the early days of land selection, squatters had managed to make themselves owners of large swathes of good country. From 1890, colonial governments began to buy back these estates and subdivide them for the small man. The process continued for many years so that the big estates disappeared or were greatly reduced. The family farm became almost universal. Australian democracy had prevailed over the big men on the land. We were not Argentina where the democracy was stymied by an entrenched land-owning class. The eastern states had become like South Australia.

In making these points I am following in the footsteps of Douglas Pike. In 1962 he published a paper called 'The Smallholder's Place in the Australian Tradition'.[3] The smallholders are everywhere he said. If you fly over Australia you see the same pattern of land holdings. Very small intensive cultivation near the cities, then the mixed family farms of wheat and sheep; only in the outback on the poorer country do the pastoralists survive. He thought the smallholders' contribution to the Australian character had been missed. This was an attack on the argument of Russel Ward's classic book *The Australian Legend* (1958). Ward said Australians had come to honour and celebrate the working-man of the bush, the shearer, or the drover, who was a hard-drinking, hard-swearing type, loyal to his mates and hostile to bosses and anyone who gave themselves airs. Pike doubted whether this legend had been very influential; he said the values Australians actually followed were much closer to the hard working, sober, smallholder on the family farms. This may well be so, but Russel Ward always had an answer to such criticisms. He said he was merely tracing the origins of a national legend which was not fully founded in fact or vastly influential.

Growing up in South Australia, I knew nothing of Ward's legend of the bush-worker. At school we did not read the works of Banjo Paterson and Henry Lawson whom Ward cited as the chief spreaders of the legend. What I learned were the deeds of the pioneers, whether they were squatters or farmers, the men who first settled the land, who worked hard to make it productive, and who battled against flood and drought and hostile Aborigines. This was a legend that celebrated courage and perseverance and invited us to honour and preserve the world that the pioneers had given us.

When I was researching the history of New South Wales and Victoria I found plenty of evidence of the pioneer legend. In 1978 I published an article with that title.[4] I opened it with the poem that Victorian school children had read over generations in the fifth grade school reader. It was called simply 'Pioneers':

> We wrought with a will unceasing,
> We moulded, and fashioned and planned,
> And we fought with the black, and we blazed the track
> That ye might inherit the land

I found the pioneer legend embodied in the works of Banjo Paterson and

Henry Lawson, which did not deal solely with bush-workers. This was the most telling riposte to Russel Ward. Here is a verse from Lawson's poem 'How the Land was Won':

> They toiled and fought through the shame of it –
>   Through wilderness, flood and drought;
> They worked in the struggles of early days,
>   Their sons' salvation out.
> The white-girl wife in the hut alone,
>   The men on the boundless run,
> The miseries suffered, unvoiced, unknown
>   And that's how the land was won.

My pioneer legend article was well received. I think I did establish that Ward's bush-worker legend was not the only rural legend that has sustained and influenced us. This was a South Australian contribution to the understanding of Australian history.

Let us consider now that other conflict in the eastern colonies that I played down when I came to look at it, the conflict between Catholics and Protestants. Religious conflict would certainly flare up regularly, but there were also determined efforts to contain it. Officially Governor Bourke in NSW made a huge contribution when in 1836, with Britain's approval, he decided to give government funds on the same basis to what he called the three great divisions of Christianity: Anglicans, Presbyterians and Catholics. The churches could never have agreed to see government support going to their rivals; this was a measure only a benevolent despot could impose. It helped social peace and was a special boon to the Catholics, the poorest group, who got many more priests and churches than they could have provided out of their own resources. It was an amazing measure for the convict colony of Protestant Britain.

At the community level it was common practice to ensure that there was at least one Irishman on the governing committees of hospitals, mechanics institutes, friendly societies, and sporting bodies. This was the inclusiveness, the political correctness, of our ancestors. The term British used more here than in Britain itself was not a nostalgic reaching back to the mother country; it was an assertion that here the community was made up of people of the three kingdoms: England, Ireland and Scotland. The Irish had some qualms about being named Britons but there is no doubt that the Australian use of the term included them.

The social cohesiveness of New South Wales society was tested when a mad Irish Catholic attempted to assassinate Prince Alfred, our first royal visitor, in 1868. Henry Parkes, minister in the colonial government, launched into an anti Catholic crusade but in every suburb and country town there was a public meeting or rally where there were three speakers, an Englishman, a Scotsman, and an Irishman and sometimes a fourth, a native born Australian as well. They jointly declared their loyalty to the Queen, abhorred the assassination attempt, and disassociated the Catholics from it. This was the joint declaration for social peace. At the great public meeting in Hyde Park in central Sydney, the Anglican bishop approached the platform to speak and was turned away by the organisers. This was a common practice: the clergy had to be kept at bay as those most likely to stir sectarian animosities.

The Catholics acquired a grievance when the state withdrew support for church schools; Victoria began in 1872 and the other colonies followed. The other denominations were content to give way to a state system of schooling. The Catholics insisted that they had to instruct their young and went on claiming that the state should assist them. For nearly a hundred years the state refused. With their own schools maintained by huge effort, the Catholics drew away from the rest of the community and in the 20th century Catholics also developed their own hospitals, friendly societies, charities and sporting clubs. Sectarian animosity peaked in World War I when the Catholic Archbishop Daniel Mannix spoke coolly about the war – he said it was only an ordinary trade war – and was a very effective campaigner against conscription. This awakened in Protestants all the old fears about Irish disloyalty. Mannix did a poor service to his people who actually volunteered to fight in the same proportion as Protestants.

But two great Australian institutions stood against sectarian divisiveness. The RSL embraced and kept both Protestant and Catholic veterans. The Labor Party was the workers party for both Catholics and Protestants. The efforts of the Catholic bishops after World War I to form Catholic parties failed.

Since sectarian bitterness disappeared only in the 1960s there are people alive who can tell us how bad it was. They always start by recounting the nasty ditties that Catholic and Protestant children shouted at each other when their paths crossed:

> Catholic dogs, sitting on logs, eating maggots out of frogs.

To which an appropriate reply was:

> Proddie dogs will always yell when they feel the fire of hell.

Since the nastiness of children is so profound and requires so little prompting I do not set too much store by this. What we should notice is that Catholics and Protestants are living in the same neighbourhood and their paths cross. The children are going to different schools but they live in the same streets. At no stage in our history have Catholics and Protestants lived separately and apart. The Irish in eastern Australia were here from the first and could take all the advantages of first comers. They were among the first settlers on the land; they were not latecomers in urban ghettoes.

People also regularly recall that there were some government departments that were exclusively Catholic and others exclusively Protestant. A sure sign of divisiveness: but of what sort? We are not looking at Protestants getting all the government jobs, not at Northern Ireland let us say. Catholics had access to government departments; indeed, they were in charge of some departments, for how else could they appoint their own kind? Protestants and Catholics were mutually suspicious and preferred their own kind so they agreed informally to colonise different departments. It was a quiet accommodation of difference.

Before the sectarian bitterness ended, Catholics were widely distributed in due proportion through the hierarchies of wealth and professional expertise. So when the Protestants and Catholics agreed they were both Christians and should stop fighting each other, this social divide disappeared instantly. There were no structural inequalities to be overcome.

I think there has been a tendency among Australian historians to show that theirs is proper history by exaggerating the extent of conflict. So you think this is an uneventful history, they say, I'll show you conflict! Of course there was conflict but we need to measure its extent, notice what softened it and consider how consequential it was. After writing his history of South Australia, Douglas Pike, as I did later, wrote on Australia as a whole. He produced a short history of the country and called it *The Quiet Continent* (1962). The title got him into trouble, particularly for seeming to downplay the violence done to the Aborigines. Actually he made no secret of the extent of violence and dispossession visited on them. And in dealing with settler society he wrote of 'angry workmen' and of Australia being 'torn by industrial disputes'. But in his conclusion, as he justifies his title, he writes 'more obvious than prolonged class war is the blurring of class distinctions. The miserly are everywhere scorned, however great their wealth. Local traditions defy the extremes of grandeur and poverty ... a very wide range remains for each man to do what he likes'.[5] Pike here is echoing the comments of some English visitors to Australia. They noticed that the rhetoric of politics was more extreme and savage than in England, though the actual social divisions were so much less. The underlying stability of Australian society allowed politicians to play with fire, to do what would actually be dangerous in a society with a desperate underclass and a privileged aristocracy. Or to put the point another way: in Australia political talk was not a good guide to social structure.

We have been looking at South Australian perspectives on Australian history. Now I am going to switch focus and look at how South Australia has been affected by its position within Australia, to which of course it is geographically connected and after Federation in 1901 politically connected. A good deal of its history, even some of its distinctive features, makes more sense if South Australia is put into this wider context. There has been a tendency to ascribe anything distinctive or unusual in South Australia's history to its distinctive origins. Douglas Pike thought that South Australia's plan for industrialisation carried out by Thomas Playford reflected a South Australian style since it was a planned colony following the formula of that theoretician of colonisation Edward Gibbon Wakefield. In his evocative history of Adelaide, Derek Whitelock sees the city's origins having a very long lasting effect.[6] It goes on contributing to Adelaide's 'sense of difference', which is the subtitle of the book. When Whitelock wrote another book on the Adelaide Festival, founded in 1960, his historical account of its origins also began with Wakefield in London in the 1830s.

The South Australian Commissioners who were responsible for the planning and settlement of the province thought that the Murray mouth would be a likely site for a capital. And no wonder. The prospects of a great commercial city at the mouth of the continent's longest river were very appealing. River vessels could carry the produce of the whole Murray Darling Basin into South Australia. Except should convict-free South Australia be encouraging connections with the convict east? When Colonel Light chose the site of Adelaide the Commissioners in London still wanted the Murray mouth to be considered, even though Light had correctly identified the key problem of the Murray; its mouth was not clear and there was no good harbour nearby. The party that supported Light in Adelaide noted that the site he had chosen for the capital gave good enough access to the Murray but 'without fear of any injury to the principles of the colony, from too near an approach to the confines of the convict settlement'.[7]

But along the Murray from the convict east came the first overlanders, bringing cattle to the new settlement and kick-starting its pastoral industry, and with them convicts and ex-convict workingmen. This created a panic in paradise because these folk continued with their old trade of thieving. At the same time, this was a reassuring development: it showed that the no-convict policy for South Australia was absolutely correct. What could not be openly acknowledged was that these newcomers taught the colonists how to make post and rail fences, wooden huts and, from their lawless camps in the Hills, provided Adelaide with palings and shingles. So, even in its beginnings, Adelaide was not completely isolated from the convict east – and to its benefit.

Henry Fox Young who was governor from 1848 to 1854 was keen to develop the commercial possibilities of the Murray. He was well placed to do so because he was the true head of the government, since self-government only came into operation after he departed. He himself visited the Murray and then offered a government reward for the first steam ship to navigate the river up to the Darling. With the gold rushes in 1851, there were huge encampments of miners in northern Victoria who were much closer to the Murray River than they were to Melbourne. Now there was a chance of making big money by supplying them with flour and other goods. Two boats successfully went up the River, Randell's *Mary Ann* and Cadell's *Lady Augusta*. Young himself travelled on the *Lady Augusta* and awarded it the prize. The river trade took off. To solve the problem of the Murray not flowing into the sea, Young built and operated a government railway from Goolwa to Port Elliot. This was the first government railway in Australia, though operated by horses rather than steam. The merchants of Adelaide would have preferred the governor to provide a railway from Adelaide to its port.

South Australia faced an existential crisis in the first months of the gold rushes to the east. Nearly all the able-bodied men left for the gold fields. Copper mining, which had made the colony prosperous, had to be suspended; business of all sorts came almost to a standstill. The bankers contrived an ingenious scheme to rescue the colony. The South Australian government would buy gold at a higher price than was being offered in Victoria; the government would run an assay office where the gold would be smelted into ingots which the banks would accept as good money. So gold would flow into South Australia and the diggers who had gone east would follow their gold home. And more or less so it turned out. Governor Young did not develop this scheme but he had to sign it into law, which was a risky thing to do since colonial governors were not meant to tamper with the currency. Young's government ensured the scheme was a success by quickly establishing the assay office and providing an armed escort, which ran regularly from the goldfields to Adelaide, so diggers could safely despatch their gold.

In dealing with the opportunities and threats in the east, Young was a bold, even a distinctive governor. Think of him as an early version of Thomas Playford. Young raised the price of gold against instructions to lure gold and men from the east; Playford operated price control on bread, pies, haircuts and other common necessities in defiance of his party's platform so that wages here could be kept lower than in the east as an attraction for new industry. Young built a government railway; Playford nationalised the Adelaide Electric Supply Company. No one, as far as I know, has attributed Young's policies to the distinctive origins of South Australia.

In 1868 a party of German farmers and their families travelled from South Australia along the Murray to select land in New South Wales. It was a great trek; 14 covered wagons and two spring carts took five and half weeks to reach Albury. The farmers had sent their harvesting machinery by paddle steamer, but for the first years they had to do without them because the river was low and the steamers were stranded downstream. As we have seen in New South Wales and Victoria, land could be bought on time payment. In 1869 Victoria joined New South Wales in allowing the selector to peg his farm wherever he liked. This is what the German farmers were able to do in the Riverina. South Australia was the farming colony but now it was easier to become a farmer in the east.

During the 1860s in South Australia the balance had shifted between squatters and farmers. Land was still being withdrawn from the squatters and put up for sale at auction. But now squatters were cashed up and they outbid the farmers. North of Clare they assembled huge freehold estates and farming was kept out. The farmers demanded that it was the squatters who must be kept out. The farmers' cry at the 1870 election was: We must have land on the same terms as in Victoria.

There was great opposition to moving away from land sales by auction, a system that had operated since the foundation of the colony. Governments liked auction sales since they brought ready revenue; time payments would initially give them much less and entailed the hassle of collecting payments. All property holders were suspicious of new land being offered too cheaply because it would lead to a general devaluation of property. But the great weapon the farmers had was that some farmers – the numbers were in dispute – were already leaving for Victoria. Reluctantly, in stages, governments changed the law: land was offered on terms, auction sales were stopped, farmers had first pick of the land, but always after it was surveyed. Selection before survey was never introduced, an anarchic principle, which South Australia did well to avoid. Under these provisions farming did develop in the mid north beyond the pastoralists' estates and on Yorke Peninsula. So farming, which had made South Australia distinctive, continued to flourish but only because of the competitive pressure coming from the success of the land reform movement in the east.

From the mid 1880s South Australia went into recession, ahead of the colonies in the east where prosperity held up until 1890. The one positive development for South Australia in the late 1880s was the discovery and development of the mines at Broken Hill just over the New South Wales border. Broken Hill's ores were transported to Port Pirie by rail and the town and mines took most of their food, equipment and supplies from South Australia. Then in the 1890s South Australia became the chief supplier of the new gold fields in Western Australia. But this new business was vulnerable because the governments of New South Wales and Western Australia had the power to impose duties which could shut South Australian products out. This fear was among the reasons why there was such strong support in South Australia for Federation, which would establish free trade between the states. The new Commonwealth government was also likely to build a railway to Western Australia across the Nullarbor, relieve South Australia of the burden of running the Northern Territory, and complete the railway north across the continent. South Australia would become the terminus of the Commonwealth rail system.

In joining the federation South Australia compromised its position as the superior Australian colony, free of the convict taint. It was now tainted by association. New Zealand could not come at this and stayed out of the Commonwealth. Tasmania was so badly tainted by convicts that it gained by joining the Commonwealth.

With the new pattern of trade and the Commonwealth to secure it, South Australia recast itself as the central state, a new distinctiveness. It was not set apart from the other colonies and states; it was at their heart. I became aware of the distinctive position of South Australia at primary school. I was gazing one day at the map of Australia hanging at the front of the class when I made a discovery. I turned to pass it on to my neighbour. 'What are you saying Hirst?', said the teacher, for talking was forbidden. I was a goody-goody student so this was a rare occurrence. 'What did you say Hirst?' 'Sir', I replied, 'I was saying South Australia is the only state that has a common boundary with all the others'. He was dumbfounded; he could make no reply. I was not caned or given lines. If he had had more presence of mind he could have said: 'You're forgetting Tasmania'.

Charles Kingston, the radical democrat premier, led South Australia into federation. He saw clearly the economic advantage of federation but he was equally keen to ensure that the Commonwealth was a thoroughly democratic polity – except of course for the small states having the same representation in the Senate as the rest. Kingston insisted the Senate must be elected directly by the people, not indirectly by the parliaments, and by all the people; it must not in any way mimic the upper houses elected on property franchises of the sort he faced in South Australia. And so it was provided. Kingston also enthusiastically embraced the democratic process of making the federation: the people to elect the delegates to the Convention and to vote at referendum on the constitution they produced. This process was agreed to by the colonial parliaments and amazingly by their anti-democratic upper houses.

Kingston looked to take advantage of this concession. His plan was to use the democratic Commonwealth as the warrant for creating a truly democratic South Australia. South Australia had claims to being the democratic colony; it had allowed manhood suffrage in its constitution from the first and was the first to grant women the vote. But South Australia's Legislative Council was still elected on a property franchise while the Commonwealth's upper house was to be elected by all the people. During the 1890s Kingston regularly sent up bills to the Council to widen the franchise of the upper house to include all householders. The Council regularly rejected them. Since the referendum had gained legitimacy in Commonwealth affairs Kingston held a referendum on household suffrage and got an overwhelming 'Yes' vote. The Council still did not budge. Kingston vowed he would not leave South Australia for the Commonwealth until household suffrage was carried. That did not work either. The Assembly voted to free him from this undertaking. His successor as premier, Frederick Holder, sent a bill to the Council to create a popularly elected Convention, along the lines of the federal Convention, which would rewrite the state's constitution. You can guess the result. The notorious flexibility of politicians was perfectly equal to allowing Legislative Councillors to permit in the Commonwealth what they refused for the state.

It was Don Dunstan who in 1973 finally got all citizens a vote for the Legislative Council. And it was the Commonwealth Senate that provided the model for the revamped Council. The whole state votes as one on a system of proportional representation. That gives small parties a chance of gaining seats and usually ensures that the government of the day does not control the upper house. This is the new way of a getting a house of review now that property as a test of voting cannot be countenanced. But I am sorry to report that Dunstan makes clear in his memoirs (*Felicia*, 1981) that he hoped Labor would have a fair chance of controlling the upper house.

Dunstan was an admirer of Kingston and like him pursued his local purposes in the wider Australian sphere, in this case in the federal Labor party. Well before he was a local leader and while still very young Dunstan made himself a significant figure in the national executive and conferences of the party. He had the handicap of being a lawyer in what was still a workers' party and never, in the words of one of the old guard, having 'used a pick or shovel in his fucking life'.[8] His aim was to transform South Australia into a progressive libertarian social democracy. But before he could do that as a Labor premier he had to have his principles adopted by the national party. He worked on the party's civil liberties platform and its policy on immigration, with he himself moving the motion at the national conference in 1965 that led to the dropping of the term White Australia. When the government he led did achieve his purposes, South Australia became an inspiration for Labor supporters everywhere. Gough Whitlam referred to the 'brightness of the light which seemed to shine from Adelaide around Australia during the Dunstan years'.[9] Dunstan was proud of the interest he aroused in Australia and naturally enjoyed the praise he received. From South Australia he had made a national reputation. 'Modesty is not your forte,' shouted a Liberal member to Dunstan across the House. 'That is quite true,' Dunstan replied. 'False modesty, however, never was.'[10]

The regime that Dunstan worked so hard to replace and subvert was that of Sir Thomas Playford, the premier who industrialised a primary-producing state and who kept himself in power by ensuring that the votes of his supporters were more valuable than those of his opponents. In short by a gerrymander or as it has been dubbed by political scientists, a Playmander. What shall we call him? A Liberal?, which was his party label. No. A conservative?, the term which historians commonly use. No. I call him a conservative moderniser. We will find his like not in the political firmament of Great Britain from where we take our political labels, but in the more backward states of Europe in the 19th and early 20th centuries, who were attempting to catch up with the major powers. Playford wanted South Australia to catch up with the industrial states of Victoria and New South Wales. It was a great moment for him when South Australia ceased to be a mendicant state, relying on special grants from the Commonwealth.

Playford had an Australian predecessor in Sir John Forrest, premier of Western Australia in the 1890s, whose control was as complete as Playford's and whose modernising was almost as systematic: the building of Fremantle harbour, the pipeline to the goldfields, a network of railways. Playford did not think of himself as unique; he told Sir Charles Court, the premier who shaped Western Australia's industrial and mineral transformation, that the states were still at that stage where they needed benevolent dictators – and, we might add, especially the smaller states.[11] It is in them we find the parallels to Playford: in Western Australia with two commanding premiers in Forrest and Court and in Tasmania where the Hydro-Electric Commission with very large powers brought industry to a primary-producing state and which its critics said came close to running the state.

I have been raising questions about the distinctiveness of South Australia. I have suggested that there are distinctions which are not so distinct, and distinctions which origins don't explain or fully explain. I am proposing that being small or vulnerable or backward in a wider system of states can lead to distinctive responses.

We can pursue this further in the lives of Thomas Playford and Don Dunstan, the two great premiers of the 20th century. Think of them for the moment not as South Australians but as men of great capacity in a small state. They are almost polar opposites in their aims and achievements, so it is unlikely that both can be understood as exemplifying a continuing South Australian ethos, as Derek Whitelock seems to propose.[12] Their commonality is their position within the Commonwealth.

Consider first Don Dunstan. He is not born in South Australia. He is born in Fiji. Most of his education takes place in South Australia but when qualified in law he returns to Fiji. He does well there as a lawyer, but then, as can happen to a young man, he wonders if his life is to amount to just this. He decides he wants to change the world; it must be possible, he thinks, to build a decent social democracy. Fiji is not quite the place to begin. South Australia will be the site of the experiment. If it succeeds, South Australia can be an example to the nation, perhaps even the world.

Thomas Playford comes from an old South Australian family and is seemingly content cultivating his orchard in the Adelaide Hills. When an old comrade from World War I urges him to go into politics, it seems a natural course to take for his grandfather had been premier of South Australia. In office, he is a fierce South Australian patriot; even his admirers are critical of his refusal to give any consideration to Australia and its needs as he battles the Commonwealth for money and resources to keep his industrial transformation going.

So how, in summary, can we compare them? Dunstan is committed to his social democratic cause and wants to make South Australia a model for the rest of the world. Playford is committed to South Australia and wants its industries to match those of the big states in the east. To model or to match: these different approaches both boost South Australia's standing in the nation and bring wide renown to the leaders who shaped them. Whether national and international renown was important to Playford, I am not sure. For Dunstan it was very important; being simply a South Australian leader was far from enough for him.

You can see why I was concerned about how my remarks this evening might be received. I began with South Australia as a distinctive colony and ended by describing it as a small state. But under the leadership of Playford and Dunstan South Australia punched well above its weight. I hope it can find ways to keep that tradition alive.

Notes on the Text

Chapter 1 • Turning Points in South Australian History

1 Martin Crotty and David Roberts (eds), *Turning Points in Australian History*, Sydney: UNSW Press, 2009, p. 12.
2 Derek Whitelock, *Adelaide 1836–1976: A History of Difference*, Brisbane: University of Queensland Press, 1977, p. xi.
3 Douglas Pike, *Paradise of Dissent 1829–1857*, Melbourne: Melbourne University Press, 1957.
4 In 1977 the archaeologist Rhys Jones termed the practice 'Fire-stick farming', see J. Allen, J. Golson and R. Jones (eds), *Sunda and Sahul: Prehistoric Studies in Southeast Asia, Melanesia and Australia*, London: Academic Press, 1977.
5 Ann Curthoys, Ann Genovese and Alexander Reilly, *Rights and Redemption: History, Law and Indigenous People*, Sydney: UNSW Press, 2008, pp. 42–7.
6 Anthony Trollope, cited in P.D. Edwards and R.B. Joyce (eds), *Australia and New Zealand*, Brisbane: University of Queensland Press, 1967, p. 179.
7 See, for example, *Adelaide and Country, 1870–1917: Their Social and Political Relationship*, Melbourne: Melbourne University Press, 1973; *The Strange Birth of Colonial Democracy: New South Wales 1848–1884*, Sydney: Allen & Unwin, 1988; *Convict Society and its Enemies: A History of Early New South Wales*, Sydney: Allen & Unwin, 1983; and his collections of essays *Sense and Nonsense in Australian History*, Melbourne: Black Inc., 2006, and *Looking for Australia*, Melbourne: Black Inc., 2010.

Chapter 2 • The Adelaide District in 1836

1 For a detailed account of the natural vegetation in 1836, see D.N. Kraehenbuehl, *Pre-European Vegetation of Adelaide*, Adelaide: Nature Conservation Society of South Australia, 1996.
2 Jean Nunn, *This Southern Land*, Adelaide: Investigator Press, 1989, pp. 11, 60, 67–8.
3 Eric C. Rolls, *Visions of Australia*, Melbourne: Lothian Books, 2002, pp. 139–40.
4 James Backhouse, *A Narrative of a Visit to the Australian Colonies* [1843], New York, 1967, p. 509; Helen Mantegani, 'Recollections of the Early Days of SA from 1836', *Proceedings of the Royal Geographical Society of Australasia*, South Australian Branch, Vol. 5, 1901, pp. 70–2.
5 31 December 1836. G. Stevenson, 'Extracts from the Journal of Mr & Mrs G. Stevenson', *Proceedings of the Royal Geographical Society of Australasia*, South Australian Branch, Vol. 30, 1928, p. 55. Also Backhouse, *A Visit to the Australian Colonies*, p. 509.
6 Sharyn Clarke, 'The Creation of the Torrens: A History of Adelaide's River to 1881', unpublished MA thesis, Discipline of History, University of Adelaide, 2004, p. 10.
7 Backhouse, *A Visit to the Australian Colonies*, p. 510; William Light, 1839, reproduced in David Elder (ed.), *William Light's Brief Journal*, Adelaide: Wakefield Press,

1984, pp. 69–70, 77, 80, 99; George Hamilton, *A Journey from Port Phillip to South Australia in 1839* [1880], Adelaide: J. Williams, 1974, p. 67; Charles Sturt, *Narrative of an Expedition into Central Australia* [1849], Adelaide: Libraries Board of South Australia, 1964, Vol. 2, pp. 189–90.

8 June 1837. Dr Everard, 'Early Reminiscences of South Australia', *Proceedings of the Royal Geographical Society of Australasia*, South Australian Branch, Vol. 5, 1901, pp. 77–8.

9 Clarke, 'The Creation of the Torrens', pp. 52–3; Luise Hercus, Flavia Hodges and Jane Simpson, *The Land is a Map*, Canberra: ANU e-Press, 2002, p. 262.

10 24 December 1836. Light, 1839, in Elder (ed.), *William Light's Brief Journal*, p. 90.

11 20 January 1837. Stevenson, 'Extracts from the Journals', p. 65.

12 12 January 1837. Light, 1839, in Elder (ed.), *William Light's Brief Journal*, p. 95.

13 Valerie Chapman and Peter Read (eds), *Terrible Hard Biscuits: A Reader in Aboriginal History*, Sydney: Allen & Unwin, 1996, p. 77; Clarke, 'The Creation of the Torrens', p. 17.

14 George French Angas, *Savage Life and Scenes in Australia and New Zealand* [1847], Adelaide: Libraries Board of South Australia, 1969, Vol. 1, p. 288; Clarke, 'The Creation of the Torrens', p. 36; Karen Moon, 'Perception and Appraisal of the South Australian Landscape 1836–1850', *Proceedings of the Royal Geographical Society of Australasia*, South Australian Branch, Vol. 70, 1969, p. 45.

15 George Blakiston Wilkinson, *South Australia* [1848], Adelaide: Government Printer, 1983, p. 45.

16 Everard, 'Early Reminiscences of South Australia', pp. 77–8; William Finlayson, 'Reminiscences', *Proceedings of the Royal Geographical Society of Australasia*, South Australian Branch, Vol. 6, 1903, pp. 43–4; James C. Hawker, *Early Experiences in South Australia* [1899], Adelaide: Libraries Board of South Australia, 1975, pp. 9–10; Kraehenbuehl, *Pre-European Vegetation*, pp. 65, 69, 72.

17 George French Angas, *South Australia Illustrated*, London: Thomas McLean, 1847, p. 1.1.

18 E. Stephens, 'The Aborigines of Australia', *Journal and Proceedings of the Royal Society of New South Wales*, Vol. 23, 1889, p. 484.

19 T. Scott, *Description of South Australia*, Glasgow: Duncan Campbell, 1839, p. 12, cited in Moon, 'Perception and Appraisal', p. 45.

20 *Ibid.*, p. 57.

21 *Ibid.*, p. 45.

22 Hamilton, *A Journey From Port Phillip*, p. 67.

23 c.1839. Stephens, 'The Aborigines of Australia', pp. 484, 494; *Report of the Select Committee on the Aborigines*, SA Parliamentary Paper No. 165, 1860, pp. 7, 55.

24 April 1838. Joseph Hawdon, *Journal of a Journey from New South Wales to Adelaide*, Melbourne: Georgian House, 1952, p. 61.

25 12 December 1837. Backhouse, *A Visit to the Australian Colonies*, p. 519.

26 Hamilton, *A Journey from Port Phillip*, p. 67.

27 31 December 1836. Stevenson, 'Extracts from the Journals', p. 55. Also Angas, *South Australia Illustrated*, pls 10, 53, 58; and Eugene von Guerard's painting *Fall of the first creek near Glen Osmond*, 1855.

28 Sturt, *An Expedition into Central Australia*, p. 244.

29 24 January 1838. T. Horton James, *Six Months in South Australia* [1838], Adelaide: Public Library of South Australia, 1962, p. 230. Also Angas, *Savage Life and Scenes*, Vol. 1, p. 48.
30 August 1838. Charles Sturt, *An Account of a Journey to South Australia* [1838], Adelaide: Sullivan's Cove, 1990, p. 19.
31 John Morphett, November 1836, cited in R.T. Lange, 'Vegetation', in C.R. Twidale, M.J. Tyler and B.P. Webb (eds), *Natural History of the Adelaide Region*, Adelaide: Royal Society of South Australia, 1976, p. 99.
32 14 February 1850. Tom Griffiths (ed.), *The Life and Adventures of Edward Snell*, Sydney: Angus & Robertson, 1988, p. 78.
33 Angas, *South Australia Illustrated*, p. 33.
34 John Morphett, 26 November 1836, cited in Rob Linn, *Cradle of Adversity: A History of the Willunga District*, Adelaide: Historical Consultants, 1991, p. 18.
35 February 1842. J. Lort Stokes, *Discoveries in Australia* [1846], Adelaide: Libraries Board of South Australia, 1969, Vol. 2, p. 402. See also George French Angas' painting *Rapid Bay, encampment of the Yankalilla blacks* (c.1845).
36 Angas, *South Australia Illustrated*, p. 49.
37 Sturt, *An Expedition into Central Australia*, p. 244. Also Chapman & Read, *Terrible Hard Biscuits*, p. 78; Simpson Newland, 'Annual Address', *Proceedings of the Royal Geographical Society of Australasia*, South Australian Branch, No. 22, 1921, p. 3.
38 Jane Franklin, 'A Visit to South Australia', December 1840, Franklin Papers, MS114, National Library of Australia.
39 August 1838. Sturt, *A Journey to South Australia*, p. 21.
40 1 December 1837. Backhouse, *A Visit to the Australian Colonies*, p. 511.
41 Light quoted in Moon, 'Perception and Appraisal', p. 47.
42 *Ibid.*, p. 45.
43 Hawker, *Early Experiences in South Australia*, p. 7.
44 1840s. Wilkinson, *South Australia*, pp. 44–5.
45 Allan L. Peters (ed.), *Recollections: Nathaniel Hailes' Adventurous Life in SA*, Adelaide: Wakefield Press, 1998, p. 25.
46 April 1838. Hawdon, *A Journey from New South Wales*, p. 61.
47 Franklin, 'A Visit to South Australia', December 1840.
48 October 1838. Hawker, *Early Experiences in South Australia*, pp. 7, 23.
49 Clarke, 'The Creation of the Torrens', p. 100.
50 F. Sinnett, cited in Clarke, 'The Creation of the Torrens', p. 102.
51 25 June 1838. Angas Papers, State Library of South Australia, PRG 175, pp. 419–22, courtesy Bernie O'Neil.
52 William Finlayson, 'Reminiscences', State Library of South Australia, PRG 290/8; Mary Thomas, *The Diaries and Letters of Mary Thomas*, Adelaide: W.K. Thomas & Co., 1925, p. 123, both courtesy Tom Gara.
53 January 1844. Angas, *Savage Life and Scenes*, Vol. 1, p. 43.
54 *South Australian Register*, 27 March 1841, p. 4, courtesy Tom Gara.
55 Concerning fire, see Valerie Campbell, 'The Coastal Archaeology of the Fleurieu Peninsula', unpublished MA thesis, Discipline of Archaeology, Flinders University of South Australia, 1988, pp. 226–40; Finlayson, 'Reminiscences', p. 41; Bill Gammage, 'Fire in 1788: The Closest Ally', *Australian Historical Studies*, Vol. 42,

No. 2, 2011, pp. 277–88; Bill Gammage, *The Biggest Estate on Earth*, Sydney: Allen & Unwin, 2011; Twidale *et al.*, *Natural History of the Adelaide Region*, p. 116.

56 Stephens, 'The Aborigines of Australia', p. 494.

57 Edward Snell in Griffiths (ed.), *Edward Snell*, p. 69.

58 Peters, *Recollections: Nathaniel Hailes*, p. 12.

59 Hercus *et al.*, *The Land is a Map*, p. 263.

60 24 January 1839. D.M. Hahn, 'Extracts from the Reminiscences of Captain Dirk Meinertz Hahn, 1838–1839', *South Australiana*, Vol. 3, 1964, pp. 120–1.

61 January 1839. Martin Buchhorn (ed.), *Emigrants to Hahndorf*, Adelaide: Lutheran Publishing House, 1989, p. 117.

62 *South Australian Register*, 26 June 1841, p. 3, courtesy Tom Gara.

63 1840s. Wilkinson, *South Australia*, p. 240.

Chapter 3 • South Australia: Between Van Diemen's Land and New Zealand

1 John Connor, *The Australian Frontier Wars: 1788–1838*, Sydney: UNSW Press, 2002, pp. 84–101.

2 *Ibid.*, pp. 79–83.

3 *Ibid.*, pp. 102–3.

4 A.G.L. Shaw, 'British Policy Towards the Aborigines, 1830–1850', *Australian Historical Studies*, Vol. 25, No. 99, 1992, pp. 265–85.

5 *Ibid.*, p. 269.

6 Alan Frost, 'New South Wales as Terra Nullius: The British Denial of Aboriginal Land Rights', *Historical Studies*, Vol. 19, No. 77, 1981, pp. 513–23.

7 Henry Reynolds, *The Law of the Land*, Melbourne: Penguin, 1987, pp. 45–54.

8 *Ibid.*, pp. 11–17.

9 Brian Dickey and Peter Howell, *South Australia's Foundation: Select Documents*, Wakefield Press: Adelaide, 1986, p. 43.

10 Torrens to Grey, December 1835, Australian Joint Copying Project (henceforth AJCP), CO 13/3.

11 Reynolds, *The Law of the Land*, pp. 81–2.

12 *Ibid.*, p. 97.

13 Charles Buxton (ed.), *Memoirs of Sir Thomas Fowell Buxton*, London, 1926, p. 231.

14 Aborigines Protection Society, *Fourth Annual Report*, London, 1841, p. 6.

15 House of Commons, Sessional Papers, 1837, 7, No. 425, *Report of the Select Committee on Aborigines (British Settlements)*, p. 77.

16 Arthur to Buxton, 31 December 1835, in *The Governor's Letterbook: 1833–36*, Tasmanian State Archives: G.O. 52/16, p. 247.

17 *Ibid.*

18 *Ibid.*

19 Arthur to Spring Rice, 27 January 1835, AJCP, CO 280/55.

20 Reynolds, *The Law of the Land*, p. 99.

21 *Ibid.*, pp. 100–01.

22 For a full discussion of the Letters Patent see Shaun Berg, 'A Fractured Landscape: The Effect on Aboriginal Title to Land by the Establishment of the Province of South Australian', in Shaun Berg (ed.), *Coming to Terms: Aboriginal Title in South Australia*, Adelaide: Wakefield Press, 2010, pp. 1–24.

23 Stephen to Gardiner, 10 December 1835, AJCP, CO 13/3.
24 John Brown, Diary, 4 January 1836, in *Papers of John Brown, 1837–49*, State Library of South Australia, item nos 36–37.
25 Reynolds, *The Law of the Land*, pp. 113–14.
26 See, for instance, I.H. Kawharu, *Waitangi: Maori & Pakeha Perspectives on the Treaty of Waitangi*, Auckland: Oxford University Press, 1989.
27 Claire Simmons and Shaun Berg, 'The Law as a Prisoner of History: An Examination of Aboriginal Title in South Australia', in Shaun Berg (ed.), *Coming to Terms: Aboriginal Title in South Australia*, Adelaide: Wakefield Press, 2010, pp. 63–4.
28 Douglas Pike, *Paradise of Dissent*, Melbourne: Melbourne University Press, 1957.
29 Ann Curthoys, Ann Genovese and Alexander Reilly, *Rights and Redemption: History, Law and Indigenous People*, Sydney: UNSW Press, 2008, pp. 37–59.
30 Henry Reynolds, *Why Weren't We Told?*, Sydney: Viking, 1999, pp. 185–225.
31 George Trevorrow, Thomas Trevorrow and Matthew Rigney, 'Preface', in Shaun Berg (ed.), *Coming to Terms: Aboriginal Title in South Australia*, Adelaide: Wakefield Press, 2010, p. vii.

Chapter 4 • No Convicts Here: Reconsidering South Australia's Foundation Myth

1 T. Horton James, *Six Months in South Australia*, London: J. Cross, 1838, pp. 39–41.
2 *Ibid.*, p. 42.
3 Letter dated 16 November 1845, quoted in Eric Richards, 'South Australia Observed, 1836–1986', in Eric Richards (ed.), *The Flinders History of South Australia: Social History*, Adelaide: Wakefield Press, 1986, p. 6.
4 For further discussion, see John Hirst's chapter in this volume, and John Bannon, 'South Australia', in Helen Irving (ed.), *The Centenary Companion to Australian Federation*, Cambridge: Cambridge University Press, 1999, pp. 130–1.
5 See, for example, Alan Atkinson, 'Four Patterns of Convict Protest', *Labour History*, No. 37, 1979, pp. 28–51; and W. Nichol, 'Malingering and Convict Protest', *Labour History*, No. 47, 1984, pp. 18–27.
6 Conditions in the penal colonies differed over time and between places, so this summary generalises objections. The Bigge and Molesworth reports, published in 1822 and 1838 respectively, provide a more complete summary of the perceived problems with the convict system. See J.T. Bigge, *Report of the Commissioner of Inquiry into the State of the Colony of New South Wales*, London, 1822; and William Molesworth, *Report from the Select Committee of the House of Commons on Transportation*, London, 1838.
7 Joanne Archer, 'Wakefield's Theory of "Systematic Colonisation"', *National Library of Australia News*, Vol. 13, No. 9, 2003, p. 6.
8 Henry Capper, *South Australia. Containing Hints to Emigrants; Proceedings of the South Australian Company*, 2nd and revised edition, London: Robert Tyas, 1838, p. 35.
9 *Ibid.*, p. 6.
10 Letter from Governor Grey to Lord Stanley, 6 September 1845, tabled in the House of Commons (UK) and included in *Copies of all correspondence between any person or persons interested in South Australia and the Colonial Office, respecting the effect upon that Province of the Official Notice of the Comptroller-General of Van Diemen's*

land of the 21st day of June 1845, relative to convicts in the colony who were holders of conditional pardons (in continuation of Parliamentary Paper, No.401, of Sess. 1846).

11 J.H. Croucher to W.E. Gladstone, 17 February 1846, in *ibid.*

12 J.H. Croucher to W.E. Gladstone, 18 March 1846, in *ibid.*

13 Letter from Lord Lyttelton, British Under-Secretary of State for War and the Colonies, to D. McLaren, Manager of the South Australian Company, 16 May 1846, in *ibid.*

14 Graham Jaunay, 'South Australian Convicts: A Study', *The South Australian Genealogist*, Vol. 22, No. 1, 1995, pp. 8–9. Thirty-one of these sentences were passed in the latter half of 1851, when legislation was being passed in the UK and South Australia to bring transportation to an end, so the prisoners ended up serving their sentences at home. These figures do not include escaped convicts who were sentenced in other colonies and who were apprehended and returned by South Australian authorities without facing court in SA.

15 *Ibid.*, pp. 7–9.

16 *Ibid.*, p. 8. The first person sentenced to transportation (for 7 years) was James Gordon in May 1837. See *South Australian Gazette and Colonial Register*, 3 June 1837, p. 5, and 8 July 1837, p. 4.

17 A.R.G. Griffiths, 'A History of South Australian Prisons', unpublished MA thesis, Department of History, The University of Adelaide, 1964, p. 44.

18 Pakington, 14 December 1852, cited in Henry Button, *Flotsam and Jetsam: Floating Fragments of Life in England and Tasmania; An Autobiographical Sketch with an Outline of the Introduction of Responsible Government*, Launceston: A.W. Birchall & Sons, 1909, p. 454.

19 South Australia, No. 9 of 1865, *An Act to repeal Act No. 18 of 1857–8, intituled 'An Act to prevent the introduction into the Province of South Australia of Convicted Felons and other Persons sentenced to Transportation for offences against the Laws,' and to make other provision in lieu thereof*, 1865.

20 Steven Anderson and Paul Sendziuk, 'Hang the Convicts: Capital Punishment and the Reaffirmation of South Australia's Foundation Principles', *Journal of Australian Colonial History*, forthcoming.

21 *Adelaide Chronicle*, 17 March 1840, p. 2.

22 *South Australian Register*, 21 March 1840, p. 5.

23 This and the other cases discussed here are examined in greater detail in Anderson & Sendziuk, 'Hang the Convicts'. For the Donelly case, also see *Southern Australian*, 16 March 1847, p. 4; *South Australian Register*, 31 March 1847, p. 2; and Alan Pope, 'Aborigines and the Criminal Law in South Australia', unpublished Ph.D. thesis, Deakin University, 1998.

24 See, for example, R. Foster, '"Don't Mention the War": Frontier Violence and the Language of Concealment', *History Australia*, Vol. 6, No. 3, 2009, pp. 68.1–68.15.

25 *Adelaide Times*, 5 March 1853, p. 3.

26 *Adelaide Times*, 14 March 1853, p. 3.

27 The proportion of those reprieved remains relatively low (46.2%) even if one includes an additional three men who *might* have had convict pasts. The difficulty in determining the backgrounds of the offenders is discussed in Anderson & Sendziuk, 'Hang the Convicts'.

28 Three of these were women, convicted of aiding and abetting their husbands who had committed an assault and robbery. At the time, leniency in sentencing was regularly extended to female offenders, especially if they were caring for children. Their cases are thus not absolutely comparable to those involving the offenders with convict backgrounds, all of whom were male.

29 See *Southern Australian*, 9 March 1841, p. 3; *Adelaide Chronicle*, 10 March 1841; *South Australian Register*, 13 March 1841, p. 2. Also see 'Judge Report of the case of John Wilson', 6 March 1841, State Records of South Australia (henceforth SRSA), GRG 24/1, 1841/85a.

30 Their crime was committed 12 years after the Curran and Hughes robbery, and it is possible that the criteria guiding sentencing had relaxed as social values and the imperative of maintaining law and order in a new settlement softened during this period. The case is reported in *Adelaide Observer*, 27 November 1852, p. 8, and 4 December 1852, p. 2. Also see 'Judge Cooper to Colonial Secretary Office, 30 November 1852', SRSA, GRG 24/6, 1852/3415.

31 *South Australian Register*, 5 September 1840, p. 4. For further details of the case, see *Adelaide Chronicle*, 9 September 1840.

32 See, for example, Maureen M. Leadbeater, 'Whaling: South Australia's Early Days', Adelaide Cooperative History, http://www.ach.familyhistorysa.info/whaling.html; accessed 12 April 2012; and Parry Kostoglou and Justin McCarthy, *Whaling and Sealing Sites in South Australia*, Adelaide: State Heritage Branch, Department of Environment and Planning, 1991. For evidence of whaling activity around Kangaroo Island in 1803, see 'Ship News', *Sydney Gazette and New South Wales Advertiser*, 8 January 1804, p. 4.

33 George Sutherland, 'Report of a Voyage from Sydney to Kangaroo Island', in South Australia Company, *South Australia: Outline of the Plan of a Proposed Colony to be Founded on the South Coast of Australia; with an account of the soil, climate, rivers, &c.*, London: Ridgway and Sons, 1834, p. 50.

34 P. Cunningham, *Two Years in New South Wales; A Series of Letters, Comprising Sketches of the Actual State of Society in that Colony; of its Peculiar Advantages to Emigrants; of its Topography, Natural History, &c. &c.*, Vol. 1 of 2 vols, London: Henry Colburn, 1827, pp. 21–2. In 1827, Major Lockyer added: 'The great scene of villainy is at Kangaroo Island, where, to use the terms of one of them, a great number of graves are to be seen, and where some desperate characters are, many of them runaways from Sydney and Van Dieman's [*sic*] Land.' (Lockyer cited in W.A. Cawthorne, *The Kangaroo Islanders: A Story of South Australia before Colonization*, Adelaide: Rigby, 1926, p. vii.)

35 Alexander Tolmer, *Reminiscences of an Adventurous and Chequered Career at Home and at the Antipodes*, 2 vols, London: Sampson Low, Marston, Searle & Rivington, 1882. See, for example, Vol. 1, pp. 287–90, 307–22.

36 Quoted in Tom Dyster, *Pump in the Roadway*, Hawthorndene, S.A.: Investigator Press, 1980, p. 24.

37 Dyster, *Pump in the Roadway*, pp. 22–3. Even the hangman who sent the convicts Curran and Hughes to their graves was described as being 'an old convict and tiersman' (see James C. Hawker, *Early Experiences in South Australia*, Adelaide: E.S. Wigg & Son, 1899, p. 66).

38 Letter from Benjamin Boyce to his parents and siblings, 22 July 1842, State Library of South Australia, D4308/1; and Eric Richards, 'A Voice from Below: Benjamin Boyce in South Australia, 1839–1846', *Labour History*, No. 27, 1974, pp. 65–75.

39 *Ibid.*; and Letter from Benjamin Boyce to his parents, 1 February 1844, State Library of South Australia, D4308/2.

40 Letter from Edward Stephens to Governor Hindmarsh, 29 June 1837, SRSA, GRG 24/1, 1837/211.

41 *South Australian Register* (25 January 1840, p. 3) reported: 'out of the *thirty* prisoners tried at the last delivery, there was only one convicted who had come to the colony direct from England; and among the twenty-five prisoners now awaiting their trial for different offences, there are but *five* English emigrants, the remaining twenty being escaped convicts, ticket-of-leave men, or emancipated from New South Wales or Van Diemen's Land'.

42 Governor Hindmarsh to Lord Glenelg, 1 November 1837, South Australian Duplicate Despatches No. 53, SRSA, GRG 2/5/1. When Hindmarsh was recalled to London in 1838, his acting replacement, George Milner Stephen, suggested that only the recently enrolled constables stood between the colonists and anarchy. He added that there were twice as many escaped convicts marauding about the settlement as there were prisoners in the gaol (then numbering 21). See Robert Clyne, *Colonial Blue: A History of the South Australian Police Force, 1836–1916*, Adelaide: Wakefield Press, 1987, p. 20.

43 Gawler quoted in Max Carter, *No Convicts There: Thomas Harding's Colonial South Australia*, Adelaide: Trevaunance Pty Ltd, 1997, p. 233.

44 *South Australian Gazette*, 30 April 1840.

45 'Evidence taken before the Select Committee on South Australia. Evidence of T.F. Elliot, Esq', *South Australian Register*, 20 November 1841, p. 4.

46 See, for example, State Library of Queensland, 'Queensland Convicts', http://www.slq.qld.gov.au/info/fh/convicts/qlders; accessed 12 April 2012.

47 An article published in the *South Australian* on 19 June 1846 was more moderate in tone but maintained the stance against convicts and expirees. 'It is true', it reported, 'cases of *extreme* depravity are rare, but the number of larceny cases (especially in a country where employment at liberal wages is so readily procurable) is such as to be really alarming, and to indicate but too plainly the deleterious ingredient infused in the shape of convict expirees from Van Diemen's Land; nor are our apprehensions on this score abated, when we reflect how readily many colonial youth may be corrupted by convict example, in the absence of any sound education, whether secular, moral, or religious.'

48 Colonial Secretary's Office to Henry Inman, Superintendent of Police, 20 August 1838, SRSA, GRG 24/4, 1838/93–4 (C, Vol. 2); and Colonial Secretary's Office to Henry Inman, 1 October 1838, SRSA, GRG 24/4, 1838/117 (C, Vol. 2). On his arrival in October 1838, Governor Gawler granted the men free pardons. See: *South Australian Gazette and Colonial Register*, 20 October 1838, Government Order No. 7.

49 Waller's case is brought to light in 'Central Police Court', *Sydney Morning Herald*, 16 February 1854, p. 5; 'Sydney Police Court – Wednesday', *Empire* [Sydney, NSW], 16 February 1854, p. 2; 'South Australia', *The Cornwall Chronicle* [Launceston, Tas.], 7 June 1854, p. 5; and Carter, *No Convicts There*, p. 266.

50 Leadbeater, 'Whaling: South Australia's Early Days'.
51 William James Hosking, 'Whaling in South Australia 1837–1872', unpublished BA(Hons) thesis, Flinders University, 1973, p. 4. Hosking nevertheless cautions against overstating the longer-term importance of whaling to the South Australian economy, noting that 'the benefits that whaling brought to Hobart Town, which prospered greatly from support industries (such as ship-building, vegetable farming, rope and tar manufacture etc.), did not come to Port Adelaide' (p. 33). Also see pp. 8–9 for further discussion of this point.
52 James, *Six Months in South Australia*, pp. 45–6.
53 John Morphett, agent to large holders of South Australian land residing in England, and addressed to those persons, 28 February 1837, cited in Henry Capper, *South Australia. Containing Hints to Emigrants; Proceedings of the South Australian Company*, 2nd and revised edition, London: Robert Tyas, 1838, pp. 72–3.
54 C. Smith, Diary (extracts; 1839–1854, transcribed by her son Duncan Stewart), Smith Family Papers, State Library of South Australia, PRG 144, p. 26; E.S. Mahony, 'The First Settlers at Gawler, February, 1839', *Proceedings of the Royal Geographical Society of South Australia*, Vol. 28, 1927, p. 56; and Hosking, 'Whaling in South Australia 1837–1872', p. 3.
55 Mahony, 'The First Settlers at Gawler', p. 56. It appears that Mahony composed most of this text some thirty years prior to publication. She lived at Gawler with her parents and siblings after emigrating from Ireland in 1838.
56 John Wrathall Bull, *Early Experiences of Life in South Australia and an Extended Colonial History* [1878], 2nd ed., 1884, pp. 56–7.
57 Except where other references are supplied, this brief vignette about Broadstock's life is drawn from Dale Gathercole, 'Joseph Broadstock: A South Australian with a Convict Past', *The South Australian Genealogist*, Vol. 22, No. 1, 1995, pp. 22–3; and 'Broadstock Family Tree', Brenton Broadstock, http://www.brentonbroadstock.com/page32/page31/page31.html; accessed 14 April 2012.
58 *Hobart Town Courier and Van Diemen's Land Gazette*, 3 January 1840, p. 4.
59 *Argus* [Melbourne], 23 February 1847.
60 Following the death of his wife, Broadstock formed a close relationship with his housekeeper, Elizabeth Eaton Braynard, and they had a daughter in 1874.
61 *South Australian Register*, 15 December 1855, p. 2.
62 *South Australian Advertiser*, 5 August 1858, p. 3.
63 John S. Levi and G.F.J. Bergman, *Australian Genesis: Jewish Convicts and Settlers 1788–1850*, new edition, Melbourne: Melbourne University Press, 2002, pp. 271–2.
64 State Records of New South Wales, Certificate of Freedom No. 068/2515, SR Ref 4/4423, reel 601; and David Solomon, 'The Crime and Punishment of Emanuel and Vaiben Solomon', 2007, http://www.oocities.org/solomon_genealogy/Trial_of_Emanuel_and_Vaiben_Solomon.html; accessed 19 April 2012.
65 Eric Richards, 'Solomon, Emanuel (1800–1873)', *Australian Dictionary of Biography,* http://adb.anu.edu.au/biography/solomon-emanuel-4623; accessed 14 April 2012.
66 Jaunay, 'South Australian Convicts', p. 9; and Eric Richards, 'The Fall and Rise of the Brothers Solomon', *Journal and Proceedings of the Australian Jewish Historical Society*, Vol. 8 (part 2), 1975, pp. 12–13.

67 The land was purchased in 1848. In order to take better advantage of the topography, a new site for the Port Pirie township was established a few kilometres north, and Emanuel's subdivision was renamed Solomontown in 1873. Solomontown is now a residential suburb of the city of Port Pirie. See Nancy Robinson, *Reluctant Harbour: The Romance of Pirie*, Adelaide: Nadjuri Australia, 1976, pp. 41–3, 74, 76, 94.
68 See Hirsch Munz, *Jews in South Australia 1836–1936*, Adelaide: Thornquest Press 1936, pp. 18–19. Also see Richards, 'The Fall and Rise of the Brothers Solomon', pp. 1–28.
69 Sarah Engledow, 'The Saint and the Merchant', *Portrait,* No. 38, 2011, pp. 30–3.
70 Richards, 'Solomon, Emanuel (1800–1873)'. One of Emanuel's nephews, Judah Moss Solomon, was also elected to the Legislative Council and became Lord Major of Adelaide. Judah's son, Vaiben Louis Solomon, perhaps had the most distinguished political career of the family, briefly becoming premier of South Australia and helping to draft the Australian Constitution before entering Federal Parliament. See: 'Judah Moss Solomon', *Australian Dictionary of Biography*, http://adb.anu.edu.au/biography/solomon-judah-moss-4930; accessed 14 April 2012; and 'Premiers of South Australia – Hon Vaiben Solomon', Parliament of South Australia, http://www.parliament.sa.gov.au/Members/Ministers/Pages/PremiersofSouthAustralia.aspx; accessed 14 April 2012.
71 *South Australian Register*, 9 January 1845, p. 2.
72 *Ibid.*
73 Boyle Travers Finniss, *The Constitutional History of South Australia during Twenty-One Years*, Adelaide: W.C. Rigby, 1886, pp. 20–1.
74 A.L. Haydon, *The Trooper Police of Australia: A Record of Mounted Police Work in the Commonwealth from the Earliest Days of Settlement to the Present Time*, London: Andrew Melrose, 1911, p. 253.
75 James, *Six Months in South Australia*, p. 41.
76 Letter from Edward Stephens to Governor Hindmarsh, 29 June 1837, SRSA, GRG 24/1, 1837/211; and Stephen Morphett cited in Henry Capper, *South Australia*, pp. 72–3.

Chapter 5 • Proclamation Day and the Rise and Fall of South Australian Nationalism

1 P.A. Grenfell-Price, *The Foundation and Settlement of South Australia, 1829–1845*, Adelaide: F.W. Preece, 1924, pp. 42–59.
2 The events of the day are described in great detail in the second issue of *The South Australian Gazette and Colonial Register*, published on 3 June 1837 – the first issue of the paper published in the colony itself.
3 While 28 December came to be observed as the anniversary of the foundation of settlement in South Australia, some have suggested that other dates might have been more appropriate. Peter Howell, for instance, points out that in a constitutional sense South Australia was created on 19 February 1836, this being the date when the Letters Patent, which defined the boundaries of the colony and brought it into being as a legal and political entity, was signed into law. See P.A. Howell, *South Australia and Federation*, Adelaide: Wakefield Press, 2002, pp. 8–10.

4 Jim Davidson, 'The Rise and Fall of Proclamation Day', *Meanjin*, Vol. 51, No. 4, 1992, p. 796.
5 *Ibid.*, pp. 796, 806.
6 P.A. Howell, 'The South Australia Act, 1834', in Dean Jaensch (ed.), *The Flinders History of South Australia: Political History*, Adelaide: Wakefield Press, 1986, pp. 26–30.
7 J.M. Main, 'The Foundation of South Australia', in Dean Jaensch (ed.), *The Flinders History of South Australia: Political History*, Adelaide: Wakefield Press, 1986, pp. 1–6.
8 *South Australian Government Gazette*, 31 January 1856.
9 Duncan Bell, *The Idea of Greater Britain: Empire and the Future of World Order, 1860–1900*, Princeton: Princeton University Press, 2007, p. 4.
10 John Manning Ward, *Colonial Self-Government: The British Experience 1759–1856*, London: Macmillan Press, 1976, pp. 291–8.
11 John Hirst, *The Sentimental Nation: The Making of the Australian Commonwealth*, Melbourne: Oxford University Press, 2000, p. 46.
12 *Advertiser*, 31 December 1895, pp. 5–6.
13 Mark Twain, *Mark Twain in Australia and New Zealand*, Melbourne: Penguin Books, 1973, p. 189.
14 Anthony Trollope, in P.D. Edwards and R.B. Joyce (eds), *Australia and New Zealand*, Brisbane: University of Queensland Press, 1967, p. 179.
15 Ken Inglis, *The Australian Colonists: An Exploration of Social History 1788–1870*, Melbourne: Melbourne University Press, 1974, p. 143.
16 Alan Atkinson, 'Tasmania and the Multiplicity of Nations', 2005 Eldershaw Lecture, *Tasmanian Historical Research Association and Proceedings*, Vol. 52, No. 2, December 2005, p. 197.
17 John Eddy and Deryck Schreuder (eds), *The Rise of Colonial Nationalism: Australia, New Zealand, Canada and South Africa First Assert their Nationalities*, Sydney: Allen & Unwin, 1988, p. 134.
18 Anne Coote, 'Out from the Legend's Shadow: Re-thinking National Feeling in Colonial Australia', *Journal of Australian Colonial History*, Vol. 10, No. 2, 2008, p. 113.
19 *Ibid.*, p. 114.
20 *Mercury*, 17 February 1873.
21 Cited in *Argus*, 1 December 1950.
22 *Argus*, 28 June 1862.
23 *Argus*, 1 July 1884.
24 *Queenslander*, 16 December 1882.
25 *Sydney Morning Herald*, 21 November 1887.
26 *Western Mail*, 9 June 1888.
27 Inglis, *Australian Colonists*, p. 143.
28 *South Australian Register*, 6 January 1838.
29 *South Australian Register*, 25 December 1841.
30 *South Australian Register*, 28 December 1857.
31 *South Australian Register*, 29 December 1857.
32 *South Australian Register*, 29 December 1887.
33 *South Australian Register*, 29 December 1887.

34 *South Australian Register*, 29 December 1857; 29 December 1865.
35 *South Australian Register*, 29 December 1859.
36 *South Australian Register*, 29 December 1885.
37 *South Australian Register*, 29 July 1863.
38 *South Australian Register*, 29 December 1859.
39 *South Australian Register*, 29 December 1884.
40 *South Australian Register*, 29 December 1871.
41 *Advertiser*, 29 December 1899.
42 *South Australian Register*, 28 December 1883.
43 *Ibid.*
44 *Advertiser*, 30 December 1890.
45 *South Australian Register*, 29 December 1892.
46 *South Australian Register*, 29 December 1893.
47 *South Australian Register*, 29 December 1879.
48 *Advertiser*, 30 December 1878.
49 *Advertiser*, 28 December 1909.
50 *Advertiser*, 28 December 1914.
51 *Advertiser*, 28 December 1886.
52 *South Australian Register*, 29 December 1871.
53 *Advertiser*, 29 December 1914.
54 *Ibid.*
55 *South Australian Register*, 29 December 1896.
56 Graeme Davison, J.W. McCarty and Ailsa McLeary, *Australians 1888*, Sydney: Fairfax, Syme & Weldon, 1987, pp. 18–29.
57 *Sydney Morning Herald*, 1 February 1888.
58 *Ibid.*
59 *Advertiser*, 26 January 1888.
60 *South Australian Register*, 29 December 1890.
61 *Advertiser*, 28 December 1892.
62 *Advertiser*, 29 December 1896.
63 John M. Williams and Clement Macintyre, 'Commonwealth of Australia', in Akhtar Majeed, Ronald L. Watts, and Douglas M. Brown (eds), *Distribution of Powers and Responsibilities in Federal Countries*, Montreal: McGill-Queen's University Press, 2006, p. 28.
64 *Advertiser*, 31 December 1901; 29 December 1903.
65 *Advertiser*, 29 December 1903.
66 *Advertiser*, 29 December 1914.
67 *Advertiser*, 28 December 1920.
68 *Advertiser*, 29 December 1921; 29 December 1926; 15 November 1835.
69 Coote, 'Out from the Legend's Shadow', p. 122.
70 For a detailed account of this gradual shift of powers, see Williams & Macintyre, 'The Commonwealth of Australia'.
71 *Advertiser*, 29 December 1926.
72 *Mail*, 7 November 1936.
73 *Mail*, 28 November 1936.
74 Davidson, 'The Rise and Fall of Proclamation Day', p. 800.

75 *Advertiser*, 29 December 1936.
76 *Advertiser*, 15 November 1935.
77 Atkinson, 'Tasmania and the Multiplicity of Nations', pp. 197–200.
78 *Messenger Eastern Courier*, 11 April 2012, p. 14.

Chapter 6 • Sex and Citizenship: From Ballot Boxes to Bedrooms

1 Cornelius Proud, 'How Women's Suffrage was Won in South Australia', *Review of Reviews*, 20 January 1895; Helen Jones, *In Her Own Name: A History of Women in South Australia from 1836*, Adelaide: Wakefield Press, revised ed., 1994, chapter 5.
2 C.H. Spence, diary entry for 17 December 1894, in Susan Magarey, with Barbara Wall, Mary Lyons and Maryan Beams (eds), *Ever Yours C.H. Spence: Catherine Helen Spence's 'An Autobiography (1825–1910)', Diary (1894) and Some Correspondence (1894–1910)*, Adelaide: Wakefield Press, 2005, pp. 317–18. On Rose Birks, see Susan Magarey, 'Sex vs Citizenship: Votes for Women in South Australia', *Journal of the Historical Society of South Australia*, No. 21, 1993, pp. 78–85. On all of these women, see Jones, *In Her Own Name*, chapters 4, 5 and 6.
3 Spence, diary entry for 17 December 1894, *Ever Yours C.H. Spence*, p. 317.
4 *Ibid.*, p. 318. On Mary Lee, see Helen Jones, 'Mary Lee (née Walsh)', in Wilfrid Prest, Kerrie Round and Carol Fort (eds), *The Wakefield Companion to South Australian History*, Adelaide: Wakefield Press, 2001, pp. 312–13.
5 *Weekly Herald*, 21 December 1894.
6 On Elizabeth Webb Nicholls, see 'Elizabeth Webb Nicholls (née Bakewell)', and Margaret Allen, 'Woman's Christian Temperance Union (WCTU)', both in Wilfrid Prest, Kerrie Round and Carol Fort (eds), *The Wakefield Companion to South Australian History*, Adelaide: Wakefield Press, 2001, pp. 382, 587–8.
7 *South Australian Chronicle*, 22 December 1894.
8 South Australia, *Parliamentary Debates* (henceforth SA *PD*), 17 December 1894, c. 2924.
9 Proud, 'How Woman's Suffrage was Won in South Australia'.
10 *Adelaide Observer*, 22 December 1894.
11 *Advertiser*, 18 December 1894.
12 This account is compiled from J.B. Hirst, 'Ebenezer Ward (1837–1917)', *Australian Dictionary of Biography, 1851–1890*, Melbourne: Melbourne University Press, Vol. 6, 1976, pp. 351–2; W.J. Sowden, 'Our Pioneer Press, *The Register*, *The Observer* and *The Evening Journal*. A History', transcript with handwritten corrections, 1926, South Australian Archives, State Library of South Australia, 1219/25A; *Register*, 28 April 1880, 29 April 1880, 30 April 1880, 1 May 1880, 5 May 1880, 6 May 1880, 7 May 1880, 11 May 1880, and 5 December 1895; *Adelaide Chronicle*, 7 October 1911; *Express and Telegraph*, 9 October 1917. Also see Magarey, 'Sex vs Citizenship', pp. 75–8.
13 SA *PD*, 17 July 1894.
14 See Susan Magarey, *Unbridling the Tongues of Women: A Biography of Catherine Helen Spence*, updated ed., Adelaide: University of Adelaide Press, 2010, pp. 129–30.
15 *Observer* [Adelaide], 1 August 1891.
16 Jones, *In Her Own Name*, chapter 5; Magarey, *Unbridling the Tongues of Women*, pp. 148–55.

17 Jones, *In Her Own Name*, pp. 132–67.
18 All of this paragraph is drawn from Magarey, *Unbridling the Tongues of Women*, pp. 44–8.
19 Tom Stevenson, 'Population Statistics', in Wray Vamplew, Eric Richards, Dean Jaensch and Joan Hancock (eds), *South Australian Historical Statistics*, Sydney: University of New South Wales, 1984, pp. 18–19.
20 C.H. Spence, *Some Social Aspects of South Australian Life*, reprinted from the *South Australian Register*, Adelaide: R. Kyffin Thomas, 1878.
21 Jones, *In Her Own Name*, p. 29.
22 Catherine Helen Spence, *A Week in the Future*, serialised in *The Centennial Magazine: An Australian Monthly*, December 1888-July 1889, published with an Introduction & Notes by Lesley Durrell Ljungdahl, Sydney: Hale & Iremonger, 1987, especially chapter 6.
23 Alison Mackinnon, *The New Women: Adelaide's Early Women Graduates*, Adelaide: Wakefield Press, 1986, pp. 77–80. See also Anne Geddes and Margaret Hammond, 'Agnes Nesbit Benham: Sexual Reform and Socialism in Adelaide', *Journal of the Historical Society of South Australia*, No. 15, 1987, pp. 110–23.
24 Catherine Martin, *An Australian Girl*, London: Pandora, 1988, pp. 35, 85.
25 Margaret Allen, 'She Seems to Have Composed Her Own Life: Thinking about Catherine Martin', *Australian Feminist Studies*, Vol. 19, No. 43, 2004, p. 38.
26 See Susan Magarey, *Passions of the First Wave Feminists*, Sydney: UNSW Press, 2001, p. 114.
27 SA *PD*, 29 August 1973, pp. 574–7.
28 Rex Jory [interview with George Lewkowicz], 8 December 2009, The Don Dunstan Foundation, Don Dunstan Oral History Project. Accessible from http://hdl.handle.net/2328/15044.
29 Mr Gardner (Morialta), speech on 'Dr D Tonkin', House of Assembly, 22 June 2010; Andrew Parkin, 'Transition, Innovation, Consolidation, Readjustment: The Political History of South Australia since 1965', in Dean Jaensch (ed.), *The Flinders History of South Australia: Political History*, Adelaide: Wakefield Press, 1986, p. 326.
30 SA *PD*, 19 September 1973, p. 831.
31 *Report of the Select Committee of the House of Assembly on the Sex Discrimination Bill, 1973–1974*, South Australia, Parliamentary Paper No. 115, 1974, Recommendation.
32 SA *PD*, 16 October 1974, p. 1514.
33 *Ibid.*
34 SA *PD*, 11 June 1975, pp. 3296–7.
35 These commentators are quoted in Susan Magarey and Kerrie Round, *Roma the First: A Biography of Dame Roma Mitchell*, Adelaide: Wakefield Press, 2007, revised 2009, pp. 153–4, 176.
36 Parkin, 'Transition, Innovation, Consolidation, Readjustment', p. 302.
37 Typescript of article by Don Dunstan written in response to an invitation by J.A. Fitzgerald, editor, *Melbourne Herald*, 25 June 1974, Dunstan Papers, Box 23, Flinders University Library.
38 Robert Holmes, 'A Political Biography of Peter Duncan', research project essay in Politics II: Party, Party Systems and Society in Australia, Flinders University,

July 1977, in Alan Patience's notes towards a biography of Don Dunstan, Flinders University Library.

39 *News*, 12 March 1970; 'Only the Chains Have Changed' [leaflet], 15 December 1969, quoted in Marilyn Lake, *Getting Equal: The History of Australian Feminism*, Sydney: Allen & Unwin, 1999, p. 221.

40 Newsclipping, 4 March 1973, Women's Liberation Movement Archive, State Library of South Australia, WLM 1/19/4.

41 *Report of the Select Committee ... on the Sex Discrimination Bill, 1973–1974*, Appendix A.

42 Jill Blewett, 'The Abortion Law Reform Association of South Australia 1968–73', in Jan Mercer (ed.), *The Other Half: Women in Australian Society*, Melbourne: Penguin Books, 1975, pp. 377–94.

43 *Report of the Select Committee ... on the Sex Discrimination Bill, 1973–1974*, Appendix A.

44 Personal communication from Deborah McCulloch.

45 *Report of the Select Committee ... on the Sex Discrimination Bill, 1973–1974.*

46 SA *PD*, 16 October 1974, p. 1513.

47 SA *PD*, 28 October 1975, p. 1438.

48 Margaret Power, 'Women's Work is Never Done – By Men: A Socio-Economic Model of Sex-Typing in Occupations', *Journal of Industrial Relations*, September 1975, pp. 225–39.

49 SA *PD*, 30 October 1975, pp. 1560–1. The International Labor Organisation material is quoted in Hon. R.J. Hawke, 'Official Opening Speech', National Technology Conference, *Proceedings and Report*, Canberra, 26–28 September 1983, p. 5.

50 Quoted by the Hon. Anne Levy, SA *PD*, 30 October 1975, p. 1561.

51 Noni Farwell, 'Dame Roma Mitchell and the Arts', in Susan Magarey (ed.), *Dame Roma: Glimpses of a Glorious Life*, Adelaide: Axiom Publishing in association with the John Bray Chapter of the Alumni Association of the University of Adelaide, 2002, p. 244.

52 Barry York, 'Power to the Young', in Verity Burgmann and Jenny Lee (eds), *Staining the Wattle: A People's History of Australia since 1788*, Melbourne: McPhee Gribble/ Penguin Books, 1988, p. 234; Verity Burgmann, *Power and Protest: Movements for Change in Australian Society*, Sydney: Allen & Unwin, 1993.

53 Newsclipping, 4 March 1973, Women's Liberation Movement Archive, State Library of South Australia, 1/19/4.

54 Phil, 'The Wonderful, Ebullient Gay Demo', *Boiled Sweets*, Vol. 2, No. 2, 1973, pp. 1–2, quoted in Graham Willett, '"In Our Lifetime": The Gay and Lesbian Movement in Australia 1958–1978', unpublished PhD thesis, University of Melbourne, 1997, chapter 8.

55 Robyn Archer, 'The Menstruation Blues', in Robyn Archer, *The Robyn Archer Songbook*, Melbourne: McPhee Gribble, 1980, p. 21.

56 The Boston Women's Health Book Collective, *Our Bodies, Ourselves: A Book By and For Women*, New York: Simon and Schuster, 1971.

57 Personal recollection.

58 Anne Koedt, 'The Myth of the Vaginal Orgasm' [1970], in Leslie B. Tanner (ed.), *Voices From Women's Liberation*, New York: Mentor, 1970; Anne Summers, *Ducks on the Pond: An Autobiography 1945–1976*, Melbourne: Viking, 1999, pp. 261–2.
59 See, for example, Beryl Donaldson, 'Woman's Place in the Counter Culture', in Jan Mercer (ed.), *The Other Half: Women in Australian Society*, Melbourne: Penguin Books, 1975, chapter 24.
60 The Hon. Anne Levy [interview with Deborah Worsley-Pine], 25 July 1996, History of the Women's Liberation Movement in Australia project.
61 All of this paragraph is drawn from Magarey & Round, *Roma the First*, pp. 204–15. See also Dino Hodge, 'The Long Arm of the Law – The 1950s and 1960s Decades of Shame', paper presented at the 20th State History Conference, Adelaide, August 2011.
62 Malcolm Cowan and Tim Reeves, 'The "Gay Rights" Movement and the Decriminalisation Debate in South Australia, 1973–1975', in Robert Aldrich and Gary Wotherspoon (eds), *Gay and Lesbian Perspectives IV: Studies in Australian Culture*, Sydney: University of Sydney, 1998, pp. 164–93. See also Clare Parker and Paul Sendziuk, 'It's Time: The Duncan Case and the Decriminalisation of Homosexual Acts in South Australia, 1972', in Yorick Smaal and Graham Willett (eds), *Out Here: Gay and Lesbian Perspectives VI*, Melbourne: Monash University Publishing, 2011, pp. 17–35.
63 Carol Treloar [interview with Deborah Worsley-Pine], 1 August 1996, History of the Women's Liberation Movement in Australia project. Transcript in possession of the author.
64 Magarey & Round, *Roma the First*, p. 245.
65 Peter McDonald, Lado Ruzicka and Patricia Pyne, 'Marriage, Fertility and Mortality', in Wray Vamplew (ed.), *Australians: Historical Statistics*, Broadway: Fairfax, Syme & Weldon Associates, 1987, pp. 42–3.
66 Susan Magarey, 'Why Didn't They Want to be Members of Parliament? Suffragists in South Australia', in Caroline Daley & Melanie Nolan (eds), *Suffrage & Beyond: International Feminist Perspectives*, Auckland: Auckland University Press and Sydney: Pluto Press, 1994, pp. 67–88.
67 Jones, *In Her Own Name*, pp. 295, 355.
68 Bettina Cass, 'Gender in Australia's Restructuring Labour Market and Welfare State', in Anne Edwards and Susan Magarey (eds), *Women in a Restructuring Australia: Work and Welfare*, Sydney: Allen & Unwin in association with the Academy of the Social Sciences in Australia, 1995, pp. 38–59.
69 Cass, 'Gender in Australia's Restructuring Labour Market', p. 53. See also Deirdre Macken, 'Women Slip Down Pay Scale into Jail', *Financial Review*, quoted in *The Week*, 2 September 2011.
70 Michael Keating and Caroline Smith, *Critical Issues Facing Australia to 2025: Summary of a Scenario Development Forum*, Academy of the Social Sciences in Australia, *Occasional Paper*, No. 1, 2011, pp. 9, 12.

Chapter 7 • Making the Most of It

1 Don Aitkin, '"Countrymindedness": The Spread of an Idea', in S.L. Goldberg and F.B. Smith (eds), *Australian Cultural History*, Melbourne: Cambridge University Press, 1988, p. 115.

2 Rob Linn, *Battling the Land: 200 Years of Rural Australia*, Sydney: Allen & Unwin, 1999, p. 172; Don Aitkin, 'Return to Countrymindedness', in Graeme Davison and Marc Brodie (eds), *Struggle Country: The Rural Ideal in Twentieth Century Australia*, Melbourne: Monash University e-Press, 2005, p. 115.

3 D.W. Meinig, *On the Margins of the Good Earth: The South Australian Wheat Frontier 1869–1884*, Adelaide: Rigby, 1970, and J.B. Hirst, *Adelaide and the Country 1870–1917: Their Social and Political Relationship*, Melbourne: Melbourne University Press, 1973, are the classic studies.

4 Centrex Metals Limited, company website, 2008, accessible from http://www.centrexmetals.com.au; *The Advertiser*, Business Monthly supplement, August 2011, pp. 8–9.

5 Judith Brett, 'Fair Share: Country and City in Australia', *Quarterly Essay* No. 42, 2011, p. 56.

6 Jill Roe and Helen Bartley, 'Regions/regionalism', in Wilfrid Prest, Kerrie Round and Carol Fort (eds), *The Wakefield Companion to South Australian History*, Adelaide: Wakefield Press, 2001, pp. 450–1. The same book provides a map of Aboriginal Australia on p. 9.

7 Judith Jeffrey, 'Goyder's Line', in Wilfrid Prest, Kerrie Round and Carol Fort (eds), *The Wakefield Companion to South Australian History*, Adelaide: Wakefield Press, 2001, p. 232.

8 Neville Collins, *The Jetties of South Australia: Past and Present*, Adelaide: Neville Collins, 2005, p. 41; Nic Klaassen, 'Nuyts, Pieter (1598–1655)', *Australian Dictionary of Biography (henceforth ADB): Supplement*, Melbourne: Melbourne University Press, 2005, and online, accessible from http://adb.anu.edu.au/biography/nuyts-pieter-13138/text23777.

9 K.S. Inglis, *The Stuart Case*, Melbourne: Melbourne University Press, 1961.

10 Elizabeth Salter, *Daisy Bates*, New York: Cowan, McCann & Geoghegan, 1972, pp. 243–5; Bob Reece, *Daisy Bates: Grand Dame of the Desert*, Canberra: National Library of Australia, 2007, p. 147; M.E. Fenton, *W.K. Mallyon 1850–1933: A Sketchbook of Early Church Architecture in the Mid North of South Australia*, Adelaide: Libraries Board of South Australia, 1971.

11 Robert Foster, Rick Hosking and Amanda Nettelbeck, *Fatal Collisions: The South Australian Frontier of Violence and Memory*, Adelaide: Wakefield Press, 2001, ch. 4; 'Gallery in the Open Eyre', *SA Life*, Dec 2006-Jan 2007, pp. 36–8; Ellen Liston, *Pioneers: Stories*, compiled by E.A. Harwood, Adelaide: Hassell Press, 1936.

12 For members of the Mortlock family, see *ADB*, vols 5 and 11 or online, accessible from http://adb.anu.edu.au.

13 Hematite: the mineral form of iron oxide, from black to red in colour.

14 Geoffrey Speirs, 'Museums', in Wilfrid Prest, Kerrie Round and Carol Fort (eds), *The Wakefield Companion to South Australian History*, Adelaide: Wakefield Press, 2001, p. 369–71.

15 M.R. Brett-Crowther, 'Buddicom, Robert Arthur (1874–1951)', *ADB* Vol. 7 and online, accessible from http://adb.anu.edu.au/biography/buddicom-robert-arthur-5417/text9185.

16 For the Elliston mural, see Foster *et al.*, *Fatal Collisions*, p. 44.

17 John Pickard, 'Lines Across the Landscape: History, Impact and Heritage of Australian Rural Fences', unpublished PhD thesis, Macquarie University, 2010, p. 353.

18 Bob Dobbins [interview with Jill Roe], 29 July 2011; Jennifer A. Jones, 'Old Age in a Young Colony: Image and Experience in South Australia in the Nineteenth Century', unpublished PhD thesis, University of Adelaide, 2010. Bob Dobbins now resides with his family in Adelaide.

19 Janet Callen and Gisela Heathcote, 'Horses', in Wilfrid Prest, Kerrie Round and Carol Fort (eds), *The Wakefield Companion to South Australian History*, Adelaide: Wakefield Press, 2001, pp. 266–7; Jill Roe, *Stella Miles Franklin: A Life*, Sydney: HarperCollins Australia, 2008, p. 11.

20 The folk migration has yet to be studied in any detail. Sources include 'Effie' [Mrs John Durdin], *Pioneering Days: Koppio 1903*, 8 pp., n.d., publ. National Trust of South Australia, Tumby Bay Branch, c. 2000; see also Jill Roe, 'Belly-Dancing in the Bush and Other Strategies for Survival', *AHA Bulletin*, December 1998, pp. 14–17.

21 *Souvenir of the Opening of the Tod River Water Scheme*, Thevenard, June 1928, SA Government Printer, 1928.

22 Robert Murray, *Sandbelters: Memoirs of Middle Australia*, Melbourne: Arcadia, 2011, p. 24; Penelope Hetherington, *The Making of a Labor Politician: Family and Politics in South Australia, 1900–1980*, Perth: the author, 1982.

23 Daphne Freeman (ed.), *Eyre Peninsula Ramblings*, Adelaide: Lutheran Publishing House, 1985.

24 Marianne Hammerton, *Water South Australia: A History of the Engineering and Water Supply Department*, Adelaide: Wakefield Press, 1986, p. 188.

25 Joan Airy, 'Rural Life Between the Wars', *South Australiana*, Vol. 14, No. 1, 1975, p. 19.

26 Peter Stanley, *Whyalla at War*, Whyalla: City of Whyalla, 2004, p. 9. The population of Whyalla increased dramatically from 1937–1944, from c. 1350 to 7900.

27 Richard Waterhouse, *The Vision Splendid: A Social and Cultural History of Rural Australia*, Perth: Curtin University Books, Fremantle Arts Centre Press, 2005; Bill Gammage, *The Biggest Estate on Earth: How Aborigines Made Australia*, Sydney: Allen & Unwin, 2011; Heather Goodall, 'Telling Country: Memoir, Modernity and Narratives in Rural Australia', *History Workshop Journal*, Vol. 47, 1999, pp. 160–90.

28 Charles Fahey, '"A Splendid Place for a Home": The Long History of the Australian Family Farm', in Alan Mayne and Stephen Atkinson (eds), *Outside Country: Histories of Inland Australia*, Adelaide: Wakefield Press, 2011.

29 Linn, *Battling the Land*, p. 172.

30 Graeme Davison, 'Rural Sustainability in Historical Perspective', in Chris Cocklin and Jacqui Dibden (eds), *Sustainability and Change in Rural Australia*, Sydney: UNSW Press, 2005, p. 54.

31 Brett, 'Fair Share'; Jill Roe, 'Voluntary Action and the Rural Poor in the Age of Globalisation', in Melanie Oppenheimer and Nicholas Deakin (eds), *Beveridge and Voluntary Action in Britain and the Wider British World*, Manchester: Manchester University Press, 2011.

Chapter 8 • A Place to Grow: Making a Future in Postwar South Australia

1 Mark Peel and Christina Twomey, *A History of Australia*, London: Palgrave Macmillan, 2011, pp. xiii-iv.

2 Robert Dare, 'History and Historians', in Wilfred Prest, Kerrie Round and Carol Fort (eds), *The Wakefield Companion to South Australian History*, Adelaide: Wakefield Press, 2001, pp. 257–60.

3 Mark Peel, *Good Times, Hard Times: The Past and the Future in Elizabeth*, Melbourne: Melbourne University Press, 1995.

4 Hugh Stretton used this phrase in his speech launching my book, *Good Times, Hard Times*, in 1995; the tenor of this particular idea is perhaps best captured in two of his shorter articles: 'Obituary: A.M. Ramsay and the Conventional Wisdom', *Australian Quarterly*, Vol. 50, No. 3, 1978, pp. 90–100, and 'An Intellectual Public Servant: William Wainwright, 1880–1948', *Meanjin*, Vol. 50, 1991, pp. 555–78.

5 The relevant sections of Hugh Stretton's *Ideas for Australian Cities*, 3rd ed., Sydney: Transit Publishing, 1989, remain the single most important statement. Also significant are the chapters in two collections, Kyoko Sheridan (ed.), *The State as Developer: Public Enterprise in South Australia*, Adelaide: Royal Australian Institute of Public Administration and Wakefield Press, 1986, and Bernard O'Neil, Judith Raftery and Kerrie Round (eds), *Playford's South Australia: Essays on the History of South Australia, 1933–1968*, Adelaide: Wakefield Press, 1996. John Spoehr's numerous contributions include his essays in John Spoehr (ed.), *Beyond the Contract State: Ideas for Social and Economic Renewal in South Australia*, Adelaide: Wakefield Press, 1999.

6 Peel, *Good Times, Hard Times*, p. 114 and Tables A.7 and A.8, p. 242.

7 On this theme, see especially A. James Hammerton and Alistair Thomson, *Ten Pound Poms: Australia's Invisible Migrants*, Manchester: Manchester University Press, 2005. I have also drawn here and in what follows from the rich vein of new writing about British migrants and Britishness in Australia, including Sara Wills, 'Passengers of Memory: Constructions of British Immigrants in Post-Imperial Australia', *Australian Journal of Politics and History*, Vol. 51, No. 1, 2005, pp. 94–107; Sara Wills and Kate Darian-Smith, 'Beefeaters, Bobbies and a New Varangian Guard? Negotiating Forms of "Britishness" in Suburban Australia', *History of Intellectual Culture*, Vol. 4, No. 1, 2004, pp. 1–18; Carole Hamilton-Barwick, '"A Ballot Cast for Orestes": Memory and Myth, the Construction of Identity and Meaning in British Immigrant Women's Narratives, 1947–1957', *Oral History Association of Australia Journal*, Vol. 23, 2001, pp. 47–53; and James Jupp, *The English in Australia*, Cambridge: Cambridge University Press, 2004.

8 *A Place to Grow – Elizabeth, South Australia*, South Australian Housing Trust and Supreme Sound Studios, 1962, 24 minutes. A copy of this film is available for viewing in the State Library of South Australia.

9 Report of a television interview, *Sydney Morning Herald*, 7 April 1993.

10 I have written more extensively on this, and in reference to broader Australian working-class experience, in 'A New Kind of Manhood: Remembering the 1950s', *Australian Historical Studies*, Vol. 28, No. 109, 1997, pp. 147–57, and on British men's migrant narratives in 'Dislocated Men: Imagining "Britain" and "Australia"', in A. James Hammerton and Eric Richards (eds), *Visible Immigrants Six: Speaking*

to Immigrants: Oral Testimony and the History of Australian Migration, Canberra: Research School of Social Sciences, Australian National University, 2002, pp. 111–27.

11 Tony Butcher, *Elizabeth Champions*, Adelaide: Elizabeth City Council, 1994, p. 14.

Chapter 9 • Don Dunstan and the Social Democratic Moment in Australian History

1 Ross McMullin, *The Light on the Hill: The Australian Labor Party 1891–1991*, Melbourne: Oxford University Press, 1991, p. 393.

2 Dean Jaensch, *The Hawke-Keating Hijack: The ALP in Transition*, Sydney: Allen & Unwin, 1989, p. 155.

3 Quoted in Andrew Parkin, 'Looking Back on the Bannon Decade', in Andrew Parkin and Allan Patience (eds), *The Bannon Decade: The Politics of Restraint in South Australia*, Sydney: Allen & Unwin, 1992, p. 6.

4 Parkin, 'Looking Back on the Bannon Decade', p. 6.

5 The most detailed account is in Mike Rann [interview], 10 February 2009, part 2, pp. 10–14, The Dunstan Foundation, Don Dunstan Oral History Project. Accessible from http://hdl.handle.net/2328/25126.

6 Brian Chatterton, *Roosters and Featherdusters*, Castel di Fiori [Italy]: Pulcini Press, 2003, p. 206.

7 John Cornwall, *Just For The Record: The Political Recollections of John Cornwall*, Adelaide: Wakefield Press, 1989, pp. 9–10; Chatterton, *Roosters and Featherdusters*, p. 261.

8 Quoted in Craig McGregor, 'Don Dunstan: The Exile Goes Home', *Sydney Morning Herald*, 8 March 1987.

9 It seems likely that Dunstan took the job in Victoria because he did not anticipate Labor's return to power in South Australia in 1982. See John Bannon [interview], 24 June 2008, p. 20, The Dunstan Foundation, Don Dunstan Oral History Project. Accessible from http://hdl.handle.net/2328/25070.

10 See John Cain [interview], 6 June 2008, p. 15, The Dunstan Foundation, Don Dunstan Oral History Project. Accessible from http://hdl.handle.net/2328/8428.

11 Chatterton, *Roosters and Featherdusters*, p. 260.

12 Parkin, 'Looking Back on the Bannon Decade', p. 7.

13 Chatterton, *Roosters and Featherdusters*, pp. 260–1.

14 Canberra Survey, 18 February 1977, Flinders University, Dunstan Collection, DUN/Press clippings/728.

15 Quoted in Susan Magarey and Kerrie Round, *Roma the First: A Biography of Dame Roma Mitchell*, Adelaide: Wakefield Press, 2007, p. 154. The double entendre was perhaps intended.

16 The words are those of an intelligent critic, Stewart Cockburn, quoted in *Advertiser*, 8 February 1999.

17 See Judith Pugh, *Unstill Life: Art, Politics and Living with Clifton Pugh*, Sydney: Allen & Unwin, 2008, pp. 142–7, 156–65. The resulting triangular relationship included the painter Clifton Pugh, commissioned to paint Dunstan's portrait, and the account – a mixture of romance, tragedy and farce – reads like a Bloomsbury saga.

18 McGregor, 'Don Dunstan: The Exile Goes Home'.

19 Don Hopgood [interview], 20 November 2008, p. 28, The Dunstan Foundation, Don Dunstan Oral History Project. Accessible from http://hdl.handle.net/2328/3232.
20 Graham Inns [interview], 10 February 2009, p. 1, The Dunstan Foundation, Don Dunstan Oral History Project. Accessible from http://hdl.handle.net/2328/25080.
21 John Warhurst, 'The Public Service', in Andrew Parkin and Allan Patience (eds), *The Dunstan Decade: Social Democracy at the State Level*, Melbourne: Longman Cheshire, 1981, p. 182.
22 *The Advertiser*, 8 February 1999.
23 Graham Freudenberg, *A Certain Grandeur: Gough Whitlam's Life in Politics*, revised edition, Melbourne: Penguin, 2009, p. 463.
24 Mike Steketee and Milton Cockburn, *Wran: An Unauthorised Biography*, Sydney: Allen & Unwin, 1986, p. 108.
25 Don Dunstan, *Felicia: The Political Memoirs of Don Dunstan*, Melbourne: Macmillan, 1981, pp. 249–50. Dunstan's anger was compounded by the fact that he had made the pledges on Whitlam's behalf.
26 Dunstan, *Felicia*, p. 223.
27 Dunstan to Eric Reece, Premier of Tasmania, cited in Dunstan, *Felicia*, pp. 251–3. The letter is dated 17 September 1974 and was sent to all state Labor leaders. See Dunstan Collection, DUN/VF1 Drawer 3.
28 Ron Barnes [interview], 29 May 2009, p. 4, The Dunstan Foundation, Don Dunstan Oral History Project. Accessible from http://hdl.handle.net/2328/25076. Barnes went on to say, '[w]e were bowled over by what Don Dunstan had achieved' (p. 7).
29 Rod Cameron [interview], 8 September 2009, p. 5, The Dunstan Foundation, Don Dunstan Oral History Project. Accessible from http://hdl.handle.net/2328/25075.
30 Dunstan, *Felicia*, p. 259.
31 '1976 Chifley Memorial Lecture', p. 11, Flinders University Dunstan Collection, DUN/Speeches/2930.
32 *Ibid.*, p. 21.
33 Don Dunstan, 'Whitlam Lecture', 21 April 1998, p. 2, accessible from Don Dunstan Foundation, http://www.dunstan.org.au/docs/WhitlamLecture_1998_Dunstan.pdf.
34 'Whitlam Lecture', p. 13.
35 'Evatt Memorial Lecture', 1991, p. 4, Dunstan Collection, DUN/Speeches/4005.
36 '1976 Chifley Lecture', p. 13.
37 Stewart Cockburn, *Playford: Benevolent Despot*, Adelaide: Axiom, 1991, chapter 16.
38 Dunstan, *Felicia*, p. 47.
39 Cockburn, *Playford*, p. 248. I note the use of the word 'apparent'.
40 Don Dunstan to Ian Spalding, 23 July 1962, Flinders University Dunstan Collection, DUN/VF4/ Drawer 1.
41 Neal Blewett and Dean Jaensch, *Playford to Dunstan: The Politics of Transition*, Melbourne: Cheshire, 1971, p. 156.
42 Dean Jaensch, 'Electoral Reform', in Andrew Parkin and Allan Patience (eds), *The Dunstan Decade: Social Democracy at the State Level*, Melbourne: Longman Cheshire, 1981, p. 237.
43 Rod Cameron [interview], p. 6, Don Dunstan Oral History Project. Emphasis in original.
44 Dunstan, *Felicia*, p. 70.

45 John Summers, 'Aboriginal Policy', in Andrew Parkin and Allan Patience (eds), *The Dunstan Decade: Social Democracy at the State Level*, Melbourne: Longman Cheshire, 1981, p. 127.
46 Mike Rann on Don Dunstan, *Dimensions in Time*, ABC TV, 6 May 2002. Transcript accessible from http://www.abc.net.au/dimensions/dimensions_in_time/Transcripts/s549618.htm.
47 Eugenia Koussidis [interview], 2 November 2007, pp. 8–9, The Dunstan Foundation, Don Dunstan Oral History Project. Accessible from http://hdl.handle.net/2328/3239.
48 'Tourist Development in South Australia', Working Paper, January 1971, Flinders University Dunstan Collection, DUN/Box 52/50.
49 *Ibid.*
50 Robert Kosky, 'Health Policy', in Andrew Parkin and Allan Patience (eds), *The Bannon Decade: The Politics of Restraint in South Australia*, Sydney: Allen & Unwin, 1992, p. 239.
51 Rod Oxenberry, 'Community Welfare', in Andrew Parkin and Allan Patience (eds), *The Dunstan Decade: Social Democracy at the State Level*, Melbourne: Longman Cheshire, 1981, p. 67.
52 Andrew Strickland [interview], 6 March 2009, p. 36, The Dunstan Foundation, Don Dunstan Oral History Project. Accessible from http://hdl.handle.net/2328/25083. Strickland worked as a public servant in the Policy Division of the Premier's Department in the 1970s and was later deputy head of the Department for the Environment.
53 For details of some of these interventions, see Ian Kowalick [interview], 18 July 2007, pp. 21–4, The Dunstan Foundation, Don Dunstan Oral History Project. Accessible from http://hdl.handle.net/2328/15048. Kowalick worked in the Premier's Department through most of the 1970s.
54 Written testimony provided by John Mant, 28 June 2010, The Dunstan Foundation, Don Dunstan Oral History Project. Accessible from http://hdl.handle.net/2328/23553. At the time Mant was a senior adviser to Tom Uren, Minister for Urban and Regional Development, and later held a senior position in DURD.
55 Andrew Parkin and Cedric Pugh, 'Urban Policy and Metropolitan Adelaide', in Andrew Parkin and Allan Patience (eds), *The Dunstan Decade: Social Democracy at the State Level*, Melbourne: Longman Cheshire, 1981, p. 105.
56 *Ibid.*, p. 112.
57 Thatcher quoted in an interview with Douglas Keay, 'AIDS, Education and the Year 2000!', *Woman's Own*, 31 October 1987, pp. 8–10.
58 It can be argued that the immediate results of the accommodation were less happy in New Zealand. See the riveting internal account of the Lange government by the cabinet minister Michael Bassett, *Working with David: Inside the Lange Cabinet*, Mairangi Bay: Hodder Moa, 2008.
59 See generally Parkin & Patience (eds), *The Bannon Decade.*
60 Steketee & Cockburn, *Wran*, p. 130.
61 *Ibid.*, p. 334.
62 *Ibid.*

63 Allan Patience, 'The Bannon Decade: Preparation for What?', in Andrew Parkin and Allan Patience (eds), *The Bannon Decade: The Politics of Restraint in South Australia*, Sydney: Allen & Unwin, 1992, p. 350.
64 'Whitlam Lecture', p. 6.
65 Don Dunstan, 'What Kind of Competition Is This?', in John Spoehr (ed.), *Don Dunstan – Politics and Passion: Selected Essays from the Adelaide Review*, Adelaide: Bookends Books, 2000, p. 162.
66 Don Dunstan, 'The Looming Water Disaster', in John Spoehr (ed.), *Don Dunstan – Politics and Passion: Selected Essays from the Adelaide Review*, Adelaide: Bookends Books, 2000, p. 46.
67 'Evatt Lecture', pp. 11–12.

Chapter 10 • South Australia and Australia: Reflections on their Histories

1 This chapter was first presented in a slightly different form as the History Council of South Australia Annual Lecture, University of Adelaide, 4 August 2011. The historical interpretations presented here are drawn from my collections of essays, *Sense and Nonsense in Australian History*, Melbourne: Black Inc., 2005, and *Looking for Australia*, Melbourne: Black Inc., 2010.
2 *Sydney Morning Herald*, 30 March 1906.
3 *Tasmanian Historical Research Association, Papers and Proceedings*, Vol. 10, December 1962, pp. 28–33.
4 John Hirst, 'The Pioneer Legend', *Historical Studies*, Vol. 18, No. 71, 1978, pp. 316–37.
5 Douglas Pike, *Australia: The Quiet Continent*, 2nd ed., London: Cambridge University Press, 1970, pp. 225–6.
6 Derek Whitelock, *Adelaide 1836–1976: A History of Difference*, Brisbane: University of Queensland Press, 1977.
7 *Ibid.*, p. 31.
8 Don Dunstan, *Felicia: The Political Memoirs of Don Dunstan*, Melbourne: Macmillan, 1981, p. 63.
9 Whitlam cited in John Spoehr (ed.), *Don Dunstan – Politics and Passion: Selected Essays from the Adelaide Review*, Adelaide: Bookends Books, 2000, p. 11.
10 *Don Dunstan, The First 25 Years in Parliament*, compiled by Richard Yeeles, Melbourne: Hill of Content, 1978, p. 128.
11 Stewart Cockburn, *Playford: Benevolent Despot*, Adelaide: Axiom, 1991, p. v.
12 Whitelock, *Adelaide 1836–1976*, p. 307.

Index

Wakefield Press is an independent publishing and
distribution company based in Adelaide, South Australia.
We love good stories and publish beautiful books.
To see our full range of books, please visit our website at
wakefieldpress.com.au
where all titles are available for purchase.
To keep up with our latest releases, news and events,
subscribe to our monthly newsletter.

Find us!

Facebook: facebook.com/wakefield.press
Twitter: twitter.com/wakefieldpress
Instagram: instagram.com/wakefieldpress

www.ingramcontent.com/pod-product-compliance
Ingram Content Group Australia Pty Ltd
76 Discovery Rd, Dandenong South VIC 3175, AU
AUHW020910100725
413679AU00003B/66

9 781743 051191